D0821212

Voices of Hope
TEENAGERS THEMSELVES

Voices
TEENAGERS

of Hope
THEMSELVES

compiled by the Glenbard East <u>Echo</u>

advised by Howard Spanogle

Adama Books   New York

Other books in the Teenagers Themselves trilogy:

Teenagers Themselves
Voices of Conflict

Copyright © 1988 Adama Books
All rights reserved.

LIBRARY OF CONGRESS
Library of Congress Cataloguing-in-Publication Data

Voices of hope: teenagers themselves III / compiled by the
    Glenbard East Echo: advised by Howard Spanogle.
        p.   cm.
Written and compiled by reporters for the *Echo*,
a student newspaper in Glenbard East High School, Lombard, Ill.
Continues: Voices of conflict. 1987
    Summary: Teenagers present more of their views on such topics as
drugs, sex, suicide, and homosexuality and consider solutions to some
of the conflicts that divide today's youth.
        ISBN 1-557-74012-7 : $16.95
    1. Teenagers—United States—Attitudes.   [1. Youth—Attitudes.]
I. Spanogle, Howard. II. Glenbard East High School (Lombard, Ill.)
III. Echo (Lombard, Ill.)
HQ796.V636 1988   88-2049
305.2'35'0973—dc19   CIP
                                                           AC

Printed in Israel

Adama Books, 306 West 38 Street, New York, New York 10018

To future journalists,
both students and advisers,
who discern the reality
and who share the responsibility
to express the dreams
of a nation in conflict.

Acknowledgments

Completion of **Voices of Hope** was possible because of the vision and the generosity of the Village of Lombard, which provided the project a Community Development Grant; Malcolm Bilimoria, who designated the project as the recipient of a General Electric STAR grant; and the Book Benefactors: Gamit Enterprises, Grove Dental Associates, Prospect Federal Savings Bank, Standard Federal Savings and Loan Association, and Friends of the Helen M. Plum Memorial Library.

Additional assistance came from considerate librarians, who loaned us part of their air-conditioned facilities; a cooperative administration; Sharon Keller, who provided invaluable computer assitance; Lynne Doles, who fielded telephone calls and letters from throughout the nation; Ellen Steiskal, who photocopied the never-ending pages of copy and forms; bookstore manager Gerri Long; bookkeeper Blanche Knight; helpful secretaries; and supportive colleagues.

Hundreds of publications advisers as well as numerous scholastic journalism associations and high school principals provided essential assistance in conducting the discussions and in gathering the national reactions. In addition, *The Echo* is grateful for the support of its printer, CompuComp Corporation; the Youth Communication offices; the Glenbard East art department; and the north campus art department of Lyons Township High School in LaGrange, Illinois.

The staff especially thanks its travel agent, June Chapek of Gary-Wheaton Travel, and the families throughout this country who contributed to the project by serving as generous hosts and by assisting in the research process.

National reactions were gathered during 1986–1987 by the National Teenage Research Project, which was conducted by the *Glenbard East Echo*, a high school student newspaper in Lombard, Illinois. The opinions represent the diverse ideas expressed by nearly 4,000 teenagers. Though all individuals signed their comments, some names have been withheld because of the sensitive nature of the information. Editing changes have been made only in punctuation and spelling.

The discussions come from tape-recorded interviews. These interviews, conducted by *Echo* researchers and editors, were conversations with teenagers and adults in more than 35 cities throughout the United States. Adults have been distinguished by giving their last names to avoid confusion. Opinions expressed do not necessarily represent the views of their organizations or positions. Editing changes have been made only to avoid repetition or misrepresentation of an idea.

Contents

Editor: Greg Jao
Associate Editors: Gina Nolan and Dave Seng
Copyeditor: Diana Slyfield
Contributing Writers: Eric Kammerer and Erik Landahl
Staff Writers: Doug Addison, Chris Anderson, Tim Burke, Sara Corrough,
 Doug Elwell, Julio Flores, Michelle Jao, Cathy Mau, Dave Palomares,
 and Kim Peirce
Computer Coordinator: Robert Hester
Researchers: Mark Cerepa, Kevin Ellerbruch, Dave Landahl, Paulette
 Polinski, Jeannie Ryba, and Laura Ulfers
Research Assistants: Don Gomez, Chris Gorman, JoAnn Vasbinder
Art Editors: Mark Peaslee and Pete Mandik
Artists: Students from art departments at Glenbard East High School and
 Lyons Township High School-North Campus
Book Design and Opening Decorations: Irwin Rosenhouse

Preface

Out of questions and concerns, hopes and discouragements; from an often ignored but continually persevering source—teenagers themselves—came the impetus to examine the nation, to discern the difference between the appearance and the reality, to dream that honest communication builds the bridges to solution.

That honest communication began long before the Glenbard East Echo worked diligently to compile the Teenagers Themselves trilogy. As adviser for more than two decades, I view *Voices of Hope* as a continuation of a tradition: challenging assumptions and serving readers. I remember editors insisting on thorough reporting and candid writing. I also remember them asserting, "Every story has to expand people as human beings." The concerns for honesty and people translated into books with similar priorities—presenting the diverse sounds of a nation and telling the story in an intriguing way.

As I look back, I realize the tradition began long before my involvement with the Echo. To the surprise of my students, there is a pre-Echo era in my life, and that era also involved a national outlook. I remember collecting, as an ambitious elementary school student, postcards of all the state capitols and of other major cities in the United States. Maybe that project provided unusual training for collecting thousands of written responses and planning hundreds of tape recording sessions throughout the nation.

Voices of Hope is an extension of *Voices of Conflict,* the second book in the trilogy. The methods—tape recording hundreds of interviews throughout the nation, collecting thousands of written responses, and shaping free-form essays and artistic interpretations—were the same for both books. *Voices of Hope,* though, portrays conflicts with specific institutions and with abstract values. Of more importance, it concentrates on the second emphasis—solutions, both pragmatic proposals and idealistic dreams.

Each book in the trilogy provides the next step to expand communication between generations. This third book completes the journey teenagers began in the self-examination of *Teenagers Themselves* and continued in the investigation of their peers in *Voices of Conflict. Voices of Hope* extends the investigation to the world in which they function. However, the third book ends by returning to the inner perspective, one of dreams for themselves and for the nation.

Now it is your turn. Listen to the voices—both of conflict and of hope. Expect contention, but anticipate solution. Respond to the clamor and to the counsel. Recognize the way things are, and discover the way things could be. Then share the dreams for yourself and for the nation.

Howard Spanogle
Adviser, Glenbard East Echo

Conflict with Authority

Teenagers find innumerable dead ends as they career down endless passages through the labyrinth of life. Stalked by parents, they flee from the rules and lack of trust at home. Some attempt to escape by entering the streets, only to find dead ends in prostitution and drugs. Others attempt to leave the maze through education, but they discover that school walls lead to new mazes of punishment and confusion.

Some teens seek work to map a path out of the maze. Inevitably, however, the map leads them into greater clashes with parents and teachers. Work schedules corral teens into continual conflict. As they begin to search for shortcuts to freedom, they run into walls of prejudice in law and politics. When teens attempt to go to the media for help, they are ignored or misrepresented. Hoping to find rest and relaxation, teens try to escape from the labyrinth by immersing themselves in entertainment, only to be confronted with a gross specter of stereotypes. Once they begin to understand the immensity of the maze, technology changes the ground rules.

With maturity comes the knowledge that there is no escape from the maze. Maturity teaches teens that communication helps them circumvent the dead ends. Maturity also teaches them that communication can create a satisfying life within the paths that control their lives.

Chapter 1.

Kids and Parents

"Ma, I'm home," Jenny screamed as she walked through the door to the apartment. She threw her books on the hall table and checked her reflection in the mirror on the opposite wall. "Not bad," she thought as she pushed her curly dark hair out of her brown eyes. She checked her smooth skin for any sign of blemishes. When she didn't find any, she breathed a sigh of relief. "No zits, it's Friday, I have a hot date with Billy tonight, and my geometry for Monday is already done. Yeah, it's going to be a good weekend."

"Ma? Where are you?" Jenny asked the seemingly empty apartment. "That's funny, she should be home," Jenny thought. "Lord knows she can't hide in this tiny dump." Jenny glanced around the cramped apartment. "Ma already ate—the dishes are in the sink. Shit, what a pig. I'm glad I'm going out to eat. I'll probably have to clean this, but at least I won't have to eat it."

Just then, Jenny heard the water running in the bathroom. She walked over and stood next to the door.

"Ma, are you in there? Why didn't you answer me?" Jenny asked.

The knob on the door turned slowly, and Jenny's mother emerged. Rosalee Hamilton was only 32, but she looked much older. Years of hard work etched deep lines in her forehead, and years of hard partying painted dark circles under her eyes. Jenny was used to seeing her mother in almost any condition, but she was shocked when Rosalee turned to face her.

"Ma, what happened to you? How did you get that bruise on your arm? And that cut on your face? Ma, what's going on?"

Rosalee shut her eyes in an attempt to block her daughter's questions. She took a deep breath and tried to gather the courage to face Jenny. "Damn," Rosalee thought, "I expected her to be at the library for at least another hour."

"You've got all your homework done already? Gee, honey, that was fast."

"Ma, cut the shit. What's going on? Was Martin here again?"

Rosalee cringed as her daughter mentioned his name. She knew how much Jenny hated her on-again, off-again lover.

"That bastard was here, and he beat you again. Ma, why don't you just tell him to get lost?"

"Now, Jen, Martin means well. He just loses his temper sometimes. You know how tense things are for him at work."

"Work?" Jenny screamed, "You mean all the work he does waiting around the unemployment office for some fantasy job that is no work but great pay? Ma, he's nothing but a bum! The only reason he comes around here is because you give him free food and free sex. He's an asshole," Jenny yelled.

"Shut up! I don't need to hear this from you. Get to your room." Rosalee's dark eyes flashed as she screeched at her daughter.

"Are you kidding? Do you think I'm waiting around for that jerk to come back? He's probably gone down to the liquor store to buy some cheap bottle of wine. He'll bring it back up here and apologize for nearly killing you. And, of course, you'll welcome him back. And the whole damn thing will start all over again. Sorry, Mother dear, I'm not waiting around for this little scene. I'm going out with Billy tonight."

Rosalee drew her breath in sharply. "Billy, that little sex-starved punk? You are not going out with him. Believe me, Jenny, he's only out for one thing. And I will not take care of your baby!"

"Oh, Ma, give it up. Billy is clean. No drugs, he's not in a gang, and he even has a part-time job, which is more than you can say for Martin. Besides, what's wrong with a bastard baby? I was one, wasn't I?" Jenny cast a vindictive glance at her mother.

"You shut up. I was married when I had you. You are as legit as the Constitution. I would not have a baby out of wedlock."

"No, that's why Granddad threatened to kill Daddy if he didn't marry you. No wonder he stuck around so long. I'm surprised that Daddy lasted all the way until my sixth birthday."

With that parting shot, Jenny spun around and grabbed her coat off the couch. Then she snatched her purse, threw open the door, and rushed out, right into Martin.

"Where are you going in such a hurry, little lady?" Martin asked in a voice dripping with sweetness.

"Get out of my way, you idiot. I'm going out," Jenny snapped.

"You're not going out with that punk your mother doesn't like, are you?" What's his name, Billy?" Martin's questions were now becoming sharp.

"If I am, it's none of your business. At least Billy has a job and can afford more than a bottle of foul Gallo white wine," Jenny retorted.

She didn't see Martin's hand until it was crashing against her face. She fell backward into the dank, unlit hallway. Rubbing her chin, Jenny looked up at her mother. Rosalee had rushed forward to protect her daughter but was held back by Martin.

"You know, Ma, I really love you, but sometimes I just can't like you."

Jenny picked herself up and sprinted down the hall. "Another great weekend this is going to be," she mumbled.

Diana Slyfield

The Weekend Routine

It's another Saturday morning for Steve, a typical American teenager. As he shuffles downstairs to the breakfast table, he can already hear his parents griping. "Great. Here we go again," he thinks.

He tries to say good morning, but the parents strike too fast. Mom is the first to start the interrogation.

"What time did you get home last night, young man?"

Trying to answer is futile. When Mom is mad, Steve can't get a word in.

"I thought I told you last week that you were to be home by midnight. That doesn't mean 1:30 in the morning."

Actually, it was more like five minutes after one, but Steve doesn't want to start any arguments. He has enough on his hands already. Now it's Dad's turn.

"Where were you, son? Were you at that party I told you not to go to? You know, the one I heard you talking about? The one with two kegs? I'll bet you were."

His father is right. Steve had been at the party.

Dad continues. "Didn't I tell you that I don't want you going to those crazy parties? You know how I feel about you kids drinking. I won't put up with it. I don't care if all your friends drink. I won't tolerate any teenage alcoholics in this home."

The statement makes Steve burn inside. His father doesn't know what goes on at parties. Steve drinks socially, not to the point of sickness like the rest of his friends. Not wanting to risk a fight, though, Steve bottles up his feelings. His mother starts in again.

"Just who was at the party? Was what's-her-name there? You know, the sleazy little blonde who's always calling this house. I don't know what you see in her anyway. Maybe I don't want to know what you see in her. Do you think I don't know what goes on at these parties? You kids get so drunk and make promises you can't keep. The next thing you know, you're having sex in someone's bedroom. I think some of the things you teenagers do are disgusting. Don't you have any morals at all?"

Again Steve just sits there. He knows there is no point in trying to say anything. He's heard it all before. His parents will never change.

Dad rattles on. "Do you think life is just one party after another? Where are your priorities? You don't even have a job. How do you expect to pay for college? You can't even pay for your own car."

Steve knows what's coming next. His father will take away the car privileges.

"Do you think I'm going to let you use the wagon forever? Right now, I don't think I should allow you to use it at all. A vehicle is for someone who can show some responsibility and respect. Until you show some to your mother and me, you can consider the car off-limits."

Steve sighs. The clash is over. It always ends with punishment of some sort. No big loss. Steve knows he will get the car back for the weekend.

But next week the argument will start again. Steve will come in late, and once again he will hear his parents' assessment of the typical teenager.

Tim Burke

Conflicts

I don't know about other teenagers' parents, but I know mine are still back in the stone age. . . .

When they were young, the girl never asked the guy out or paid for the date. Now girls ask guys out all the time, pick them up, and pay for the date, too. I don't look at that as being tacky, but my parents sure do. . . .

I need money almost every weekend. . . . My parents always tell me, "You should do something that doesn't cost money. I always did." There isn't much to do anymore in my town that doesn't cost money, but there is no way to convince my parents of that. . . .

I wish my parents could get it through their heads that both boys and girls can "get themselves into some sort of trouble." My brother is four years younger than me. On some nights, he can stay out later than I can. . . .

I know my parents are only looking out for my well being, but sometimes I just don't understand their rules. Times change, moms and dads. So instead of trying to stop them from changing, how about moving with them?

> 15-year-old female
> Iowa

Even though we have the same last name, my father doesn't like me. He's very conservative, and I'm kind of punk. I wear wild clothes compared to him. I listen to music too much, and I don't work enough. All we have to do is talk. I think we could close the gap if we both gave in a little.

> Tom Fedro, 16
> Arlington Heights, Illinois

One time I went out with a couple of friends and drank a little too much. I got grounded for three months. My parents told me I was supposed to be setting an example for my little brother and sister. But my dad comes home drunk, and it is no problem. . . . What kind of example is that for me?

> 15-year-old female
> Texas

When I ask my mother where she is going, she usually tells me "out." She almost never gives me a number to call if something comes up. A lot of times she's late, and I'm the one who gets gray hair from the situation.

If I ever told my mom that I was just going "out," I wouldn't leave the house until she knew exactly where I was going and precisely what I was going to do. Also, I better be back when I'm supposed to, or else.

> 15-year-old female
> Massachusetts

If the parents knew exactly what their teenagers did, the teenagers would . . . not be allowed to go out anymore or would be asked to leave the house because they are disgracing the family name. If parents want to close the communication gap with their teenagers, they should be more of a friend and less of a concerned parent.

> 16-year-old female
> Illinois

To my parents, everything is so important. For me, it's . . . live one day at a time and have as much fun as you possibly can. . . . In the past month, there have been so many fights about my attitude on life and school that I have moved out of the house, quit school, and become totally independent.

> 16-year-old female
> Washington

My parent's unwillingness to change has directly affected me. I will be getting married this May 17. The wedding is an arranged marriage. Being Asian Indians, my parents also had an arranged marriage. Even though they have lived in the U.S. for twenty years, they still hold fast to this Indian custom.

My parents fear that I will make a mistake if allowed to marry on my own.

> 16-year-old female
> Iowa

Parents are too overprotective. I can understand caring, but to want to know every minute of your life is a little out of hand. Parents don't call, . . . they just stay out. If kids do that, they get grounded and beaten.

> 15-year-old male
> Texas

The automobile is the universal center for argument between a parent and a teen. . . .

I asked my sister why our parents . . . refused to let me use what I thought had been the family car. My sister was quick to deaden my hopes by explaining the family history to me. . . .

My parents both grew up during the Depression. . . . As children, they were taught to save money, and they didn't have as many luxuries as I know. . . . They are extremely well off now.

My sister pointed out that the two cars in the "family" belong to only two people—my mother and my father. The cars are their possessions just as my stereo is mine. But what my parents don't seem to understand is . . . to keep up with the pace of life now, an automobile is essential . . . I guess after fifty years of penny-pinching, it is hard to convert to the materialistic attitude of today. So . . . it's off to work I go.

> 16-year-old male
> New Jersey

My parents say to me when they are mad, "I put in nine hours today." All I can think of . . . is, "So what?" I got up this morning at 6:30 to do a paper route. Then I prepared and went to school. At 3:15 track practice begins. I usually don't get home until after 5:30. By this time I'm sometimes too tired to eat, but they say they work nine hours a day—that's bullshit.

Their nine hours consist of sitting at a desk answering a phone and having an occasional errand to run. You can tell just how hard work is for them by their fat asses. . . . I would like to see them go through two weeks of conditioning for any active sport.

If more parents could listen to my point of view without blowing up, I don't think they would see us as such lazy people.

> 15-year-old male
> Minnesota

I was picked up by the cops for having alcohol. . . . My parents couldn't believe I'd actually do something like that. They had lost touch with me. . . . They didn't even realize I drank. I had been drinking for about three years. . . .

After that incident, they were ashamed to have me as a daughter. When I tried to explain why I drink, all they did was yell. They don't think I need to drink to be popular. To them, it's just a waste of money and a good way to ruin my life.

They think because they don't drink, neither should I. They are right, but why can't they understand what I'm going through?

> 16-year-old female
> Iowa

I come from a family of 11. I am the second youngest. I cooked, cleaned, and did all of the rest of the housework. My father, when he would come home, would come home drunk and do disgusting things to me, such as have oral sex and beat me. I did not think anything of it because I did not know it was wrong.

My mother would hardly ever be home. She would spend the day over at my grandmother's house. She would help out there instead of at our house. . . .

I moved out about three years ago. I have never gone back. Right now I do not like them, any of them. The year I moved out, I was in school and got hurt. The people at school called over to my grandmother's, where my mother was, to ask if they could send me home so I could go to the hospital. She told them she did not have a daughter named "Sandy." So they called over to where my father works, and he said the same thing. My family disowned me.

> 19-year-old female
> Michigan

The gap between parents and kids has become so severe that . . . millions of kids run away every year. They can't make their parents understand their problems. I have seriously thought about running away sometimes. Me and my step mother don't even speak to each other anymore.

> 14-year-old male
> Texas

Discussion

Runaways

Seattle
Orion Multi-Service Center

Female runaway: My mother is an

alcoholic. My dad is a crazy, screwed up Vietnam vet. When I was 13, I was having difficulty dealing with their divorce and the oncoming step-parents.

Male runaway: I had a hard problem dealing with being adopted. My dad was never there. My mom was crazy. They got divorced. I went onto the streets. It was a mutual decision for me and my mom. Everything built up, and it was like, "We need time away from each other. Goodbye." My first thought was, "I'm glad I'm out of there."

Female: I left because the pressure built up so much. My mother was still drinking, and that had to stop. I couldn't deal with the divorce. I couldn't deal with the step-parents. I was living with my dad, but I wanted to live with my mom. She couldn't take me. Something just snapped. Finally, I said, "I can't deal with this anymore."

When I first left home, I didn't believe that I had done it. It was kind of fun. I had run away before, and I thought my father would take me back in a couple of days. The first couple of days it was really nothing. When I finally called home, they said, "You're not coming home." My first thought was, "To hell with you. I'll show you." I showed them, but I didn't show them how I wanted to show them. That's when I started to get scared and to not know what I was going to do.

I ended up coming downtown. I never got into prostitution, thank God. But I hung around with the kids down there. They always took care of me and made sure I had some place to stay.

Male: When I went out on the street, I was having a lot of fun. I was drinking and doing a lot of drugs. I was involved in prostitution. I didn't really realize what was happening until about a

year ago when the fun started to end. I started getting sick. I stopped the drugs. Drugs screwed my life up. Drugs made me think weird things, and I've done weird things because of drugs. I don't want to mess with them anymore because I don't want to die. I want to live. When I was doing drugs, I never looked for the future. I started looking at the future after I started coming off drugs.

Female: The day-to-day thoughts were more questions with no answers. "Where's the money going to come from? How am I going to get through today?" You don't think about tomorrow on the street. You have to focus all your attention on making it through that day—finding someplace to sleep, finding someplace to eat, finding some cash for whatever you need for it. It was a day-to-day survival thing. There were periods when I couldn't comprehend what was going on because the thoughts were so confusing.

In January last year, things took a turn for the worse. I got pregnant and denied it. I didn't want to face up to it. I didn't go in and get a pregnancy test until I was three and a half months along. By that time, it was too late to get an abortion. I carried through with it, but I didn't have anywhere to live.

Male: I don't think I could ever go back home. I visited my mom this past weekend. We fought all weekend. Our views on things are so different.

Female: There is no way I could go back home. In four years, I haven't said one word to my dad. I've made attempts to contact him. I've sent birthday cards, Fathers' Day cards, and things like that. He just doesn't want to have any contact with me. It creates a problem because my little brothers still live with him. I still see them,

and they get in a lot of trouble. My dad thinks that I'm going to corrupt them into the kind of lifestyle that I'm in. If anything, I'm trying to prove to them, "Man, don't leave home. Just stick it out. Don't get yourself into the mess that I got myself into."

My mom is still married to this man whom I don't get along with. I'd go back if my mom were ever to leave this guy, but not while he is around.

Male: Two summers ago I was in San Francisco, and I wanted to get off the streets. I went to the Larkin Street Youth Center. They referred me up here. I like helping out with physically and mentally handicapped individuals. I'd like to get into art, dance, and theater.

Female: I came to the Orion Center because I was getting hassled by a bunch of pimps in a McDonald's one day. That was about the time the Guardian Angels were running around all over the place. One of them rescued me and started asking me a bunch of questions. They brought me down here.

I'd like to go into criminal psychology. I've been going to college for three quarters now. I want to get married and have a couple of kids. If I have kids, I wouldn't make everything taboo. My parents would say, "You can't

do this." I would automatically go out and do it just to see why I couldn't do it. I hope to be the kind of parent that my kids can talk to.

I would advise kids to try and work things out. Don't consider the streets as the only option because there are other options. The street is the option that is going to ruin you the most. Try and work out a compromise. Parents have to understand their kids are going to rebel. They need to sit down and hear their kids' views and compromise. Be willing to listen. Find time for your kids. Get involved in their problems.

Male: I'd say try and stick it out at home. But I have to say I've learned an enormous amount by being on the streets. I've learned to take care of myself and make decisions. The streets are a good learning experience, but it is hard. It scars you for life because you will always have that in your past. Parents should get to know their kids instead of letting them grow by themselves. Parents should also let their kids know them.

Female: There is still a lot of

confusion, anger, and pain. I need to work through stuff that I've held in. A lot of the anger is directed towards myself—anger for letting myself be this way, hurt because of the things I've done with myself.

My life now is fulfilling. The experiences have been bad, but they have helped me realize things I never would have realized at home. I appreciate things a lot more because I know what it is like to have absolutely nothing.

San Francisco
Huckleberry House

Johannes Troost *Program Manager:* In the past, there were young people running away to experience life. People are still trying to sort their lives out, but in the context of a lot of physical or drug abuse in their family.

Some people run away from home because they're testing their boundaries. They're bumping up against the family's notions of independence. That creates conflict. One of the ways to resolve conflict in a situation like that is to run.

Other kids leave home because there is a good reason for leaving

home. I don't know too many people who want to stay around to get beaten or sexually molested. Running away is a real positive step for them, by saying, "I'm not going to take this anymore."

Another group of kids we see are those who've been pushed out or thrown out by parents so overwhelmed with their own problems they cannot respond to their son or daughter. And they may genuinely love that kid.

The most important thing that we can do is to convince a family that they can make a difference. Parents need to reinvest in their young people, and that's hard to do. There is a definite link between how we see young people, how we encourage them, and the productivity that they're going to give society.

Atlanta
Police Department

Ted Hall *supervisor, youth and missing persons unit:* A number of kids who run away from home have legitimate reasons. They have very abusive parents. A lot of psychologists and sociologists have gone so far as to say, "You show me a runaway kid, and I'll show you a kid who's got a real problem at home."

Families in this country are undergoing tremendous pressures. Fathers are out of the homes, and mothers are the only providers. This is causing a great deal of stress for young people.

Theresa Price *investigator:* It might be an alcoholic parent, incest, or child abuse. The kids just can't deal with it so they leave. They will stay with a friend, and most of them will return home within a couple of days.

With some of them, there isn't enough money in the household. Somebody comes along and says, "Hey, come along with me. I'll take you out to dinner." So they leave. Some of those kids get involved in prostitution. They hook up with a pimp.

Hall: I think that in a lot of cases, the kid wants to make a statement and wants to show the parents that he's committed to making the change in the family. We fool ourselves into believing that the kids will be back when they get hungry. They have to decide between eating and the dangers of the street.

You ask some runaways, "Why did you leave home?" They say, "I can't get along with my mother. She wouldn't let me go to the party." Parents don't have enough trust in their children to let them go to the store or go to a party and come back at a reasonable hour. Therefore, the children get angry and run away. When the parent tries to clamp down on them and they can't handle it, the kids leave.

How can teenagers help solve these problems?

Hall: A solid bond of mutual trust is very important. I would just love to see kids be able to trust their parents, and their parents able to trust the kids. Trust is something that young people must earn. I don't think it is automatic. Once it's earned, it's very important to keep nurturing that relationship. There is nothing better than for a teenager to be in the situation where his parents actually respect him as a person who can make correct decisions. Teenagers should also be understanding towards parents' problems.

Seattle

Ray Jager *counseling coordinator:* The Orion Center serves street kids, particularly those involved in prostitution. We send caseworkers on the streets to contact the kids

and get them into the center. Once we get them into the center, we can provide them with housing and food and mainstream them into their old school.

The kids are in lots of pain. They have been physically abused. They have been sexually abused. They have been neglected. They have been emotionally abused. They have been abandoned. They have been deprived of the basics in life. The problem cuts right across socio-economic standards, race, creed. We have Catholics, Buddhists, Hindus.

Upwards of 80 percent of our clients have been physically or sexually abused at home. One young woman has been on the streets since she was 14. She was physically abused by her father and sexually abused by her mother. She was put in a foster home and was molested by her

foster father. She hit the streets and got into prostitution.

One person that we talked to was a well-dressed, nice-looking guy. He needed money to fix something so he came down to turn a few tricks and get the money he needed. Then he was going to go home, and life would go on until he needed more money.

The kids learn how to get into prostitution from the media. The older ones do it on their own. There are certain areas of town where older prostitutes teach the younger ones how to do it. We were in an area where a 19-year-old woman who had obviously been on the streets for some time was showing a 13-year-old how to walk and how to stand at the street corner—how to advertise. Pimps get involved as they see new faces on the streets. They pick kids up and take care of them.

I think kids initially choose prostitution because they see it as glamorous. It gets them out of abusive situations. Prostitutes will talk about making $300 a night. We have an active caseload of 200. Probably more than fifty percent are male. Some of them are gay, but a few non-gays will do some sort of sexual activity for money. It is either prostitution or starve.

One young man was physically abused a lot by his mother. He still has some scars. She couldn't cope with his being homosexual. He ran away and hit the streets. He became very involved in prostitution and very involved in drugs. But he wants to go home.

Drugs are a form of survival on the streets. It starts with pot. The biggie now is crack. If kids do come here strung out, they will be taken away and their friends will be asked to leave.

Dealing with the drug problem while they are still hustling on the streets is putting the cart before the horse. Once they are committed to change, have different housing, some good food and clothes, and are off the streets, then we can deal with the drug problem and the long-term abuse they have suffered.

One of the solutions is education. I don't think the public is aware of the degree of the problem. A lot of people see it as a choice—the kids choose to get into prostitution. Prostitution is their survival. We see prostitution as child abuse, and I don't think that the general public sees it as that.

We need to look at options. We have kids who have been through nine or ten foster homes. Rather than look at the options, we take them out of one foster home and stick them in another.

Somewhere the kids have fallen through the cracks of the system. They are viewed as hopeless, but I don't think that we can condemn them to a life on the streets.

Communication

Dallas
Wilmer-Hutchins High School

Sheila: My friends have a hard time talking to their parents because they'd rather talk to a friend their own age.

Gary: They'd rather talk to somebody in their own peer group because they go through some of the same things.

Jacqueline Turner *parent:* The parents have gone through the same things you're experiencing. If students would give parents the opportunity, they'd find out that parents could relate to the same thing. It just happened at a different time.

To keep our kids from making the mistakes we did, we parents hold on a little bit tight. Listening to kids, parents hear the same things they said 20 years ago. I thought my parents were old-fashioned. "I'm young, and times are different." I'm sure my daughter says the same thing about me.

Doris Strickland *parent:* A lot of parents don't have time to get close to their children. They want to, but they don't. Then the child becomes too old, and it's too late.

Parents are working now and are real busy. They're not home during the hours their children can talk to them. This is one reason kids talk to their peers rather than to their parents.

Turner: We are losing our children because of the material things that we try to get for them. We give our kids everything they need—that's how we show our love. "I'm going to give my child what I didn't have." Instead of just taking her in my arms and saying, "I love you," I chose to work, work, work to give her everything. But I lost

her. All kids want is love and understanding.

Martin: In our family, most members are home about the same time. When my father comes home from work, I try to find a time to talk to him. But he reads the newspaper, eats, and watches a movie so I don't know when to break in.

Gerald Henderson *parent:* Don't you think he would stop and hold a conversation when he comes in and sits down with the newspaper?

Martin: He probably would, but you don't want to take that chance. He could say, "I'm tired, and I've been working. Give me a chance to sit down." So you say, "Okay, I'm going to let him sit down for a little while and take a break."

Sheila: Almost every night before we get ready to go to bed, I go up to my mom and say, "Mom, I love you." And we just start talking.

Turner: I could talk to my dad about a boy, but I couldn't talk to my mom. I'd just mention a boy's name, and she'd go wild. "You better not do anything. I am not taking care of any baby." I wouldn't say anything to her.

Sheila: I think it would be neat if your mother would tell you something about herself and ask you to tell her something. You could bring out your inner selves.

Strickland: The communication lines should be open early. Then it wouldn't be a last resort when we have to talk. If communication starts when the kid is young and has an open mind, then we can talk any time.

Lombard, Illinois
Glenbard East High School

Brad: I communicate fairly freely with my parents, but my parents come from a different era. They don't think quite the same.

They're also gone a fair amount of the time.

Sue: There is no communication gap between my parents and me. I tell them everything. They trust me. When I go out, I tell them exactly what I do. They don't have any problems with that because they know I'm telling them what really happened.

Sharing your lives is the basis for preventing the communication gap. If I went home and my parents weren't interested in what I did, we would have a bigger communication gap.

Magnus Seng *parent:* I don't share, nor do I want to share, all the things that my teenager goes through. Nor does he want to share all the things I go through. I think that there should be an atmosphere that we can share when we want to share. One of the problems is we've got to be there at the same time to communicate. When we come home from work, we're shot. Sometimes he's shot.

The way I approach his social life and the way his mother approaches his social life are radically different. His mom goes into great detail: "Who'd you go with? How many were there? What did you do? What time did you get home?" And my question is, "Where've you been?"

Womazetta: Sometimes you get aggravated because you get tired of being told to do things. Then Mom says, "God, you are in a grumpy mood." But in my house you do not raise your voice at your mother. You do not talk back.

Seng: Shouldn't kids be able to tell their parents to go shove it?

Womazetta: I think so, but that's definitely out of the question at my house.

Kris: How many times do you tell your parents, "I have a real tough problem, and I have to talk to you about it?"

Womazetta: There are things that I can tell my mother, but there are things that I cannot. There are a lot of things you can't talk to anybody about.

Dave: "Gee Ma, I don't feel well. My stomach is upset"—that's about the limit of my explanations for things. I never come home drunk, and I never get in a fight at school. So there's trust.

Brad: The cool part is when your parents have experienced things. The one thing I still can't talk to my parents about is drinking. They are not able to relate to that because it wasn't a part of their childhood.

Kris: That's true. My mom went to Glenbard East, and only the guys drank. They'd drop the girls off and then go to someone's house and drink.

Seng: It's an entirely different phenomenon. When I grew up, we didn't have to deal with booze at parties.

Brad: You need an open mind. One of the coolest people I know is my adopted grandmother. She's 80 or so, and she's able to talk about anything—sex, drugs, or whatever. She hasn't gone through it, but she's open to talk, which is something that my parents still aren't able to do.

Minneapolis
South High School

Jon: My parents never know what's going on in my life. They want to know when I go out and where I'm going to be, but other than that . . . . If I'm not home for dinner, they usually don't know where I am—whether I'm at work or at school.

Mary: My parents started very young with my brother and me about sexuality and knowing our bodies and the different stages we go through. I'll probably do it with my kids.

Jon: I get this little confirmation book every once in a while. When I was in junior high, I'd go up to bed and there would be a little book on my bed. I'd throw it on my shelf. I can't talk to my parents, and I've never been able to.

Adam: My parents were just remarried. My stepfather is 66, and my mother is 43. He's brought up three children so he doesn't want to deal with the teenager and loud noise. As far as going to him for advice, sure, as long as it's not personal.

Mary: My parents and I get along fine, but there is a communication gap because my dad's 67 and my mom's 53. They kind of understand, but it seems like they've forgotten what they've gone through.

Brian: My friends are more on my level. My parents forgot what they used to do when they were little. They used to be just as bad, but they don't remember that.

Tammy: I can talk to my mom but not my dad. I think my dad was the same way with his parents. He never talked to them. He doesn't want to talk to anybody.

Jon: My dad was brought up not talking to anyone, and he doesn't communicate well. Try to convince him he's wrong. God forbid.

Kyle: You can see that it's wrong, but he'll go, "No, it's not wrong." If he finally decides he's wrong and can't argue the point anymore, he'll usually walk away and mumble something. You can't get him to say that he's wrong.

Los Angeles
Zion Baptist Church in Watts

Philip: There is a communication gap between all parents and all teenagers. The parent should try to understand how the child feels, and attempt to meet the need and the love that the child requires.

Sherry Smith *parent:* As a parent, I want my children to confide anything that happens to them. Having been a child myself at one time, I know teens can't always do that. I would never tell my mother a lot of things because of the way she might react.

Paul Henderson *parent:* A typical father says, "I wouldn't want my daughter pregnant out of wedlock." So if the daughter becomes pregnant, she already knows how the father feels about it. So she may hide it as long as she can because she knows it is going to hurt her father.

The father is not going to disown the child, but hiding the pregnancy indicates that the child didn't trust the father and didn't care enough to tell the father. On the other hand, if a child does tell a parent everything, the parent isn't going to approve. But I think the parent and child can work things out.

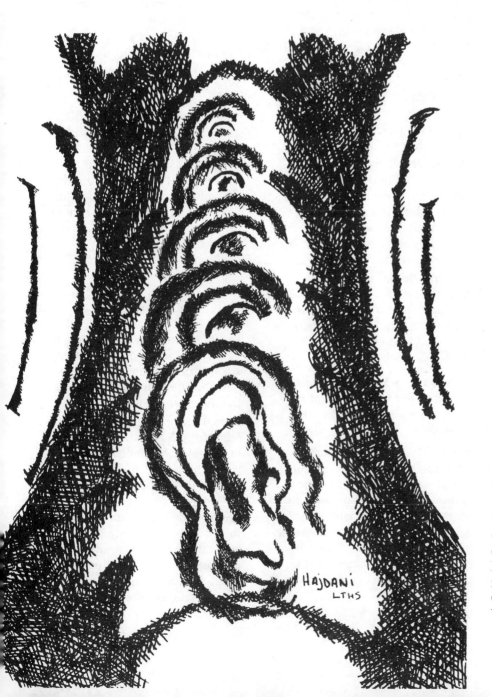

Red Oak, Texas
Red Oak High School

Dawn: Anytime I go to my dad, he says, "I don't really have time to listen to this." When I get something, I ask him what he thinks about it. "I don't care. It's yours."

But when my mom gets mad at something, he jumps on my case—like when I get a bad grade in school. When I get good grades, he doesn't really care. When I do anything bad, he crabs at me.

My mom said, "He cares, but he just can't show it. That's the way he was brought up." I think, "Gosh, sometimes he could show it instead of ignoring me." For my birthday, he has never gotten me anything. He walks in, "Happy birthday." Walks out.

Washington, D.C.
Family Research Council

Jerry Regier *executive director:* For teens to communicate with their parents, a reservoir of trust has to be built. If we have a pattern of letting our children tell us everything that is going on and then being caring, teens will continue to confide. But if there is any sense that acceptance is contingent upon their actions, then it is very difficult for children to confide honestly.

When communication breaks down, families need a third party. There is a stage when teens think other people know more than their parents. It's very important to have other people to talk to, whether it be teachers, youth leaders, or sports stars.

I think mutual respect comes from communication and consistency. If parents are consistent, the kids respect them. For instance, I don't believe kids respect shallow religion in parents. Or rules that don't make sense. You have to be able to trust each

IN ONE EAR AND OUT THE OTHER

other. You have to be open and fair.

Teenagers want to know what the parameters are. Rules give kids an option to say no to their friends, even if they have to blame their parents for it. Sometimes teens want to say no to one another and want an excuse. One of the best excuses is, "My parents won't let me do this." They may be mad, but inside they are glad.

A parent's view of the family is the view of responsibility. "I'm responsible for these people. I brought them into the world. I'm responsible to make sure they are ready to face the world." Also, the parent is concerned about leadership. "How can the whole group be strengthened, be happy, and have their needs met?" A child's view of the family is more self-oriented. "How does this family help or hinder me in doing what I want to do?" The teen years are when people move from that idea to "What can I contribute to this family?" By the end of those years, there is a sense of responsibility.

Trust

Dallas

Martin: I think that parents should know about the person you want to take out—to a certain point. But I also feel that I'm not getting married to her. I just want to take her out to see if I really like her.

Turner: The only time I wanted my dates to meet my parents was when I felt that I really cared

deeply for the boy.

Sheila: I should think every boy would want to meet their girlfriend's mom. Then they can say, "I've got her mom all in a bag, and I can take my girl anywhere I want." If they don't want to meet my mom, I say, "You're gone." I want to meet his family, too.

Martin: I feel that if I want to have any sexual activity or if I want to date, it is up to me. I don't want my parents to know because I have such respect for them.

Sheila: I think my mom should know when I'm doing it. My mama found some contraceptives in my sister's purse. She didn't say too much about it because she said, "I'd rather see her with them than without them."

Turner: I think I want my daughter to tell me, but in reality I wouldn't want to know. I don't think a girl would tell her parents that. And I don't think a boy would either.

Gary: Parents know on their own. Nobody's got to tell. I want my mom to know, but she knows anyhow.

Sheila: My mama always says, "You can't fool Mama. I'm going to know anyways. Just let me know so I can get you some birth control pills." But it isn't easy to tell your mama that you are ready for birth control pills. When my neighbor's kids become 12, the parents put them on birth control pills. They don't care if they need them or not.

Lombard, Illinois

Gerri Long *parent:* When I was growing up, my parents trusted me greatly. I had a lot more freedom than maybe some of you have, but I feel it's because I earned their trust.

Kris: When I started high school, my mom said, "Who were you with? Why were you with them? What were you doing? What time will you be home?" It's her business because I'm her child, but I felt like, "I don't even want to tell you."

I don't like her telling me, "Be home at that time. You can't be five minutes later." Also, I don't like her asking me why I'm with certain people. We had a lot of fights my freshman and sophomore years. Junior and senior years she started letting up.

I can tell her, "Yeah, I was at a party. Yeah, there was beer." And she is like, "Oh, all right." She trusts me, and that makes me feel better. I'm not saying the more she lets me do, the more I like her. But the more she trusts me, the more we coincide.

Sue: A lot of times, when I get a letter from a friend, I'll toss it on my dresser. My mom thinks she owns the world so she goes in and reads a little bit of the letter.

One time I had beer tabs on my dresser. My mom said, "What are these?" I said, "Mom, those are beer tabs. I took them off the cans and put them on my dresser. What are you doing in my room?" She doesn't like me to go in her room.

During the summer I was dating this guy. My parents thought he was pretty bogus. I was losing weight, and my mom thought I was on drugs. When I wasn't home, she'd go look in my room to see if she could find something. I could tell she'd been in my room because I'd leave things a certain way, but she wouldn't put them back the same way.

Tammy: My parents have always trusted me and my sisters. They went to San Francisco and left me with both cars. I had a set of car keys before I was 15, before I had my learner's permit, just in case.

Jon: When I say I'm going to be in at a certain time, my parents just go to sleep. If I'm not in, they never know the difference unless I am loud. I don't abuse that trust. If I'm 15 minutes or half an hour late, I don't worry about it. But if I'm later than that, I call.

My parents encourage me to drive when I go out with my friends because they trust my judgment. But they don't necessarily trust my friends whom they don't know. My parents pay for gas, insurance, repairs— everything. They just want me to know that they trust me. Knowing that, I don't abuse that trust.

Adam: My parents will go to the cabin for a weekend and leave me alone. They say, "Be in by 12. We might call." I know they're not going to call so I have the liberty to come in at 3 in the morning. Maybe that's abusing the trust.

Silver Springs, Maryland
A private home

Norma Irvin *mother:* I told our kids that we trust them until they prove they really can't be trusted. A little lie now and then—I'm sure everybody does that. The basic goal is truthfulness.

Ben, Jr. *teenager:* I hope that they have enough trust in me to think that I'm not going to do anything foolish. So I don't have to explain to them what I did on a date. But I guess I'd tell them if they'd want to know.

Norma: Parents have to realize that teenagers are no longer children. They have to be responsible for their own actions. That is very hard for parents to accept. As we get older, we don't have control over them. Teens have to learn what they should and shouldn't do on their own. Hopefully with the teaching at home, they're not going to make many mistakes.

Rules and punishment
Dallas

How effective are rules?
Sheila: I think they're very effective. It isn't like my mom sat down and told me, "I don't want you to do that." But I know what I'm supposed to do. If my mom lets me use the car, I'm not going to mess around because I want to use it again.

Martin: When parents don't enforce rules they have set, that leaves an area between the parent and child which needs to be bridged. If you set a rule but do not enforce it, that's not fair.

Why do parents treat sons and daughters differently?
Henderson: The father says, "As soon as that boy turns 17, I'm going to take him down to the drugstore and train him right."

Turner: A girl is just the opposite. Gerald is going to take his son after someone else's daughter. But if a young man comes for Gerald's daughter, he is ready to kill him.

Henderson: It's a chauvinist attitude. I want my son to grow up and be able to take care of his household. He'll be able to satisfy a woman.

Kris: My mom says, "I'm the mother. I make the rules. You obey." It's like a communist dictatorship.

Womazetta: When I go out with a bunch of friends, my mom never tells me what time to be home. She says to use my judgment. I think she's really afraid of me growing up and going away and never coming back. But she pretty much lets me do what I want.

Brad: I was fortunate that I had two older brothers so my parents were already broken in. They had already gone through the problems of having kids come home late and knowing about what goes on. I'm in drama, and so was my brother, so they let me stay out all night at cast parties.

Seng: If I had a daughter, I'd probably worry a lot more. When I was growing up, my mother was always down on my five sisters. I had no restrictions.

Brad: I have some friends whose parents will ground them if they're two minutes late. It's ridiculous.

Maybe we'd be better off without curfews. When I was a little kid, my parents let me stay up as late as I wanted. They figured I'd learn when I couldn't get up in the morning. They still made me get up and go to school so I got the idea. I think maybe if we didn't have curfews, we'd learn on our own.

Dave: The rules are necessary, though. We have to live within guidelines all our lives.

Seng: Rules are not a teaching tool as much as they are for the peace and comfort of the parent. I like to know when my son is supposed to be home. I don't worry ahead of time, but if my son is not home on time, then my wife wakes me up to worry with her. So I get mad at him for being late because I get disturbed.

Meaghan: My parents have always told me that they set the standards because they want me to know that they care. They've seen families where the parents didn't tell the kids when to come in and didn't give them any sort of responsibility. The kids resented the parents: "You don't care about me. You are not worried about me."

Brad: Aren't there other ways to show that? I think they show that through talking with you and being very honest with you. I don't know anyone who has felt neglected because of a lack of curfews.

Womazetta: When I go pick up a friend, I hear their parents say, "Be home at this time." Then we go to my house, and my mom says nothing. I feel like, "God, she doesn't even want to tell me what to do." So it sounds good to be able to do whatever you want, but if you lived with it for 16 years, it's not that great. Sometimes you do feel that you aren't loved. My mom would buy me pretty much everything I wanted. It was like she bought this stuff so she wouldn't have to give me any love. I've felt like that for a long time.

Long: If you know that you have parents who care, you are not going to go against them, out of respect. However, what happens in that family where the children feel that their parents don't care?

Kris: Curfews are just like more of the rules you have to follow. My mom always says, "You have to be in at this time. You have to clean your room before you go out." Otherwise, my privileges are denied. Sometimes I can work around them. For example, I can do my chores the next day, but they have to be done.

Decatur, Georgia
Mt. Carmel High School
Allison: My parents have five

kids, and they were different with every one. My parents were really strict with me because the first three kind of freaked out. They always came down a lot harder on me. It was confusing when I was a kid, but now I'm kind of glad for it.

Jodie: My parents weren't very strict with my brother. He's not really bad, but he's mischievous and gets in a little trouble. It seems that they are being really strict with me. I'm an entirely different person from my brother. They just don't see that.

Allison: Whenever my brother got punished, he'd get a restriction for six months and be off in three days. But if I got a restriction, I'd get on it for six months and be lucky to be off it in seven.

Amy: I always get blamed for whatever happens. If something is missing, if something goes wrong, it's always me, it's never my brother. I don't think it's fair.

My brother is a straight-A student. He's never gotten in trouble. He's never told my parents a lie, and he doesn't cuss or drink. I'm kind of the opposite of that. They expect me to be as good as he is. It drives me crazy. It makes me hate my brother, and it makes me hate my parents. I

think they should treat us equally.

How should parents correct behavior problems?

Allison: A couple of years back, my parents were having real problems with me. I got in trouble one time, and they put me in a juvenile detention center. They just left me there. I don't think I ever did anything wrong again.

Amy: I think they should sit down and have a long conversation. Get out all their feelings. I don't think they should send you away. My parents sent me to boarding school. I didn't think that was a very good way of handling the problem.

Allison: Does it work to talk? My parents used to talk to me, but I'd sit there and nod and smile and say, "You're so right." Then I'd go out and do the same thing again.

Divorce
Lombard, Illinois

Is divorce justifiable?

Kris: My parents were married for twelve years. I'm glad they got a divorce because now everything is better in their lives. Maybe not in my life or in my little brothers' lives. I wish they were still together, but they can't possibly be together. Divorce is a horrible experience.

Seng: If you are able to fall out of love, you should be able to fall out of a marriage. There are some marriages where the relationship just deteriorates and where it's doing more harm than good for the kids.

Long: Young people are getting married saying, "Well, if it doesn't work out, we can get a divorce." When we were growing up, divorce was not prevalent. There were some who did divorce, but they were looked down upon.

Meaghan: When you get married, you should stay married. If you realize that marriage is a commitment and you have to make it work, then you can make it work. Instead of saying, "How can we make this work? How can we keep our relationship and our love for each other strong?" Divorce makes it easier to say, "I don't love you anymore," because there is a way out.

Sue: But why live miserably? You can't stop two people from growing apart.

Pat Meyer *teacher:* It is too easy to get out of a relationship now. But I don't think people should stay together just to stay together. That's very damaging. Among my friends who have gotten divorces, marriage and divorce just seemed to be the right thing to do. "Oh, let's get married." Two years later things didn't work out well "so let's just head off to the divorce court." Maybe people should live together for a few years.

Kris: I was talking to my grandmother about living together. I said, "Would you buy a pair of shoes before trying them on? Would you buy a car without test driving it first?"

How does divorce affect children?

Meaghan: If you grow up without a father, you have very little identity.

Sue: I know a lot of people whose parents are divorced who have a very good identity. I don't think that people who don't love each other should be forced to live together just because some priest is saying divorce is wrong.

Minneapolis

Mary: When I was little, all my friends' parents were divorced. When mine came home from work, I asked, "Why can't you be divorced like everyone else?" Now I consider myself lucky.

Kyle: When I was really young, my mom used to drive off when she was mad. I was really worried that my parents were going to get a divorce. But now that I've talked

to them, I realize that they have a really good relationship. I don't worry about it anymore.

I realize that parents fight, and I say, "Okay, I'll get out of the house. I'll be back in two hours when you guys are talking again."

Los Angeles

How does divorce affect teenagers?

Philip: Most people just go on about their own business. Some people isolate themselves from other people. They may slack off in school, and they may have few friends.

Henderson: Single parents are not as strict, and they don't want to discipline because they don't want the child not to love them.

Seattle

What are the problems caused by divorce?
Sister Vera Gallagher *principal of Good Shephard Sisters Homes:* The

children of divorce never know when the current mom or pop is going to split. Divorce causes the inability to trust anyone, the feeling that they had better get the better of other people before other people get the better of them, and a great deal of anger which results in aggression.

Sometimes there is fear of losing the person the child loves. Sometimes there is fear of loving a person lest they should lose that person. A kind of rootlessness—if the home doesn't stay together, what does? Another problem is suicide. The loss of a mother or father or the inability to tolerate a new mother and father can cause depression.

Sometimes divorced parents try to play the children off each other. Dad may try to give better presents than Mom. The children learn that they can manipulate everybody. Sometimes parents disappear. The family becomes

'IT'S HALF PAST... OH, YOU BASTARD!'

very poor so the child lashes out. Sometimes the parent marries someone with whom the child is not compatible so the teenager decides to move out. There is no way to get a job so the child ends up involved either in theft or in prostitution.

I am inclined to think that a great deal of divorce is due to the lack of religious values and to the lack of a sense of fidelity. Americans want gratification fast. We aren't willing to work over ten or fifteen years to make something work. "If it doesn't work, why not try the next one?"

Also, the lack of moral and religious values causes family breakdowns. We made a study of 150 children sent to us from the juvenile department. Most of them didn't have a religion. It is hard to get through life if one doesn't have some philosophy. It often seems to teenagers that everything has fallen apart. Religion gives them a sense that there is something stable in life.

Families don't do enough with each other. Both parents work. I know they are tired and need to take time for themselves, but if they aren't giving time to their children, there isn't going to be interaction. It doesn't depend on piles of time but quality time.

The only profession in the world for which no one gets any training is marriage. I would like to see good courses on marriage in the school.

I wish there were after-divorce counseling available for parents.

And maybe after-divorce support groups so that they can talk out their anger and not have to lash out at the children.

I think love is missing from a lot of homes. I've been asked, "Do you think that love can cure all?" And my answer is, "Yes, I do."

Washington, D.C.

What causes divorce?

Regier: Increasingly we see parents who are looking for their own self-fulfillment rather than the family's fulfillment. That attitude leads to the easy disintegration of the family. "If this family is not meeting my needs, I don't have to take this." There is an attitude of not sacrificing for the family—on both sides.

The root of divorce is misunderstanding coupled with lack of commitment. If you go into marriage as a lifetime commitment, you can go through a lot of tough times. But if you go into marriage with an attitude of, "We'll see if it'll work," the grass looks greener on the other side of the fence.

How does divorce affect children?

Regier: I think we will not know the total implications of divorce on children for another generation. But research has shown that kids who come out of separated families face more questions relating to self-esteem. Many times kids experience guilt. There can be a lot of resentment built up against the father or mother. I think kids have coped phenomenally well. It is a miracle that kids are as well adjusted as they are.

Divorce can also lead to entering marriage tentatively. There is a tendency to do the same thing the parents did. Like in child abuse—those who were abused as children tend to abuse their child. Kids are going to say, "A breakup is not going to happen to me." But when they face tough times, they will get divorced unless they have a source beyond themselves.

Even though I strongly believe that divorce should not take place, it doesn't mean that single parents can't be successful. But I don't think there is any way to replace the influence of the other parent. For single parents to say, "We're successful without a father" is a delusion. Single families work out of default and determination of the single parent. A single mother can perform what's necessary—provide for the needs and emotional support—but she cannot be a father.

The lack of a parent may make kids resentful that they don't have that support. It can also make them more determined to succeed. Having two parents presents a

model in terms of the development of a child sexually and the view of human beings, life, and family.

I don't think that death affects a child as much as divorce. Research bears this out. In divorce, you have a parent absent but somewhere else. In death, the parent is absent, but there is some finality to it.

How can divorce be controlled?

Regier: According to a survey, the top characteristics that make families strong are spending time together, communicating, dealing with crisis situations, and having some religious component to family life.

A religious component contributes a base for their value system, a strength outside of the family for dealing with crisis, and a bond in a common purpose. Families that do not have any religious component can come up with that kind of purpose and goal, but I don't think that it is as strong.

Influences

Dallas

How do parents influence their children?

Turner: My parents forced me to go to school, but I didn't want to go to school. My greatest ambition was to become a prostitute. That was all I ever wanted to do. I would have been a prostitute had they left me alone, but they wouldn't leave me alone.

I had to dress a certain way, act a certain way, and talk a certain way. I was not an individual. I was Jack and Theresa Anderson's daughter. I wanted simply to be Jacqueline Anderson. But I wasn't because of what they were trying to make me. They were trying to mold me and make me be something I wasn't.

Henderson: I won't bother my kid about playing sports even though

he can play. I was basically determined that my son was going to play ball. Now he even hates to watch it on TV. It was a case of me instilling in him what I couldn't finish.

Turner: You can badger them, but that makes them choose the opposite. I made the same mistake. Why not let a child determine his own future? Parents can be the guiding force, but they should let the child choose what he or she wants to be. Let them say, "Whatever your great aspirations are, I can't fulfill them for you. You can advise me and tell me examples or different choices, but let me make the final choice. Don't impose anything on me."

Silver Spring, Maryland

Ben Irvin, Sr. *Father:* Religion plays a major role in the life of our family. Ever since the kids were small, they've been taught by my wife and me and reinforced by the church to know what's right and wrong and what's an acceptable code of conduct and behavior.

We have four children—two girls who led good clean lives and two boys who never got in trouble with the law. That's unusual in this day. That's all interrelated to the values that are taught by the family and reinforced by the church.

If a parent says one thing but does another, the children will do what the parent does and not what the parent says. If the parent says, "Don't drink alcohol because I don't want you to turn out like me," but drinks all the time, the kids will probably end up drinking alcohol.

The goal of a parent is not to protect the child but to prepare the kids to go out. Even though it's hard on a parent when their children leave, that's really what parenting is all about—to prepare children for life.

Compiled by Christine Anderson

"MY BAGS ARE PACKED. IM LEAVING YOU FOR A TALLER WOMAN."

Solutions

If we just do what our parents say, there would be a lot less problems with our parents. Just because they're our parents doesn't mean they're always wrong or always against us. They really do know our best interests.

Julie Adams, 18
Arlington, Texas

Teenagers wanting to be independent need time alone and . . . privacy.

Parents have to trust their kids enough to leave them alone.

Frouwkje Gilkey, 16
Chicago, Illinois

The communication gap can be closed by setting one or two nights a week down for discussion. There can be a set dinner time when discussion takes place instead of watching the television or reading the newspaper. If parents wouldn't always give their children the third degree . . . when they go out

and not ground them for coming home five or ten minutes late, they would receive more respect. . . . If children would listen to their parents and respect what they say, teenagers will soon understand what their parents say . . . is for our own good.

Liz Link, 14
Dubuque, Iowa

More and more parents are trying to get to know the teenage sons and daughters better and the kind of pressure they go through. And more teenagers are opening up to their parents and telling them how they feel and care. I think the gap can be closed by having parents and teenagers show their true feeling toward one another.

Pat Maloney, 14
Dubuque, Iowa

With both parents working now, it is very hard to talk to your parents. The parents usually talk to each other about what they did during the day. Do they ask the kids about their day? No, and that's why most teenagers become further apart from their parents. Parents need to realize their child has problems, too. We go to school, and some problems develop during the day that we'd like to talk about.

16-year-old female
Illinois

My family, although our conversations sometimes end in heated arguments, tell each other what is on our minds. Even something like, "Dad this chicken is overcooked" may lead to a discussion, but it's the discussion about the comment that is important. It brings it all together.

Claire Baldikoski, 17
Elmhurst, Illinois

I think more authority is needed in the home. Parents are shy and unsure of how to communicate with their children. This causes the children to feel unloved and as though nobody cares about their accomplishments. In homes where the parents take authority, there is a closer bond between parents and children.

Kids need to be taught

responsibility and how to grow up. If they are unsure of their parents' values, it is very difficult for them to set their own values straight. I think more than anything else, more communication is needed in the homes of children.

Jennifer Allen, 15
Brookfield, Connecticut

Both the teen and the parent should look at each other more as friends than family. By doing that, it is easier to talk to one another.

I wish my mother would be able to be my friend instead of an authority. Why can't some parents understand that kids would like to have a friendship with them?

16-year-old male
Illinois

Teenagers think that if they attempt to share a true problem with their parents, their parents will . . . lose respect for them. . . . It is just the opposite. If you come to your parents and talk to them and be open, they will be glad to hear the truth from you. They will also know more about what to expect from you. . . . If you just communicate more with your parents, you will win the trust and respect that you were scared you'd be losing.

Loria Thatcher, 16
Hinsdale, Illinois

If parents and children smoked more pot together, they could open the routes of communication more easily and just basically get along better.

17-year-old female
Michigan

What students don't realize is that parents are usually doing what's best for their children. They also don't realize that their parents were kids, too. They know where they made their mistakes. They want their kids to avoid the same ones they made.

Eli Marks, 17
Clearwater, Florida

As soon as I turned 16, I started having major problems with my parents. I started hanging around people they disapproved of, . . . staying out late, and partying. Whenever I came home, they'd ask me where I had been, and with whom, and why did my clothes always smell like smoke? I'd get mad at their questions, but I'd sit there and lie my way out of them.

The real trouble came when a friend and I decided to go to a three-night party over spring break. We'd come home in the morning to shower and change clothes, but we'd go back after supper to stay all night again. By the end of the third night, I came home so bombed that my parents knew something was up. They made a few phone calls, and "Wham," I was in a whole lot of trouble.

Things were really rough at first. I started going to a psychologist, and so did they. I think it helped a little, but what really helped more was just to sit down and communicate with them like an adult—no raised voices or accusations, just a mature discussion where both sides were voiced and listened to. I started to respect them more and to want to earn their trust.

16-year-old female
Illinois

Chapter 2.

Students and Teachers

The time has come for a revelation: High school serves as a life-support system for teens.

Take away the pencils, the paper, the books. Take away the lockers, the hallways, the classrooms. Take away the teachers. Take away the coaches. Take away the administrators. Then take away all the school friends.

What happens then? What the hell happens to American teenagers then?

Let's imagine.

"Okay, boys and girls, there will be no high school today, no high school tomorrow either. In fact, no high school ever." The cheering after an announcement like this could be deafening.

But what would happen to these teenagers who were "laid off"? They could hang out at home all day. Watch TV.

No parents around to nag them about doing homework. No homework! They could invite all their friends over to party their brains out.

But wait! Once high school terminates, these teens would lose the greatest thing school has to offer: a link to other teens. In the absence of their friends who would they turn to for support? They certainly couldn't expect their parents to fill in this role.

They also couldn't count on their parents for handouts of ten dollar bills. The teenagers would have to make it on their own. Alone, they'd have to explore work, discover activities, and search for support. But this search would be only the beginning of their struggle for survival.

Not all would be able to find what they need. Hordes of teenagers who normally don't go to high school already wander the streets during daytime hours. Conflict, strife, and potential injury await the inexperienced teenagers. The real world would jolt them. Many could get lost in evil passages. Few would find a match for high school . . . .

Maybe American teenagers should re-think their situation. A foray into this fantasy could reveal to them the importance of high school in their lives.

Why? Why is high school so important?

And if high school *is* so important, why do so few teenagers really want to go? Why do they go to high school when they desire to do otherwise?

Most teenagers won't admit to their real need for high school. Ask one on the street:

Ace Whole: "Excuse me, teenager, do you like to go to high school?"

Tina Jirr: "What are you, some kind of a comedian?"

But at times teens express their need for high school through private talk:

Anne Irole: "My parents can be a real pain in the ass! What do they know? Sure,

I try to talk to them, but they're like walls, preaching walls. I must find someplace to escape to. For now, take me to school. I need to get away."

Even those who'd rather not have to study recognize the value of being in a high school environment.

Stud E. Hall: "I hate school. I hate the stupid competition for being in the top 10 percent. You get caught proving yourself intelligent, and parents think you can get good grades in everything. If it weren't for my friends, I would've given up a long time ago. What the hell, I want to enjoy school. I don't want to sit up all night trying to get a damn A in everything."

Fay Leur: "My friends are my life. They save me from hell. They are real family. They understand me. I wish we could all live somewhere without any hassle of home, school, and work."

Cliff Noats: "Who cares about school? Just keep me connected to my life. Drugs and booze stimulate my brain. Girls—sex means satisfaction. The gang—we talk, act, and dress the way we want. It's our music. It's our cruising. Freedom to do what we want. Sure, there's other things. But for now, This is what I want. With the gang, I'm a somebody, not some damn corpse in a gutter with problems."

Jack Strap: "How the hell should I know what the asymptotes of the graph of tangent x are! I can hit any ball out of the park any time. Just hand me a bat! I need baseball. I need basketball. Any damn sport will do. It's all I want. It's all I can do. Get those damn books out of my face! Let me live my life. I need the team."

Connie Fusion: "I'm afraid, What am I going to do? Is school a waste? I don't know what I want. Actually, I do know. But does it fit with reality? Will I have to end somewhere in a place where I don't want to be? I have no choice but to go to school for now. But then what? Will I do what I like? I'm afraid."

All the pencils, paper, and books. All the lockers, hallways, and classrooms. Against this background teens grapple with teachers, coaches, administrators, and themselves. Classes are only one part of the experience. High school serves a much greater purpose.

Teens learn in their own ways as their adult selves take shape and grow. Their high school "family" guides them through a maze into the real world. There they awaken to the revelation that high school served as their life-support system.

Julio Flores

Conflicts

Athletics in school are stressed far too much. Sure, they are important for social development, but often . . . young athletes' grades suffer for a winning season. . . . Is it really worth messing up one's life for one winning season?

In my school some teachers favor the athletes while others do quite the opposite. I guess what bugs me the most is how my school spends all their extra money buying new uniforms— and other sports-related expenses— while other departments are grossly ignored.

Patty Wurscher, 17
Bettendorf, Iowa

I think there is too much emphasis on athletic ability and not enough emphasis on what you do with your ability to learn. I am more interested in learning something than throwing a ball in the air. I'm not putting down athletics. If people would study as much as they concentrate on athletics, this world would be a much better place.

Lori Lehman, 18
Uniontown, Pennsylvania

I find that too many teachers do not

express a desire for the student to learn. They are not excited about their profession. . . . Right off, a student can perceive if the instructor is really interested in you as an individual, not a number. Perhaps some teachers will complain that this is too much work. . . . But if we are given a chance, maybe all that we need is a push in the right direction and a smile.

Jennifer Norton, 18
Bakersfield, California

Just because an athlete doesn't make straight A's, people will tend to think they're dumb. . . . People think because you're an excellent athlete, you should automatically be an excellent student. Just think of all the gifted students that barely have enough coordination to walk and chew gum at the same time.

Jim Dalzell, 18
Uniontown, Pennsylvania

I once had a teacher who . . . made it quite clear . . . that she could easily be taken over by her students. . . . The rest of the year she never gained control of her classroom

and was often not at school. She never had respect because she never showed she wanted any. If a teacher lets her students misbehave, then it seems she doesn't care enough about them.

Vaughne Glennie, 14
Tucson, Arizona

If someone's relative, a close one, had died, a person tends to be depressed, uninterested, and not caring about school. That's how it was with me, anyhow. One of my teachers said she didn't care, even if it was my own mom—that it's my responsibility to get my homework done. . . . That certainly didn't encourage me to learn.

14-year-old female
California

Jocks think they own the school. They go around causing trouble and get away with it. They get passed for playing sports.

I definitely don't like preps because they don't do anything all day in school. They just sit in the yearbook room all day. It's hard to tell what they do in there. Every time they come out of the room, a massive screen of smoke comes pouring out. Of course, they get away with it. . . . Most of the time they run around the halls and

talk to the principal in between classes without a pass. Nobody says nothing.

18-year-old male
Pennsylvania

No matter how much talent an athlete has, if he doesn't get passing grades, he shouldn't be able to play. . . . Last year I was supposed to be on the baseball team and start as shortstop. Because of my poor grades, I was not eligible to play. I was smart enough to realize what happened to me. So I took summer school classes to make up for what I had failed before. I feel I am more responsible. . . .

Favoritism is part of this problem. Many teachers pass student athletes so they can play in their sports even if they don't deserve it. They think they are doing a favor to the kids. But down the road they are going to realize that it hurt them more than it helped.

Joe Gill, 18
La Claire, Iowa

In my junior year, I took American history. The teacher had a bad attitude towards low grades and the "not-so-smart" people in the class. He also had the appearance of a stuffy, no-fun old man. I wasn't having a good year, and my grades showed. I started off pretty good, but then I started to drop. He criticized me instead of showing concern. . . .

His attitude towards me then made a big difference. At the time, I thought . . . it's me, I just don't understand history. But it wasn't me. It took me having to repeat a half year of history to find that out.

I aced all the tests, and it's not just that I took them last year. It has more to do with the teacher I now have. He tries to bring us up to his level. He has more pep. If you do poorly, he tries to help. When you do better, he sends his praise. . . .

17-year-old female
Arizona

I've only had one really bad student-teacher relationship. . . . She treats her students like elementary kids. . . . She'll single out and embarrass one student. I

C. HUTH ATHS

hate going to her classroom because I fear it will be me that she'll decide to make an example of today.

17-year-old female
South Carolina

A big problem with our system of education is the lack of encouragement given to students from school teachers, board members, and other school personnel. . . .

When a student is treated unjustly by a teacher or other school employee, it dulls the attitude towards school and the quality of one's work. You can't unfairly kick a person and expect him to get back up with any enthusiasm. . . .

Many students, when they do strive to accomplish, get very little or no recognition. It must feel pretty bad to try at something and then be made to feel as if what you did meant nothing.

James Robinson, 16
Bakersfield, California

There seems to be a major conflict that is mounting in schools all over the nation . . . between academics and athletics. Both . . . want a piece of you. It's like teachers are pulling on one arm, and coaches are yanking on the other. Sometimes you feel like you are going to be torn in half.

Jason Brockway, 17
Round Rock, Texas

Discussion

Student Perspective

Chicago
The New Expression office
Interview with staff members
of Project InSIDER

What makes education exciting?

Robin: In the public schools, a lot of the time, the only thing students find good is making friends and spending time with them. It is exciting if students can talk to one another. If the teacher will allow that, students will learn. That would make school more exciting.

Glibel: The best part of education for me is learning—the excitement of finding out something new.

Robin: But schools don't promote any sense of excitement. Everyone seems to be alienated in their own little task. If there was a little more spontaneity, apathy would be diminished. Of course, there are going to be students who don't want to learn, but that attitude can change if there is a concerted effort to make school interesting and develop a community.

Is there a conflict between academics and athletics?

Glibel: I don't think so. In the office of my school, they have trophies up for tennis, and they have articles all over about Whitney Young winning something in academics. This year we had an academic decathlon team. We had cheerleaders cheering for them when they went off to California. We had a pep rally for them. You don't see that very often. We have so many academic heroes now.

How important are student-teacher relationships?

Glibel: How important is a relationship between a child and a mother? When a child is in school, the teacher takes over the role of the parent. Communication is the basis for learning. If you don't have a very good relationship with someone, you really don't care what they have to say to you.

What makes a good teacher?

Robin: Every school needs someone who is able to get students to talk. Not someone who just lectures all the time, but someone who guides the students, especially in some of the more "outdated" subjects like history and math. They can bring some spice into it.

What's most lacking in the schools is a sense of community—common understanding and sharing among students. A way to do that is to get students talking—about themselves first and then about the subject material. Teachers have to let the students take more responsibility.

One of our ideals is to have a teacher walk into a class and say, "Okay, what do you want to talk about today?" I'm not saying we should ban lecture altogether. Some subjects really need it. The students can't discuss the subject unless they know it.

Glibel: A good teacher is someone who teaches you not only from the book but also about life in general.

Do teachers abuse their power?

Robin: Teachers tend to fall into being very dictatorial. But they can allow students more license to grow and learn than to just say, "Here's the material. I'm going to tell it to you, and you are going to learn it."

Some teachers don't know their material well. Some are not all together. They are going through stuff and are a little whacked-out.

Glibel: The day of the senior luncheon, seniors didn't show up in school. So my teacher said, "Bring a note or the program sheet, and I won't give you a cut." Everyone forgot except one girl so the teacher told us to do twenty pages of homework. I guess she had a bad day and wanted to show that she had authority. But I think most teachers are professional. They can leave their personal lives at home.

How can the problems in education be solved?

Robin: One way is by developing a sense of community. Another is by improving the relations between high schools and colleges. Another is by helping ease the transition between eighth grade and high school. To ease the transition from eighth grade to high school, we propose a program where high school students tutor elementary students. For improving the college relations, college admissions directors are going to help us develop a booklet by supplying us with information from college freshmen—papers, outlines. It will contain clues so that high school students can actually see what college work is like. Then they won't be overwhelmed.

As far as community, we propose that a facilitator come in and foster the communication between administrators, teachers, and students. We want new ways of student representation for two-way communication. We want a real effective voice. We need to have that kind of vehicle to be able to talk to teachers and administrators.

Glibel: Last summer, students told me that they don't think teachers care. They are just there to get paid. I think there are a lot of dedicated teachers, but they feel that they are not supported by anybody. If there is a community feeling in a school, if there is a feeling that everybody is supportive of everybody else, that will be a big improvement.

Teacher Perspective

Nashville, Tennessee
A private home

What makes education exciting?

Gary Harvey *math/science teacher:* There is no way an individual is going to be excited about learning anything unless he is self-motivated. I disagree with the people who say it is my responsibility to motivate every student. If a student doesn't learn, it's not my fault. I can talk until I'm blue, but it will do no good. What makes learning exciting is individuals striving to accomplish something.

Is there a conflict between academics and athletics?

Harvey: I really resent athletics because they have such a detrimental effect on the intellectual part of the school. I resent how athletics has priority over everything. I can't get a cheerleader to spend more time on geometry than on her cheers. She stays up all night learning her cheers but won't spend five minutes learning her geometry. That irritates me.

The person who is an excellent athlete very rarely will be an excellent student because he is only concerned about athletic scholarships. The reason is the money that is paid to professional athletes. You pay a man $4 million to dribble a ball around, but you will not pay a teacher more than $20,000. Our priorities are screwed up.

How important are student-teacher relationships?

Harvey: Extremely. I'm very friendly with my students. In fact,

I get too involved. I'm not trying to say that I maul them or hug them all the time. But I really love them, and I'll bloody well tell them that.

I'm concerned not only about how they do in my class but also about their lives. And if I can help them in any way, I will. If a teacher and I were at odds, I didn't learn as much as I could have. So I try to be flexible so that the students can tolerate and possibly even like me.

If teachers are dictators, it will not work. All they feel from the student is resentment. The students feel imprisoned.

To me, math is boring. It's not something that the students dig. But for me, it's not very difficult to get students to listen because I'm so outgoing. I'm not at all hesitant to be stupid or crazy in class. If I get them laughing, then they're relaxed. Then I've got them where I want them.

In the hall, at the ball games on Friday nights, if the students want to come up to me and want to joke and laugh, we'll do it. In the classroom, that's when you've got to get serious for that one hour. If a student is out of line, I'm not hesitant to send his little tail out of there.

What makes a good teacher?

Harvey: A teacher has to be tolerant because these are children you're dealing with. Only very seldom are you going to have someone even close to your own maturity level. It's hard for me to tolerate student apathy. I can't even believe a student does not want to learn.

A teacher has to remember what it was like when he was in school. A teacher must realize that geometry is not for everybody. You've got to be sympathetic. Patience and tolerance may be the most important things.

Do teachers abuse power?

Harvey: I've never seen a teacher sexually abusing a student or propositioning a student. But find one incident in this country where a teacher propositions a student, and suddenly all teachers are lechers. Why is it the media want to concentrate on the negative?

But students are abused when they have trouble learning something and the teacher jumps on his butt. That's ridiculous. Students need time. They can't learn two-column proofs in geometry instantly. Teachers abuse students by going so fast that students can't keep up or can't fully learn something.

I always resented it when a teacher would not say, ''Hey, I was wrong.'' A teacher is not a supernatural being. A teacher is just a normal human being who makes mistakes. When I teach my advanced physics class, I say, ''Y'all watch me because I make mistakes.'' I want them to stop me before I get myself all messed up. There are teachers who will not admit they make mistakes. It's bad for the teacher-student relationship, and it just messes up things.

How can the problems in education be solved?

Harvey: I don't totally agree with the idea of educating everybody. The idea that I'm going to take a student with an IQ of 50 and teach him elementary algebra is preposterous. We should have a system advocating survival of the fittest. In other words, if the student does not have the intellect to proceed to the ninth grade, he should not be pushed just because we don't want to mess with him. If a person does not have the brains to do what it takes to get a high school diploma, he should not receive one.

Everything is watered down if

you do that. What does a high school diploma mean today? Virtually zero. If you want to get a job that is desirable, you're going to have to go to college for four or eight years. If we push a person with a 50 IQ through and give him a high school diploma, what is he going to do? He's going to go hang chickens or work at McDonald's.

There is nothing wrong with education that money can't fix. If you would pay teachers a salary comparable to those of other professional people, you wouldn't see the public education system out begging for people. They have to hire people off the streets and give emergency certificates to people who aren't qualified to teach. High quality people would be waiting in line to get teaching jobs if they could make $35,000 a year. But it will never happen. Society is not willing to spend money on that.

There also has to be teamwork between teachers and administrators. Everybody is at odds with one another. We all need to work for the common good of educating children instead of working on our own individual progression up the ladder. Why is anybody here? We are here to give children their education. We have to get together and pull in the same direction.

Motivation:
Interest vs. Apathy

Newark, Delaware: I'd like to see more incentive on the part of the students. Some kids really want to take the tough courses. They view high school as an opportunity. At the other end of the spectrum, we have a lot of kids who view high school as a hurdle, something to get through on the way to getting somewhere else. A lot of kids are simply not willing to put out the effort to get some benefit out of high school.

How can teachers motivate students to learn?

Maria: Talk to them. Tell them what kind of work they have to do, what has to be done.

Christi: Most teachers say you have to respect them, but it's hard for a student to respect a teacher if the teacher doesn't respect the student. I had one teacher who treated you as though you were in kindergarten: making you write sentences to be quiet, turning the lights on and off, and making us put our heads down on our desks for punishment. How can you have respect for a teacher who treats you like that?

I've seen about two interesting teachers ever since I've been going to school. Because teachers don't get paid well, they say, "Why should I teach well?"

Nicki: A good teacher should have a good attitude towards young people, be willing to get to know them, and be willing to teach them, not just sit around and give out papers and say, "Here, do this." They have to give 100 percent. It's rare for a teacher to be interesting.

Maria: Interesting teachers joke around a lot, and they're outgoing. They're never in a bad mood, and they're always talking to you.

Nicki: We should work harder. Then maybe they'll look at our work and say, "These people are making an effort. Maybe I should make a better effort to teach them."

Maggie: We should talk to teachers, get to know them, and let them see a different side of us.

Dave: What makes the class interesting is interaction. When you participate in a discussion, you feel like you've given something to that class.

Brad: Teachers need to know how to work with students. They need

to compel the class. What makes a good teacher is the ability to control the class and to motivate them.

Magnus Seng *parent, college professor:* The material the teacher presents is like a script. You've got to time it right and be sensitive to the audience. It comes down to preparation. You have to work your butt off to see that it goes right.

Dave: If the teacher is up there and just babbles on about nothing, you just drift off and stop paying attention. I find myself taking notes of exactly what my teacher is saying but thinking about going fishing. There's no thought process involved. It just involves writing down information and then spitting it back.

One time I asked a teacher a question. Before I could finish my point, he simply answered, "No. Next question?" If any person has a different viewpoint, his idea will be thrown out of the class.

Pat Meyer *teacher:* It's hard to motivate students in my class. They always come in with closed minds. What we've got to do is get students to come in the door with open minds, and then we can go from there. I could come in as Lady Godiva, and the students would never notice.

Gerri Long *parent:* Is it really up to the teacher to do the motivating?

Dave: You can't learn anything unless you want to learn.

Meyer: Learning should be encouraged by the home.

Dave: Home has to be the starting point. If there isn't somebody pushing that first domino, it's never going to go.

Boston
South Boston High School

Bob Green *guidance counselor:* The key to education is what's going on in the home. If you have an environment where parents talk about current events, it's very easy to trigger interest in any subject. When that spark is not at home, it's very hard to motivate kids.

Good parents should make a big thing of education when kids are young. How many households do you think talked about the hostage situation? We'd be talking about geography with Beirut—where is it? You can talk from an historical viewpoint about why Lebanon is the way it is. You can even bring in theology and the different religious groups. If you have the stimulus and the foundation in the home, the sky is the limit on what you want to teach. If that foundation and motivation are not there, then you can talk about all these wonderful things, but that person is not excited.

But I'm not sure that education should be all that exciting. When you go to college and graduate school, most education is boring. It's up to the individual to make it exciting. The onus of education in this country is on the teacher. It should be on the students. Why shouldn't students make education exciting?

Priorities:
Athletics vs. Academics

Oakland, California: I'm not really a sports fan, but for some kids it really is a good thing. However, it does exclude a lot of students. They should have something else that is equally exciting. If I had my way, we would have more personal sports like tennis, skiing, and jogging.

How important are athletics compared with academics?

Michele: You have to have sports. Your body is just as important as your mind. Why not be in sports and academics?

Monica: But this is a school. You came here to learn.

Michele: But sports is a part of learning. Being competitive and all that garbage.

Steve Hamberger *physical education teacher:* I have a lot of students who are burnouts. I'm interested in school activities, but they could care less. I try to get them to make connections between them and the school. I don't care whether they're in the radio club or whatever, but they need to fit in. Extracurricular activities keep some students in school.

Michele: Could you imagine going to school without having anything to do but study? Yuk.

What activities receive the most attention?

Monica: The school favors football very much. It seems like they get most of the money.

Jennifer: The football team has brochures printed up for the next season. They're cool. Of course, everybody knows when the football players have a game.

Tucson, Arizona

Nicki: There's one assistant principal who's really excited about sports and athletes. He walks down the hall and says, "Hi, how's it going?" But if you're not in sports, he won't say hi.

Maggie: If a teacher is in sports, then athletes get special treatment.

Nicki: Athletics are really

important. I play a lot of different sports, but it's really hard because you have to supply the time for it.

Maggie: If you really love a sport, you'll keep up your grades so you can be in that sport. Most of the time when we have a game, I just put my homework aside until the game is over. That does not leave me a lot of time to do my homework.

Lombard, Illinois

How important are extracurricular activities?

Dave: You can accumulate an incredible amount of knowledge and theories, but when you try to go out and be personable to people, you end up being the most boring person they've ever met. Anything outside of the classroom, including athletics and clubs, seems to give people a lot more knowledge about life. You need to be able to deal with people and to learn about life and how to handle yourself.

Kris: Sports, for example, are a good way to instill teamwork, sportsmanship, and social interaction. You learn discipline, and it's just a great extracurricular activity. You learn how to win gracefully and to accept defeat.

Plano, Texas
Plano High School

What is the purpose of competition?

Sherman Millender *Principal:* I believe in competition. If you get enough competition in many areas, you can really touch a lot of kids. You need to create different ways for kids to be in competition because it's a competitive world. But it goes beyond where it should in many areas.

We have girls trying out for the drill team who have been taught ballet and dance since the time they were five or six years old.

The drill team performs in Texas Stadium and a lot of big stadiums with 35,000–40,000 people attending the games. A lot of parents will do almost anything to get their girls on the drill team. You have some kids who really get discouraged.

How effective is the "no-pass, no-play" law?

Millender: It needs some fine tuning. Some of the things are almost absurd because it's all based on a six-week period. Here's an example: student makes a 99 percent the first six weeks, makes a 98 percent the second six weeks, and a 69, one point below failing, in the third six weeks. His overall average may be 89 or 90, but because he failed that one six-week period, he has to lay out of sports for six weeks. If you're a football or basketball player, the season is over by the time you get back.

Tucson, Arizona

What's the value of extracurricular activity?

Eduardo Nuenez *assistant principal:* Extracurricular activities have a very important function because of the social learning the students undergo. Learning to lose with a little bit of dignity. Being able to win with dignity and to respect the other team. Working with people provides social interaction.

I'd say the top ten percent of the students are primarily involved in some sort of extracurricular activity. I wish we could involve students in the 40 to 80 percent range in some sort of activity. That way, we could get them more academically involved as well.

What conflicts exist between academic and extracurricular activities?

Nuenez: Academics and athletics go well in hand together. As a matter of fact, we have a lot of cooperation from the staff. For instance, sometimes our athletic teams have to perform at 3:30. Classes are out at 2:40, but if they have to travel somewhere, it means they have to leave their last hour early.

Teachers are pretty cooperative about that. It is, however, the student's responsibility to get make-up work ahead of time. If you can get a student excited about what he's doing after school, and he knows that he has to be in his classes, that will help keep a student in school.

Relations:
Students vs. Teachers

Tucson, Arizona: It seems that teachers don't get the respect that they should. I remember when the teacher walked in, you were quiet, and you did your work. Today I see more of a pal situation. The fact that a student can feel very comfortable going to a teacher, talking about very personal things, and building a much closer relationship may be a sign of an overwhelming amount of respect.

Irving, Texas

How can teachers be encouraged to inspire students?

Hamberger: If somebody came up to the teacher and said something in a sincere way, then I think that the teacher would be willing to listen. But you put a teacher on the defensive if you say, "You can't teach. You don't know anything. I'm not getting anything out of this."

Monica: If you've got the guts to talk to them, the problem might be solved. My way is different because I'm a smart aleck. I just make some rude comment, hoping they'll realize the point. I get real embarrassed trying to say, "Well, I don't like the way you treat me."

Usually I just get myself in trouble.

Michele: Teachers need more respect. In other countries, teachers are highly respected.

Monica: Teachers are not going to give you respect if you don't give it to them. There are, of course, some teachers who don't return it no matter how much you try to please them.

Michele: If they've chosen teaching as a career, they've got to give every student a chance. My chemistry teacher knows that it's impossible for me to get tutoring after school because I have to work. But he will not be here any earlier in the morning than 8:10, and that's too late. He owes it to the students to be a little early.

Hamberger: Whenever we start a new year, all the teachers should go in with a positive attitude, willing to give every student a chance, an opportunity, and some respect. They should allow for individual differences. But teachers have feelings. They form opinions just like anybody else. They just can't be neutral all the time.

Cleveland
National Scholastic Press Association convention—with teenage delegates

What makes for a good student-teacher relationship?

Connie *Calabasas, California:* It's nice if you can talk to teachers, but they shouldn't be your friend. You should be able to go to them and tell them if you have a problem with the class.

Julie *Vernon Hills, Illinois:* There's nothing wrong with being friends, but teachers should still have some authority. What makes a good student-teacher relationship is respect.

I have this teacher who always cuts loose and tells us about his dog and his kids who always throw up all over the place. He

also likes to talk about his neighbors, who he thinks are real scummy. He can get down to our level, but he can stay at his level too.

Connie: In all-girls schools, you have these pervert male teachers sometimes, and it's really hard to have any respect for them at all.

Julie: One time in ninth grade I came up to a teacher's office, and he started describing this poem and its sexual imagery in detail. It was really uncomfortable. And he said, "Isn't this fantastic. Oh, you aren't upset, are you?" Then he said, "Don't tell any of this to the administrators."

What kind of relations do students have with administrators?

Julie: The only time we ever see an administrator is when we do something that upsets them. But if we have a problem with them, it's like "Well, sorry."

Connie: They just pretend to listen. Then they don't do anything. I went in to talk with the headmaster and to tell him about some problems we have, but he just doesn't listen. It's in one ear and out the other. "We're working on it." That's their famous phrase. I tried talking to them again this year, but I finally gave up. Nobody listens. It's really frustrating.

Lombard, Illinois

Meaghan: To do well, I have to like my teacher. The teacher I hated most was fresh out of college, and he had no control over the class. The principals were always up there, and it was always so easy to cheat or pass notes. I got a low grade in that class.

Brad: Teachers I am friends with are friendly and intellectual people so we can sit down and become friends.

Sue: You're the type of person who would try to make friends with the teachers. There are a lot of students who don't care what their teachers think of them, and those are the students who probably do poorly.

Dave: I'm friends with some teachers, but it's not like I went in there and attempted to make friends. But there are quite a few people who go out of their way to be "Sally Sunshine." They don't care about really liking the teacher. They just think that they would get a better grade. Quite often it doesn't work that way.

Brad: I've never found an honors teacher yet whom I could brown-nose. But if a teacher is not very intelligent, brown-nosing works.

Dave: In that case, the teacher definitely has character flaws and needs to be patronized.

Sue: I can sit in the back of some classes and make jokes the whole hour, and the teacher will laugh along. But in some classes the teacher gives you a look that says, "Shut up or die."

Meyer: That's part of the difficulty. Some teachers don't like high school kids. They don't think that high school kids have any intelligence. They feel their role is to feed the kids with all their knowledge.

Sue: People with that attitude shouldn't be teaching.

Brad: There are some teachers out there who just want to spite the students—gym teachers for instance. Gym teachers really get off on it. There are a lot of gym teachers who live for giving out after-school make-up sessions.

Dave: Some PE teachers say, "Drop and give me fifty!" The only thing the kid can do fifty of is Oreo cookies.

Brad: There are times when you can have a really good viewpoint, and you can present it well, but the teacher just sits there and says, "No. You're wrong." What can you do? In our English class, we were supposed to write an

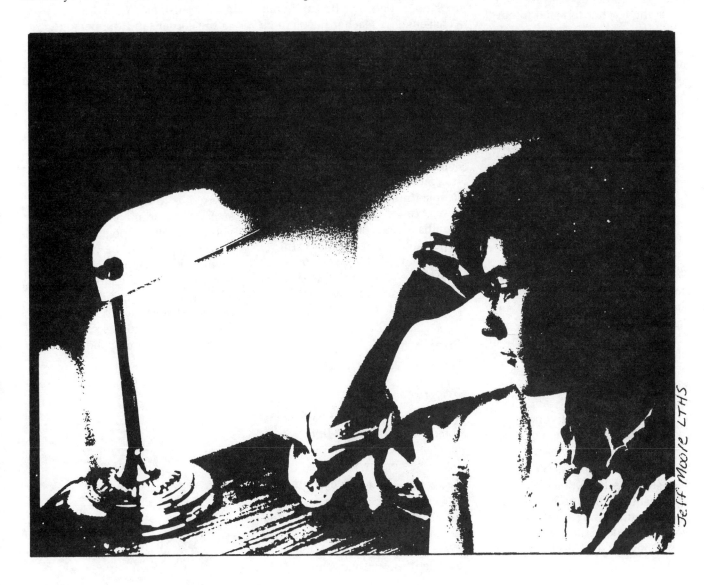

Students and Teachers   43

opinion essay, and we wrote well-supported opinion papers. The next day when we got our tests back, our teacher said, "No, your opinions are wrong."

Sue: Then he started telling us the answers we should have had, and only the people with the opinions he wanted got good grades. He justified his opinion to the extent that it was believable, but he wouldn't look at the other side.

Brad: Whenever we talk about a book we're reading, he will only talk about the plot. If we try to come up with anything deeper, he says, "No, I'm sorry, that's not in there." So the only thing you can do in that class is shut up or just sleep. There was no way we could coerce the teacher to listen to our opinions.

Sue: When you go down to your counselor and say, "Well, I don't get along with my teacher," the counselor says, "Uh huh. Sure. You have a personality conflict. Go back to class."

Los Angeles, California
University High School

Joanne: A good relationship with a teacher helps to create more motivation to do better in that class. If you hate a teacher, you want to do things just to spite her.

Dohee: I know this teacher who doesn't like me. When I'm in his class, I try to do things as he would like to see them rather than what's really me. When I'm in my English class, though, it's really relaxed. You're free to say the things you want to say, and the teacher won't laugh at you. A good relationship brings out the potential in a person.

Mina: Some teachers don't let their students have that relationship. If the teachers tried to reach out, I think more kids would respond. Students are afraid they will be rejected by the teacher.

Joanne: The teacher just gives out all the information and the students swallow it.

Julie: The teachers I like the most teach the classes I like the most. I can identify with those teachers as people. They can open up and show that they have lives, too.

Washington, D.C.
American Federation of Teachers office

Ruth Whitman *public relations director:* A teacher has to be a person who is compassionate and who cares. The better teachers are those who are loving people and show that outwardly. Another talent of a good teacher is to know their stuff. A third talent is to be the kind of person who can initiate a challenge. A teacher needs to be a team leader, a spirited person. You have to be a performer to be a teacher. You have to be able to personalize, but sometimes working a classroom with 35 students doesn't allow you to do that.

A good teacher has to be someone who can stand a very frustrating and demanding job. People think that teachers have it easy because they are off three months a year, but after grading papers and doing all that extra work, they actually work more than those who work 9 to 5. You have to be able to have that patience and that tenacity.

Punishment: Laxness vs. Strictness

Irving, Texas:

Teacher: In one of our bathrooms somebody painted, "Hitler is a fag" and "Nazis." You want to catch the person and lynch him.

Teenager: A student brought a loaded gun to school last year.

Teacher: He should not be in this school today. A gun is where you draw the line. He should be expelled from public school.

Winfield, Illinois
A private home

Joanne Wheatley *teacher/parent:* Children today are much more brazen. They don't hesitate to tell you what they feel so they're a little bit harder to discipline. Before, you might have said, "Sit down," or "Take your seat," and they would. But now, they simply reply, "Why?" They question your authority. I almost like discipline today better because you have to treat your kids fairly. You can't put a silly, stupid demand on them because you want to.

My one big beef with high schools right now is the manner in which they handle suspensions and expulsions. A child is put over in the corner, and the person in charge says, "I'm going to call your parents." They may call the parents before they turn the tape recorder on or call the police in first. Usually they do the latter.

I'm against the school district calling the police or taping a statement from a child before they have first notified the parents. That child has a right to be advised as to what to do. If it's such an important situation that you must call the police, or you have to tape what the child is saying, then by gosh, he should have some sort of counseling. When they get the child in the office and start hitting him on all four sides, the kid is scared to death and says things he probably shouldn't.

There is a trend of parents wanting the school to become very strict and to take care of all the discipline that home used to. That's a basic need now because of split homes and because mothers are working. We have to pick up a lot of that slack.

Cambridge, Massachusetts
Cambridge Rindge and
Latin High School

Edward Sarasin *principal:* We've had a lot of racial conflict. In 1981 a student was stabbed and killed.

We solved the problem on several levels. First, we said that as an institution, we demand that you show a certain degree of respect for your fellow man, whether that be your teacher or another student. After the stabbing we had a lot of small group discussions. We talked about how we perceive various races in the high school.

We made a conscious effort in our curriculum to deal with the issues of multi-cultural education. We started a teacher advisory program so every incoming freshman had an adviser. If I see a kid having a problem, I can have someone shadow that kid and see what's going on. As soon as we hear about a problem, we sit down and talk.

There was a famous gang that virtually controlled part of the campus. They completely annihilated a teacher's car. We sat down and let the kids vent a lot of their anger and frustration. Quite honestly, it ended up as a therapy session with quite a lot of negotiating. As long as we had the kids talking, they weren't vandalizing.

The conflict was the result of anger, frustration, and the inability of a system to respond to their needs. We tried to deal with that on a daily basis, and we tried to implement programs which served

as an escape valve.

When I'm dealing with a student and he raises his voice or begins to use profanity, I try to keep my voice under control and say, "Listen. Give me what I give to you. If I give you a certain level of respect, you have to give it back. If I start yelling at you, you can yell at me."

When teachers do not use good judgment concerning levels of anxiety and frustration, you let teachers know it: "Perhaps the student led you on, but the reality is that you're a professional at this high school." If teachers are abusive to any student, they're in big trouble. If teachers have sworn at a student, they're down in my office. Providing an atmosphere of respect is essential.

We've gone through tragedy, but we try to maintain a humane environment. We try to make it a responsive environment.

Improvements:
Present vs. Potential

Oakland, California: One of the things that worries me is that as a nation we are not educating for education's sake. We are educating children for more specific jobs. We are being more of a tool to industry. We forget that you should be allowed a lot of freedom of direction and choice.

Washington, D.C.: Schools are having to compete for talent. If I'm a senior in college and a chemistry major, I could go be a chem teacher at $16,000 a year and have fifteen years of slow increment raises. Or I could take a job with IBM as a paper shuffler making $25,000.

Lombard, Illinois

Sue: I have a class in which the teacher gives us two workbook pages to do every day. It's not very stimulating, but you also have to understand that there are

other people who have to do those workbook pages to understand it. You have to consider students who can't learn as easily as others do.

Brad: But a good teacher has to provide for the needs of all the students.

Dave: If students learn at different speeds, I don't think they should be in the same classes.

Long: But that makes for an interesting class.

Brad: Not in my classes. It didn't work. The people who were really intelligent sat around and talked the whole time.

Dave: The main problem with education is that we've lost imagination in learning. When a student can't have any imaginative thought, it decreases the chances for learning. I hate it when you come up with your own idea and the teacher says, "What kind of a stupid comment was that?"

Washington, D.C.

Whitman: Education is in a state of flux because of changes in the economy. We are now finding that the person who has access to knowledge will have access to power. There will be more looking at education as an economic investment. When businesses consider going to a new area, they no longer look at what the tax base is but at what the education in the area is like. It's not just because the workers want their children to get a good education but because they know they are going to need skilled employees.

Teachers in the future will have to be more flexible. They will have to make more room for sharing ideas and working as a team. Now, a lot of teachers will show you their "scars" from when they tried to be different and learned to keep their mouths shut.

Teachers have to be empowered

to be the educational expert, not the factory worker. If you're trained as a professional, you should not be slapped on the wrist every time you do something different. The teacher is the center. You can have a good principal and a concerned parent, but if a teacher is no good, it can ruin the class for the student.

Parents need to become more involved in terms of being informed and becoming active. Principals and administrators could learn more about how to be principals and administrators. In the same way, teachers could learn how to be better teachers.

Finally, the burden is ultimately on the student. I don't believe that kids don't care. I see a lot of dynamic young people. But they're turned off with schools because we're not reaching out to them.

Winfield, Illinois

Wheatley: There needs to be a broadening of the curricula, but there is a narrowing instead of a broadening. You have to look towards the future—where students are going and what they're going to need when they get out there.

If you talk to any business people who are hiring, one of their major complaints is, "The kids have good grades and do well in college, but they cannot write a good business letter. They cannot communicate on paper." This is something high school has to hit. It's a skill that takes a long time to develop. High school students should be required to take four years of writing.

Boston

Maria Grace *guidance counselor:* The best way to solve problems would be to get all the people who are making all the big decisions to come and spend a year in a high

school. They should find out what's really going on. Things are being solved by people who don't know what the heck is going on.

Green: One of the only ways to get these city kids to survive is to pretty much take them out of their homes. Put them into a system similar to what they run in Israel, a kibbutz type of system where you have trained professionals who deal with these kids all the time.

Right now, most of these kids are not properly cared for. Simple basic needs—medical attention and proper meals—are not being met. There are one-parent homes, and there are a lot of children. The environment at home is not conducive to education.

Education in America has dropped, whether in the suburbs or in the city. A good example of that is the way this country's scores compare to other countries in math and language. We've ranked in the 20s in math. We can't compete anymore. The reason for that is a breakdown in American society as a whole.

Plano, Texas
Administration office
  of Plano Independent School District

Larry Guinn *director of student services:* Since we instituted five or six new programs at Plano Senior High School, our average SAT score has gone up 48 points. Our A-Team had something to do with that. Athletes receive a lot of recognition, but a lot of math, English, foreign language, and computer students who were good in their area of interest receive no recognition. So we created a situation where for two hours after school one day a week students would come together with some people with whom they had a common interest and go beyond the classroom without the grade pressure. It's learning for learning's sake.

Oakland, California
Office of Peggy Stinnet

Peggy Stinnet *former Oakland school board member:* We should pay teachers a lot more than we do. But at the same time, we should require that they are highly qualified to teach our kids.

Education goes back to Socrates. Greek society saved its very best to become teachers because they recognized that passing on the wisdom was the way to continue. We don't do that now. We give teachers what is left over. We make babysitters out of them. We have class sizes that are too big. We give them all kinds of problem kids. We don't give them enough books or help so they don't want to stay in that environment. They can go out into another environment and be paid well and have satisfaction. The teaching profession has lost its attraction for many young people because of the lack of reward in the classroom.

Newark, Delaware
Administration office of
  Newark School District

Michael Walls *superintendent:* If society doesn't expect a very good education, the kids are not going to get it. Now society is saying, "Hey, education is really important, and we need to spend more money. We need to have better teachers and better schools."

Educators themselves are to blame. We got lazy. I've had teachers who are strictly going through the motions. They really didn't care about their jobs or the kids. They were just biding time until they could retire.

The colleges have to come in for some of the blame as well. They've admitted people into education programs who just weren't high quality people. They have graduated them and put them on the market.

DARIN WALSH LTMS

And certainly schools have to take part of the blame. And the government. Teachers can start around $15,000 with a science or math degree, but you can walk over to DuPont and start working at $22,000 or $23,000. We're going to need a million new teachers. We're going to be replacing close to half our teachers. It's no big secret why people are not going into teaching.

We are not getting the cream of the crop of the students. That has to change. The people coming out of the colleges are not the top quality people who should be teaching the kids.

What really irritates me is that the colleges have dropped their standards. They let a lower quality of student in, and then they complain that the public schools are not doing their job. The

answer to me is simple. If they don't want to teach remedial reading, don't let unqualified students into college. Keep the standards up.

What can solve these problems?

Walls: I think we will have a voucher system. Parents will be given a slip of paper that says that their children can go to the private school down the street. That voucher will be worth "X" amount of dollars, and those dollars will go to that school. Public school educators are just petrified of that happening. They know a lot of people who are now in the public schools will probably opt to go to private schools. I'm not against it. If public schools cannot compete, then someone else should do the job.

*New York City
Dome Project*

Tom Brown *director:* The Dome Project observed that a lot of black and Hispanic young people were not getting adequate education services in the New York public school system. They couldn't read or do simple arithmetic. No one was dealing with their psychological and emotional problems. We took five of these particularly alienated young people and began an alternative classroom which paid a lot of attention to individuals.

We have three alternative junior high schools where we take young people who have been truant, kicked out of school, or been arrested. We put them in a situation where we can keep the student-teacher ratio about 8 to 1. If this young person were in a traditional classroom, he would not be given that kind of attention, tutoring, or counseling. In a New York City junior high school, the typical student to teacher ratio is at least 25 to 1.

Why is a low student-teacher ratio important?

Brown: A low student-teacher ratio allows students to get to know teachers as people, and it also allows the teachers to get to know the young people. It allows the teacher to perceive the young person as a whole person and not just as someone who waltzes through a classroom at 9 o'clock and goes home at 3.

The teacher in the normal New York City junior high school does not have the time to deal with people who have a special set of problems—students who have come from very poor economic backgrounds, from families that might have histories of drug abuse or child abuse. We feel that the student-teacher ratio should be as low as 10 or 8 to 1.

We deal with about 60 students in these three alternative junior high school classes. The students may have attendance rates of 20 percent and be three years below grade level, but after two years at the Dome Project their attendance rate is usually up around 80-85 percent. Their grade scores on standardized tests usually jump two or three years.

*Portland, Oregon
Administration office
of Portland Public Schools*

Alcena Boozer *director, Project Return:* Project Return is an effort to identify the truant population, to physically locate the truants, to determine the reasons they are out of school, and to begin a problem-solving process. I didn't find the truants out on the streets. I found them at home watching television.

We asked the Board of Education to fund a transitional classroom—a place where students who have been out of school too long and can't easily be returned can go. If a student has been out for four months, they aren't going to just walk in the classroom.

We had one young man who had been out of school because he felt low self esteem—he weighed over 300 pounds. We sent him to a high school with a health clinic where he could have assistance with weight control, and he stayed in school the entire year. He's returning for a second year.

What are the major reasons for dropping out?

Boozer: There are a series of factors. The things reported by students were, "I didn't like school." "I was bored." "I felt the teachers didn't like me"—we heard that one very often. "I don't think school will get me anyplace." In some areas of the city, kids have role models who seem to be doing quite well without going to school. Kids haven't figured out that when these people disappear, they are doing time in jail.

For some dropouts, it's the lack of the economic support to go to

school. Some of the kids lived a bit far. In the winter we found families who had been out of school because there was no heat in the house. The kids had been farmed out to relatives and a place where it was warm. Also, we have some kids who are substance abusers who come from parents who are abusers.

How does Project Return change the truant's attitudes?

Boozer: We begin by doing a lot of listening and by making suggestions. The kids who stay away from school don't feel competent as students so the most successful method of changing attitudes is helping them achieve success in an area where they feel incompetent. Structure the curriculum so that it is a smaller bite, easily chewed and digested. Then, "Hey, I can do that." It takes one-on-one. The common denominator in most successful

alternative programs is a caring, humane environment.

I have yet to talk to any young person who doesn't aspire to a good quality of life. We help them establish the connection between what you do and how you end up. Most often I'm dealing with terribly apathetic 14 or 15 year olds. "I ain't doing nothing. I ain't going to school."

You ask what things they like to do when they don't go to school. Then we'll get around to, "What kind of place do you see yourself living in? How do you think those things are coming?" Sometimes we go through the want ads, look at the qualifications, and begin to see where things that happen at school help one meet those qualifications. We've found that by not being judgmental, people will listen.

Then it's a matter of systematically identifying what the barriers are. "It's too far to go to

school, and I can't get there." "Well, how about if I give you bus tickets?" "I don't have any clothes." "Well, how about if we find some clothes and help you find a part-time job?" That problem is gone. Pretty soon there's no excuse not to go.

They may not want to go back to the traditional high school, but they want to go into some educational program. Kids really don't feel good sitting home.

Compiled by Doug Elwell

Solutions

The best way to encourage student achievement is through positive reinforcement. . . . The student will not try to achieve if he believes . . . the only thing that awaits him is failure. Too often we place all of the praise on the already motivated, active students and ignore the average students. When someone is told that

Students and Teachers

they have potential, they are much more willing to improve.

Alison Little, 17
Shaker Heights, Ohio

Most of the teachers I've had in the past were not very interested in me as an individual. For example, a teacher should notice if a student is falling behind and then try to help that student catch up. . . .

I've had teachers who really care, who make a point to try and help students, whether it be after school, before school, or in class.

Teachers could encourage students by making the class more fun. That way the students will stay attentive and will get more out of the class. Teachers could also give extra credit for those students who wish to excel.

Mark Weiss, 15
Wheeling, Illinois

To have a good student-teacher relationship, you have to have a good friendship.

Sean Kenneally, 16
Columbia, South Carolina

I think that teachers need to do something besides giving grades to students. They need to give awards like ribbons, plaques, or candy to the people who have the highest grades.

Corey Hummel, 16
Waverly, Nebraska

I think the best way to get students to achieve is by punishment. . . . I had gotten into trouble because I was goofing around in class and not doing my work. The principal called my parents and made me explain what

was going on. When I got home, both of my parents met me at the door. We had a long talk. Then my dad took me out into the garage. Boy, did I get it.

But after that I went from a D average to an A average. I think that when a student gets out of hand, that person should be punished in school or have the parents notified so it can be taken care of at home. If not, that person might just keep on doing wrong.

Eric Littlefield, 14
Galesburg, Illinois

Schools are becoming more strict. Students are not able to be as independent. . . . If a school doesn't already have a student council, they should get one immediately. The students, then, would have a say in what is happening around their school.

Tom Nielsen, 16
Iowa City, Iowa

If a student and teacher may have an honest, open discussion . . . about class-related subjects, then a good relationship is evident. This differs from when a student will say only what he thinks . . . his teachers want to hear. A relationship may be improved by teacher initiative in open discussion.

Tina Cassidy, 17
Cranston, Rhode Island

Teachers and administrators can encourage students' achievement by making sure that the students are getting the best education they can get. They can set higher standards for the students to meet, thereby forcing

the student to work harder to pass.

Marianna Hann, 17
Cleveland, Ohio

The subjects that we are all forced to take in order to survive in the real world are all stuffy, boring, and often times totally unapplicable. . . . On-the-job training should become available to high school students as it is to college students. Teenagers should be given a good background in everything from balancing a checkbook to working with computers. Life skills training should become a mandatory part of a high school education.

Lisa Martin, 17
Bakersfield, California

A good student-teacher relationship consists of a comfortable atmosphere where neither feels . . . insecure or inferior. Both the student and the teacher should be on an adult level so they can exchange ideas.

Brian Kristofek, 18
Winfield, Illinois

A few teachers are under the impression that the students are at school so the teachers can have a job. . . . This problem may be solved if teachers could be paid by merit and a system of evaluation could be conducted by random members of the student body. . . . If a teacher fares well on the merit and evaluation, the teacher should get a raise. But if a teacher doesn't fare well, the teacher should have some sort of severe reprimand to face. I feel these two changes would solve the problem of apathetic teachers.

Alvin Heggie, 17
Irmo, South Carolina

Chapter 3.

Employees and Employers

Clothing Corner has three teen employees: Lisa, Steve, and Caramella, under the management of Chip Lipshitz. At Clothing Corner, as in any store, the teens' never-ending quest to find the perfect manager is equalled only by the manager's struggle to find the ultimate employee.

Worklog:

3:00—Ringing up a purchase on the register, Lisa confronts a seemingly endless line of waiting customers. Chip the manager approaches.

Chip: Lisa, could you come here for a minute?

Lisa: I'm busy with a customer.

Chip: It's important.

Lisa (apologizes to customer): I'm sorry. What is it?

Chip: The general manager is coming to inspect the store tomorrow.

Lisa (confused): So what's the point?

Chip: The store has to be spotless. I want you to rehang all the crumpled clothes, clean the dressing rooms, work the counter, wash the display counters, and arrange some shirt and sweater combinations for the display racks. Thanks.

Lisa: What?

Customer waits impatiently.

Chip: Oh, and I've been so busy helping you that I haven't balanced the sales yet.

Frustrated customer storms out.

Chip: Now look what you've done.

Lisa (to herself): Helping me? More like sitting around and watching me work.

When the manager turns his back, Lisa expresses her lack of affection for him with a raised finger.

3:25—In his office, Chip plays with his new swivel chair. The sales book lies abandoned on his desk as he turns his mind to employee matters.

Chip (talking to himself): That Lisa girl can annoy me. I tried to be nice to her, but what do I get—decadent insolence. She probably steals, too. Damn teenagers. If they didn't work so cheap, I'd never hire 'em.

3:30—Steve, a stockboy, lounges in the store's stockroom. Reclining on a stack of boxes, he eats a Snickers bar. Noticing a shirt he likes, he stuffs it in his backpack to take home.

Lisa: Are you taking that?

Steve: Well, I prefer to think of it as a 100 percent discount. Besides, Dip-Shitz hasn't given me a raise yet, and I've been here more than six months. It's only fair I should make up what he owes me.

Lisa: But don't you ever worry about getting caught?

Steve: No, of course not. I keep inventory so I just mark it off as sold. The only way I can get caught is if someone rats on me.

Lisa: Don't worry, I won't. I can't stand him either. He blames me for everything that goes wrong. Usually it's his fault, of course.

Chip (over intercom): Lisa, what's wrong with the air conditioner?

Lisa (laughs): Not again.

3:45—Lisa and one of her friends lean on the counter. They are engrossed in conversation.

Chip: Lisa, I don't pay you to talk.

Lisa: Sorry. But she is buying something, and you did tell me to be friendly to our customers.

Chip: Friendly does not mean spending ten minutes talking. If she wants to buy something, fine, but if not I'm afraid she'll have to leave.

Lisa: All right. (Flips him off as he leaves.) Let me see. Three shirts at our "super VIP discount" comes to, oh, say $5. How's that?

Friend: Sorry, I only have $3.50.

Lisa: Like I said, that comes to $3.50. Thank you. Come again.

3:55—Business has screeched to a halt. Steve, who has a crush on Lisa, has strategically arranged his workday so he'd be near the counter. Finally, he builds up his confidence.

Steve (nervous): So, Lisa, when do you get off work?

Lisa: In about five minutes. Five minutes until I'm away from Chip.

Steve (twisting his hands agitatedly): Doing anything tonight? I mean, would you like to go out?

Lisa: Well, I have to baby-sit tonight, but sure, I'd like to go out sometime.

Steve: How about Friday?

Lisa: I'm free. Sure.

Steve (racking his brain for some point of conversation): Who works after you tonight?

Lisa: That Caramella girl.

Steve: Oh no, the whore of Clothing Corner. And I have to work two more hours.

Lisa: Good luck. See you Friday.

4:30—Steve is lounging in the stockroom when Caramella, wearing a miniskirt and low-cut shirt, struts in.

Caramella (looking at her paycheck): Ooh. I got another raise. Only ten cents. I'll have to talk to Chippy about this.

Chip (sauntering in): Caramella dear, you're finally here. Oh, that rhymes.

Chip and Carmella laugh heartily and then embrace.

Chip: Watch the front counter, Steve. Caramella has to . . . uh . . . help me balance the sales book.

Steve: But I'm only halfway through the worklist you gave me.

Chip (clamping his hand on Steve's shoulder): Thanks, buddy. I knew I could count on you.

As Chip turns his back, Steve imitates Chip's swaggering stride.

4:35—Fumbling the keys on the cash register, which he'd never been trained to use, Steve is attempting to take care of a customer. Suddenly a loud moaning emanates from the office.

Customer (to himself): Hm. Should I buy this jacket or . . .

DAN O'BRIEN
LT HS

Intercom (moaning): Yes! Yes!
Customer (to Steve): Excuse me.
Intercom: (deep moan)
Customer: Are you all right, young man?
Intercom: Yes, I feel so good.
Customer: Huh?
Intercom: You touch me in places no one has ever reached.
Customer: What?
Intercom: Knead my buttocks.
Customer: I beg your pardon. I'm afraid I'm going to have to report you to your manager.
Intercom: Yes. Yes. Make it hurt so good.
Steve (racking his brain): I'm sorry, sir. We're having problems with the, um, piped-in music.
5:15—Steve is marking new prices on sale items in the stockroom while Caramella reclines on boxes.
Caramella: How can I repay you? Want to buy some pot? (She pulls out a joint and lights it.)
Steve: Sorry, I don't get high on the job. Actually, I don't get high at all.
6:00—Finished hauling in new stock, Steve arranges a window display with original combinations. Caramella, in preparation for the night crew takeover, tallies the day's sales on the cash register. Chip, as supervisor, paces back and forth to check up on them.
Chip (glancing at his watch): Well, that's it. Time to leave. See both of you Friday.
Steve (panicking): Friday? I don't work Friday.

Chip (checks schedule): You're listed to work. Is there some problem?

Steve: I kind of have a date for Friday night.

Chip: No problem. You can take the day off if you work Saturday from 9 to 4.

Steve: Thanks.

Chip: Steve? Did you do the window display?

Steve: Yeah. Is something wrong?

Chip: No, I kind of like it.

The workday ends as employees prepare for the cycle to begin again tomorrow.

Dave Seng

Conflicts

If a girl is good-looking, then she may make sexual advances toward her boss. I have seen a girl get a $2 an hour raise because she laid her boss. I tried this once and got a small raise. I commented on how sexy and nice looking my boss was. She seemed to get off on it.

> 16-year-old male
> North Carolina

I am employed at a chicken restaurant where mostly teenagers work. . . . Teenagers have stored alcohol on the premises. Also, there have been instances of employees coming to work stoned or drunk. This happens quite frequently, and it impairs their working ability.

Food is taken. People have gotten stoned in the restaurant, and there have also been drugs sold out of the store by a teenage employee.

> 17-year-old female
> Idaho

People on the jobs have it too easy. They will complain about the littlest things. They just don't know how good they've got it. I live on a farm in northwest Iowa, and I have to do things that would make most city kids puke. I have to haul manure when it is five below zero outside. I think we should have special privileges like a paid vacation.

> Harold Wieringa, 15
> Sheldon, Iowa

The bosses treat you like garbage so I get back at them. . . . I was on a cash register, and the customer was arguing with me. I told the fussy customer to shut her face and go argue some place else. . . . She got real upset and asked for the store manager. I pointed the way towards his office.

Later the manager came to me and told me about what had happened. I told him he never told us to be courteous to customers. . . .

Another time he had given me a break for half an hour. I took an hour and a half. He never knew, and I never told. I did this many other times.

There is a snack-bar at the store. My friends and I always took food and candy. . . . We kept taking food because we worked there and took advantage of the fact that the security guards were guarding the front doors. The managers were too busy dealing with customers or merchandise.

> 17-year-old male
> New Jersey

I was hired as a "secretary" . . . but I ended up as your basic cleaning lady. . . .

When I first started, I learned how to answer phone calls, take messages, and to file things. But then I didn't learn anymore new skills, and then slowly I began to take on cleaning chores. So now, instead of typing, I

vacuum, dust, or mop.

My mother says that I should be satisfied and be glad that I have a job. I'm not sure if I agree with her.

> 15-year-old female
> Oregon

The boss was supposed to be there at 8:30 a.m., but she didn't arrive until 10 a.m. So I had to open the store and start making cookies. At 9 a delivery came with about fifty boxes of supplies. I didn't know where to put anything.

When the boss came in, she started yelling at me, saying I should have known where to put the supplies. Nobody told me where to put them.

Here I had opened the store, counted out the cashier's drawers,

56

baked the cookies, and accepted delivery. . . . It was impossible to have lunch . . . and dinner.

I was scheduled for a half-hour break in addition to my missed lunch. . . . When I informed my boss that I was leaving for break, I was told I would be getting docked because of leaving. When I explained what happened, she fired me.

17-year-old female
New Jersey

So many businesses don't hire minorities such as blacks, Mexicans, and Chinese. Some bosses shy away from minorities because they dislike their race and in the process, . . . qualified workers are turned away. . . . If minorities are hired, they work under poorer conditions and are paid a lower wage than whites. More bosses should look at the qualifications, not at their outside.

15-year-old male
Iowa

If you are under 18, they won't pay you time and a half for overtime worked. If you say something to them, they will simply tell you that there are others waiting for your position, happy to fill it.

There are laws that say minors can only work until 9 p.m. or 10 p.m., but most minors don't know about it or don't have the courage to say anything—sometimes I'm the only one there, closing up at 1 a.m.

Ellen Kilcourse, 17
Waterford, Virginia

Bosses take advantage of teenage employees by having them do work that doesn't pertain to the job that they applied for. I applied for work at a pizza and pasta restaurant as a cook, but half of the time I was out working in their so-called garden—weeding, watering, etc. I was out sweeping the sidewalk or painting the walls in the restaurant.

Then one day I had gotten up in the morning and didn't feel good. I called

in to tell the owner I didn't feel good and wouldn't be able to make it. He fired me.

Paul Parson, 17
Maple Valley, Washington

Working at a local supermarket, I see . . . my co-workers trying to find some new method of getting away with things. For instance . . . one day the manager . . . noticed that the new girl had subtracted money from her bill. Somehow she had discovered the code and was pocketing the money.

On another occasion, there was a young man . . . no one would ever consider him a thief . . . taking money from the customers. Instead of giving the customer the correct amount of change, he short changes them and takes the difference. He is still working there, and the manager does not suspect.

I also somehow take advantage of certain situations. . . . At times if a friend comes through my line, I will discount the items which they buy. This way you are still charging them but not fully. Somehow teenagers find a way of taking advantage of their employer.

17-year-old female
New Jersey

I am often nervous and worried about asking for a day off or pointing out mistakes in my paychecks. I always feel as if points are being deducted and my job is in jeopardy. . . .

As a receptionist at a vet clinic, I'm supposed to answer phones, deal with owners, etc. Does that entitle my boss to ask me to clean out a bathroom? . . . He even has help in the back to clean up. Why me? I feel compelled to, though, because I feel that I need to keep my job safe.

16-year-old female
Virginia

Lower salaries, harsher duties, and altogether pessimistic attitudes are thrown our way. The younger generation is a pawn that the older generation uses to push around when

it is unable to push each other around.

Sean Szatkowski, 18
North Plainfield, New Jersey

As a golf assistant at a country club, I have realized that my boss would rather believe . . . a member . . . than believe . . . his employee even though the boss knew what happened.

For instance, a golf cart had been left on a tee, and it had started to roll down the fairway and hit a water fountain, which was completely destroyed, and the assistant got the blame. In turn, he had to pay for the damages.

16-year-old male
West Virginia

Cheating bosses can range from stealing their products to leaving a baby unattended. . . . Almost everyone has taken advantage in at least small ways. I think that teens do this because they think it looks cool, to get attention, they don't care one way or the other, to see what they can get away with, and, in some cases, they need extra money to keep up their drug habit.

Katie Storck, 15
North Plainfield, New Jersey

Over the summer, I worked in a deli. The boss usually left for a few hours during the day. . . . As soon as the boss drove off, and if there were no customers, we would sit around and eat the food. We'd also do poor jobs of cleaning the windows or sweeping the floor. It wasn't unusual for us to give our friends free food, or even sell alcohol to people we knew were under 21.

16-year-old female
New Jersey

Teenagers leave earlier than they are supposed to. Some lie and call in sick many times for work. Many give away free merchandise or steal and sell it. They steal money. Some come late for work or don't even show up.

Heather Bradley, 15
North Plainfield, New Jersey

I've done some babysitting and worked on a farm. I usually charge $2 an hour, but sometimes they pay me less. I'm too shy to ask for more.

When I worked on the farm, I was 13. Most kids that worked were 13-15. . . . We worked about twelve hours a day picking strawberries and only got a dollar a flat.

It was the only job we could get because we were under 16 so we didn't quit. Our employer knew we could not find a job anywhere else because of our ages so he took advantage of the situation.

> *16-year-old female*
> *Washington*

For almost a year I've been working at a semi-formal restaurant. My position is bus girl. Although I love my job, I often find it frustrating that my bosses take . . . advantage sometimes. . . .

On "Superbowl Sunday" morning, my boss called me up and said, "You're working today, right?" I replied, "You never mentioned anything to me about working, and I have to cocktail waitress my aunt's party today. I'm sorry." He said, "Well, the next time there is a party or holiday—come to us and ask us if we need you."

I don't think my boss would have "ordered" anyone of the older workers . . . like that. It's not fair.

> *16-year-old female*
> *New York*

Discussion

Olympia, Washington
Evergreen State College
Summer Journalism Workshop

What are the disadvantages of working?

Carrie *Auburn, Washington:* Some disadvantages were working until 11 p.m. on a school night. When it would get very busy, the owner of a local ice cream store would stand behind you and wait for you to make a mistake. As soon as you'd make a mistake, he'd take you back into the kitchen and yell at you. All the customers could hear, and it was very embarrassing. He never offered to help.

I also had to wash dishes every night in bleach water, but I have eczema. The water irritated my hands, but they still made me do it.

Monica *Sumner, Washington:* At the burger place where I work, the managers are really bad about breaks. You're supposed to get two ten-minute breaks for every eight hours. Sometimes they forget to give you your break. So you have to remind them, and they still don't give you your break.

They take advantage of us because we are just kids. Don't we have a curfew? But they have us working closing shifts so we get home at 2 a.m.

It's the kind of job that you treat shabby because they treat you shabby. When you don't want to work anymore, you don't show up. One time the manager said, "Charlie didn't show up today. I guess he quit."

Sometimes they even try to punch you out on the time clock before you are done closing. I won't let them.

Carrie: Where I work, they give you an hour to close. If you are done in an hour, that's fine. If you are not, you don't get paid for the extra time. Before they used to have one person to clean the front, one person to wash the dishes, and one person to clean the grill while the manager does the ice cream machines. Then they changed it so one person does the dishes and the front. It must take an hour and forty-five minutes, but I am sure they are only getting paid for an hour.

Stephanie *Auburn, Washington:* I worked at one of the nicest restaurants in Auburn. I worked seven-hour shifts but got zero breaks. I lasted two weeks.

Are there ever problems with sex discrimination?

Carrie: I haven't had a problem, but I noticed there was one girl who couldn't make change even with a machine telling her how much to give out. But she was really pretty and really nice to the owner so he liked her. She wasn't fired even though the cash register was $20 short every time she touched it.

Stephanie: I know an ice cream specialty shop that wouldn't hire guys because once before one guy kicked in a freezer. Where I work now, they only let girls be waitresses. All the boys are dishwashers or bus boys.

Monica: My boss always starts the guys at the grill, and they have to work to the front. I don't see why. Is it more appealing to be served by a girl?

Carrie: It's that way where I work, too. Even though they'll teach boys to do the front, they don't ever do it.

Monica: That's why they hire kids—they know we won't say anything. They know they can get away with it.

Leslie *Mercer Island, Washington:* I'm not as concerned with sex discrimination as age discrimination. If a mom was bored and decided to work, would this happen to her?

Why do you work?

Stephanie: It started out with parent pressure. My parents were always like, "Get a job. Get a job." I work so they don't have to pay as much. I don't think I have saved any money. I don't know where it goes. I don't think I spend so much. I think I am skimping on stuff, but I never have any money.

Leslie: I worked for college—

anything it takes to impress the school.

Kelly *Auburn, Washington:* College is expensive though. My dad is not going to pay for my education, and he makes too much money for me to get a grant or a loan.

How does work affect school?

Carrie: I got a job in the June before my junior year. I worked all summer, and I needed the money. They were willing to work around my volleyball schedule. I would go to school until 2:30 and have volleyball practice until 5:30. At 6 o'clock, I'd go to work until 10 or 11 p.m. Then I'd go home. I'd work two nights a week, and then two nights I'd have volleyball games. I had Wednesday night to do homework. I never got any sleep.

Everything suffered. I was always cranky. At work I wasn't doing good. At volleyball I wasn't doing good. My grades went down.

I was really irritable because I felt like I was being forced to do things I didn't want to do. I was losing freedom. I was more tense, lashing out here and there.

Leslie: I found it very easy to negotiate with my boss. I worked at an office. If I didn't feel like working, I would say I had homework. She'd say, "Okay, do your homework, and get your A."

Stephanie: I had no friends. I didn't call anybody. I didn't do anything with anybody outside of school. I felt like I existed, but that was it.

How can teenagers improve relations with employers?

Stephanie: The government ought to start regulating the businesses.

Monica: They have all these laws, but do they enforce them? No.

Carrie: Even if you try really hard to get along, try to be good, and try to say everything you're supposed to, employers reward you by taking you back into the kitchen to yell at you.

Leslie: If people put their own personal satisfaction ahead of making money, some of the younger generation would be much happier about working. It's the difference between being happy where you are and making money.

Why are teenagers treated poorly?

Monica: The managers want to do their jobs well so they can get promoted and get out of there.

Leslie: How can managers make themselves look good when they are treating you like this piece of crap? You are not performing as well as you could so they are in effect making themselves look worse.

Stephanie: If you want to be a good boss, you have to have the respect of the people who are working for you.

Monica: It has to be a mutual exchange—not just respect because you are below them—but they shouldn't treat you like you're not standing there.

Carrie: Teenagers are reasonably intelligent people, but the managers assume you are really stupid.

Cleveland
Jane Addams Business Career Center

Do parents influence the decision to get a job?

Eva: They want you to get work other than just sitting around the house watching TV and talking on the telephone.

Michael: They might want you to learn more responsibility and how to handle yourself financially. My mother suggested that I should get a job because I like to spend money. I spent a lot of it so she told me to get a job so that I can know what it's like to have to pay all these bills and support somebody else.

Yolanda: They want you to make your own money.

Kevin: If you have a job, you'll have management over money so you'll be able to spend your money wisely. You don't go out and buy everything.

Are teenagers treated differently than adult employees?

Bernard: Bosses think we're just pushovers.

Yolanda: When I had my summer job, I really didn't like the supervisor. Of the three days we were there, she came in twice. When she came in, she stayed in her office. The lady under her had this attitude: "You're going to do what I tell you to do, or you can go home." We just got fed up with it. All she did was stand in the kitchen, smoke, and talk to her friend.

Kevin: It's often looked upon as, "They're teenagers. They're glad to get the $3.50." They figure you are satisfied.

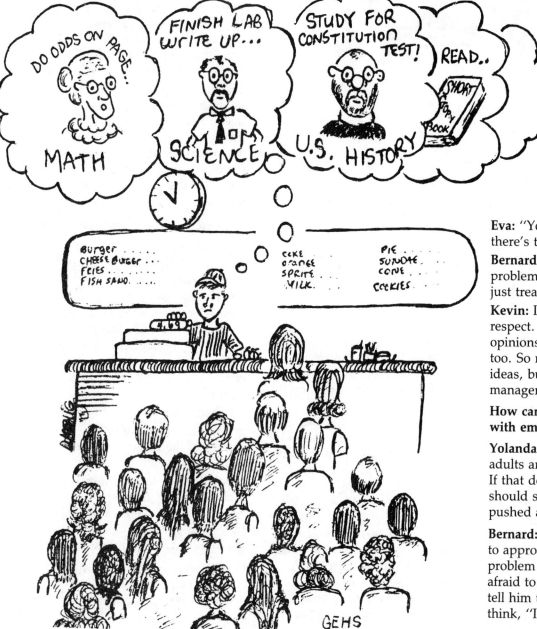

Eva: "You'd better be satisfied, or there's the door."

Bernard: The majority of the problems would be solved if they just treated us as adults.

Kevin: If they gave us a little more respect. When they're considering opinions, they need to listen to us too. So many of us have good ideas, but you can't tell the managers.

How can teens solve problems with employers?

Yolanda: They should talk to the adults and tell them how they feel. If that doesn't help, then they should show that they can't be pushed around.

Bernard: You have to know how to approach them. The main problem is that most teenagers are afraid to go to their employer and tell him the problem because they think, "I'm here making minimum wage, and he can go and get somebody else to fill my shoes."

Michael: The only thing that we as teens can do is to talk with our bosses. If that doesn't work, then I don't know of any other way to express ourselves.

Eva: Maybe we should be better at doing our work. Never be late, and really work yourself up to the boss's desk. He could really get to like you and get to know you personally. It will be a lot better. It's not brown-nosing. You're just doing your job.

What are the problems of working?

Yolanda: You can't go to work, come home at 11 p.m., and do your homework. You have to get to bed. You can't bring in your homework if you haven't done it, and you don't understand what's going on.

Bernard: Jobs are another cause for poor attendance. I have a class with kids whom you might see two or three times a week. You ask them where they've been, and they'll say, "I couldn't make it. I had to work until 3 in the morning. I just couldn't get up." I don't think employers take into mind that the kids have to go to school the next day.

Kevin: If they're going to hire teenagers and adults, they should work it so that the teenagers get the reasonable hours.

Yolanda: At least we could get home by 10:30 or 11 p.m. so we can attempt to do our homework.

Irving, Texas
Irving High School

Michele: A lot of teachers gripe that so many kids work. I'm about the only person I know right now who doesn't work. Everybody comes to school dead tired. My parents won't let me work during school.

Steve Hamberger *physical education*

teacher: Some people pull an eight-hour shift after they get out of school.

Monica: They work until one in the morning, get home, and then do their homework.

Hamberger: I know some guys who don't end their jobs until one o'clock in the morning and then try to get up for school.

Monica: But then again there's just no way to please. I guess you could just work on the weekends, but I wouldn't give up every one of my weekends for school. Besides, working on a Sunday is just like working on a Monday.

Oregon, Pennsylvania
Oregon Dairy Grocery Store

Why do people work?

Glenna: I needed a job during school. Whatever hours I want, they can give me. If I didn't have this job, I'd just be sitting around at home. This way I'm making money, and I'm learning to get along with people.

Kim: I'm going to college in the fall. When I leave, I will have a job when I come back on breaks. Having that means a lot. A job helped me to get organized with school. It helped me budget my time.

What qualities does the ideal manager possess?

Glenna: He talks to you and asks how you're doing every time you see him. They're not just up there sitting in the office, but they come down and help out. I like some respect. If you have a question, they respect you enough to answer it.

Kim: Many times my boss has bagged groceries for me, or he'll be running a register next to me. You'll say something to him, and he's really friendly about it. One time I had a problem, and I said, "I need to talk to you." That very day, he called me up there and

said, "Hey, you wanted to say something. What was it?" He was concerned about me.

What is the most important thing about a job?

Glenna: The number one priority for me would be that I enjoy it. But if I can enjoy it and get more money, hey, why not? But I'd much rather enjoy what I'm doing. I spend a lot of time there. Eight hours a day is a long time. It can only get worse if you don't like what you're doing.

What is an employee's responsibility to the employer?

Glenna: My responsibility now is to work. I don't call in sick when I'm not sick. I don't ask off if I don't have a reason. When I'm here, I put in my all. And when I'm ready to leave and move on, I'll give them sufficient notice to hire someone else. I don't just walk out the door.

Minneapolis
North High School

Why do teenagers work?

David: Money.

Kary: You get a lot of offers, meet a lot of people, and someday you might meet the right person who can help you, and you get paid for it. It's not only for the money.

David: My mom started working at Litton's on an assembly line, but they started closing up. We needed extra money so I helped out my mom and dad and got a little bit of money for myself. I'd rather work or do something than sit in the house all day.

Kary: I got my job because people kept saying that I should put my skills to use. I'm enjoying it, and I'm getting paid for it.

Mae Mae: I want to go on trips. I want to go out of town with our marching group and do certain activities.

Phil: I got it for a few reasons.

One, I needed the money. Two, I wanted to get a taste of what it was like working eight hours a day. It's a good time to start saving money and preparing for my future.

David: I always wanted to get a job. All I ever thought about was the money, but there are other things you have to look at. You have to think about how you can help their business.

What do teens dislike about their jobs?

Mae Mae: When my boss came in mad, he would get out on everybody. I would just want to go home. When I answered the phone, he influenced me to become mad.

Kary: I used to get mad at my boss, but I never showed it because he had the power to tell me to leave. I used to hate it when I would just make one mistake and he would get mad because he knew I had the talent but wasn't giving 100 percent. He used to really push me and stand over me.

Phil: I have to give up a lot of things because of my job.

David: Being with your friend, or sometimes you just want to relax.

Mae Mae: Basketball games, baseball games, track meets.

Phil: The hardest thing about my job is to have to work even though I don't want to work. I'm really tired, but I know that I've got to go to work.

How hard is it to get a job?

Phil: I went down everyday for about two weeks for an hour a day. I just kept bugging the managers. It seemed to take a long time, but I finally got the job.

Kary: You have to bug them sometimes. The manager got tired of it so he said, "Okay, I'll look at the application."

Being a teenager is a disadvantage because a lot of interviewers ask if you are in any extracurricular activities and what time you will come in. When something like football season comes around, they think that you will not come in. A lot of people use that against you.

How do employers treat teen workers differently?

Kary: When I worked for the city laying cement for the sidewalks, they expected me to be the fastest one because I was the youngest. "You're the young one. You go ahead and lay that block by yourself."

Phil: I work with security guard and maintenance guys. We all have our break room in the same area. The security and maintenance guys all had keys to it. The teenagers aren't issued keys. We have a break room, but it's three blocks away. But I do get a lot of respect because I help out a lot.

How can teens earn the employer's respect?

Mae Mae: Work harder. Be more active, communicate more, and know what is going on. Talk more with the people who work around you so that you can help them out. Then they can help you out.

Kary: Give a good first impression. You have to give out more than 100 percent.

David: I can't control what impression they give you, but I can give a little extra myself, or give advice, but that's about all I can do.

How does working affect teenagers?

Phil: It has affected my schooling. A few times I had to work late, one time because one of the pipes busted. I had to help clean up. I got home at 12:30. I didn't even hear my alarm go off.

Mae Mae: Work also affects friendships. You don't want all the time to be tied up working, but you want money. You still want to have friends and go places with them.

Phil: I like to spend time with my friends just for a change of pace. Working all the time, you get sick of the same old building, and you want to spend time away.

Is the subminimum wage fair?

Phil: It would create a lot of jobs. It would be real positive.

David: But it would be less money.

Kary: It would be opening more jobs for people, but the price of living is going up. Your check would be gone after buying one pair of pants.

Lititz, Pennsylvania
Weis Market

Have you ever been discriminated against?

Male 1: I just got a week off because of my earring. They won't let me wear it in here. They told me not to wear it, but I kept wearing it. Then they told me I have a week off. It's not fair. That's why I kept wearing it in the first place. But it's their store. They can tell me what they want.

Male 2: They tell us how long our hair can be and how we have to dress. I guess they can fire us for that too.

Male 1: I'd like to see my boss, instead of telling us what to do, come in and do it with us. Teenagers don't have job security because it's easy to find somebody else if they need the job. It's not like we have any kind of skill or anything. We can be easily trained in a week.

Olympia, Washington
Evergreen State College
Summer Journalism Workshop

How do you want to be treated by an employer?

Sarah *Mercer Island, Washington:* My first boss was really cool. She was really nice and treated me like an adult. Now where I work, they are really rude to me. The ideal boss would be one who respects you and has authority but doesn't take it out on you if he or she is having a bad day.

Leslie *Lynnwood, Washington:* My boss is really good. She talks to me like I am a person, not like I am just a kid. She treats me like

an equal though she is my boss. I can always come to her with a problem. It's very open.

What type of working conditions do teenage employees encounter?

Sarah: I have a horrible environment right now. The bathroom doesn't work. It smells. When I used it, I didn't know it didn't work so I had to fix the toilet before it flooded.

Crystina *Bremerton, Washington:* When I was a telephone solicitor, I worked in a dark room. If you shut the door, there was hardly any light. There was just a lightbulb on the ceiling. We'd work on commission, which was under the table because they were passing cash. The floors were always dirty, and there were spider webs on the walls. I was only 14.

How are teenagers taken advantage of?

Crystina: We start closing at 9:15 p.m. We're expected to have everything done by 9:45. But there are things that we have to have done, and if we are not done by 9:45, we have to work until they are done. We just get paid until 9:45. Sometimes I work until 10:15, and they don't pay us.

However, if we are a minute late, our pay starts at the next quarter hour. Everything is punctuality, speed, accuracy, and attitude. The bosses get on your case a lot.

What rights do teenagers have?

Sarah: I take advantage of my rights. They are having a hard time keeping people on, and they are really low so I took two weekends off. The boss said that was the last time so I said, "Fine, if you won't let me do it, I'll quit." She said, "No, you can go."

One of my friends worked at a fast-food restaurant. She got off at 12 o'clock at night. And she would have hours of homework. Sometimes she wouldn't get home from work until 3 a.m. and have to get up for school at 6. She had to work for college.

Leslie: I get a lot of respect from my boss. But if my co-workers want the day off, they ask me—it doesn't matter if I work an 11 or 12 hour day—because I am younger. Or they'll write it in the schedule and just leave a note for the next day. There should be no difference in teen and adult rights if it is the same job.

Tony *Battle Ground, Washington:* I think it would be better if teenagers were considered adults when it comes to the work force

because we are providing a service just like everybody else.

Crystina: When you're a teenager, you're so disposable. They can find another worker in five minutes. There are thousands of teenagers who are eager for your job. Your boss can just hold that over your head. Getting rid of you might be worth the cost of re-training. If there is something you don't like about the job, you don't have much say because they'll just get rid of you if you complain too much.

Lombard, Illinois
Glenbard East High School

What is good about working?

Sue: I meet a lot of nice people. I've had my job for about two years. It's not so much the money anymore. It's the people.

I have respect for a lot of the managers I work with because it seems like they care about your friendship. Even with the head store manager, we're still on a first-name basis. When the executives come in, we're still on a first-name basis. That's something I would definitely do if I were the manager because it makes you feel more comfortable. I would be offended if I thought a manager didn't care about me. It's kind of a feeling of mutual respect.

Is money or job satisfaction more important?

Sue: It depends on the situation. If you're our age and you're out looking for money to go to school, then money might be more important. If you're out looking for a career, you don't want to be stuck in it.

Boston
Humphrey Resource Center

Shelly: I worked at Bradley's, and I didn't like it because I worked so late. I didn't get out until 10:30. I wouldn't have enough time to do my homework, and then I'd be behind in class.

Is the subminimum wage proposal fair?

Jose: The government is crazy. I feel sorry for my little brother.

Shelley: I'm not going to say no to a job. Some money is better than none, right? I would take a job.

Jose: If I need a job bad, I'd start with $2.50.

Shelley: But as they want to lower minimum wage, the price of clothing is getting higher. At $2.50 an hour, you have to work for a whole month to buy a pair of jeans.

Oregon, Pennsylvania

What type of teenagers do you hire?

Curvin Hurst *manager:* I hire teenagers who are willing to work, and I hire on a trial basis. They have to come in and prove themselves for at least a month. If they're cutting it, then they're here on a permanent basis. In general, if the person is dedicated, willing to work, and has the energy, then we're usually willing to have him as a part of our team.

Why do teenagers work?

Hurst: Twenty-five percent are after the money, and 75 percent want to do a nice job. I would rather see teenagers come in to be part of a learning experience. This is just a stepping stone for them while they're finishing college or high school.

How should employers treat teenage employees?

Hurst: I'll go the third mile with a teenager versus an adult because they're learning. I also consider whether I know something about the family background. There are some teens who definitely have not had the chance I had. They were not brought up the way I was—being taught to think,

taught responsibility, taught discipline. I'll be more patient with them.

Sometimes I help just by listening to them. I feel I have the right, once it starts affecting job performance, to know what is wrong. Sometimes it's related to the job. Sometimes it's a terrible self-image problem or a problem at home or at school.

Grace Reed *manager:* They definitely have the right to a lunch and a break. They have the right to be treated reasonably. If they're sick, they shouldn't be forced to stand there for four hours. I don't think they have a whole lot of rights because they are working for someone else.

What is the ideal manager?

Hurst: My responsibility is authority because I'm the manager. My ideal is to be their big brother, yet still the boss.

How should employers reprimand teenagers?

Hurst: It varies. Some just have to be set down and looked at eyeball to eyeball. Others need to be encouraged, complimented more. One thing I stress with all the managers here is that if you have to reprimand someone, but the person is improving, the compliment is twice as important as the reprimand.

Is a subminimum wage fair?

Reed: I would resent it if I were a teenager and had to work for less than the minimum wage.

Elton Horst *manager:* They work hard and should be compensated for it. I resent the attitude of anyone who says, ''I'm only making $3.35 and only have to do this much. I don't have to give my full potential.'' You give your full potential regardless because that affects your whole future as a teenager. It would be nice to pay good kids good money, but it's just not possible economically.

How does work affect teenagers?

Reed: I know some students who were pretty irresponsible when they came here. Through having to hold a job, they have grown up a little and have learned some responsibility. It makes them a little more independent and gives them some spending money.

How can employers make teenagers responsible?

Horst: Hound them. Some kids have come and weren't that good, but through some work, turned into productive people. For some, it came down to, "Either you'll shape up or ship out." Some people have even been dismissed and been rehired—they came back much better.

Do employers condescend to teenagers?

Reed: There are probably two reasons why they do. One, that's human nature. Two, if you have two out of three teens who are messing around, it's hard to treat the other one well.

Horst: Also, teenagers are dispensable. I'm sure other places treat their kids poorly for that reason. "If you don't like it, I'll hire somebody else."

Do teenagers call in sick to get a day off?

Reed: That probably doesn't happen too much. I've already had to question some people about why they weren't here, and sometimes it's a semi-legitimate reason. There's one guy who said he wanted a lot of hours. We did our best to work around him. He turned around and didn't come in for a whole week. It was obvious he had something better to do.

Horst: Some kids like to call in Friday night and say, "I'm not feeling well"—only to go to a concert that night. I'm going to have a hard time accepting what they say because they lost their integrity. I'd feel much better if

they called up Friday afternoon and said, "I've got this concert to go to. Is there any way possible?" I'd break my back to get them off work.

How should managers treat teenagers?

Reed: Somewhere between getting along and keeping them in line. You can do both. You want to be understanding and see where they're coming from, but at the same time there's work to be done and it has to be done right. You have to let them know when they're out of line or when something needs to be done differently. You can't sit back and expect them to do it right if you don't tell them how. People try to live up to your standards, and if you don't set any standards, they don't live up to them.

Horst: An ideal relationship is one of being their equal. Be friends with them because that's what teens need. Yet there are times when you have to assert your authority—to be the boss. When kids work for me, I like to relate to them—to talk about their music and what they're doing in school. But I like them to respect me as a manager when the time comes.

Seattle
Public Schools Center
for Summer Work Programs

What are the most common employer complaints?

Karen Bradford *intake and support service supervisor:* They complain about absenteeism and the lack of dependability. If teenagers are going to be late, they don't call. They are here one day, gone the next day, and back for half a day.

Judy Yasutake *enrolling specialist supervisor:* Promptness is a problem too. Kids come in late and do not call ahead of time. Teens leave after breaks or lunch and don't come back.

Joyce Vail *eligibility supervisor:* A

complaint is not showing up for their interview.

Jennifer Burd *job development supervisor:* Teens are not on time for their interview. Or once they get there, they don't appear interested or excited to be there.

What causes the problems?

Bradford: The kids we work with are from low-income families. They have not had structure in their lives. They have never learned the importance of being somewhere on time. They've had no role models to pattern themselves after.

Many kids think problems will be acceptable if they make up excuses: "I'll just call and tell them that my mother was in an accident."

Yasutake: Someone got a call, "I couldn't go to work today because I broke my arm." But the next day the teen came to work with nothing wrong.

Carolyn Wells *summer adviser:* I had one student tell her supervisor that she was going to be leaving the job early because her mother had planned to go to Canada. Twenty minutes after the student left, the mother called to talk to her. It was a pay day, and the student wanted to cash the check.

Bradford: Teenagers take things very literally, but adults do not remember that. They say, "You can go on your break, and I'll see you back here in an hour." The kid forgets that the manager told them to go down to the file room and file. The kid goes on the break for an hour because that's what they thought the supervisor said. The managers have to communicate very carefully and specifically.

Vail: Appropriate dress is a big problem. Last year I had one kid go on an interview at the Seattle Center in a bathing suit. It was a very strict job site. I asked the supervisor, "Did you ask the boy why he was there in a bathing suit?" He said, "Yes. He said he was going swimming after the interview." Nobody told that kid how to dress to go to a job interview.

Burd: Kids need to think and be innovative. If they notice that they are late for their interview, they should think, "I should go to a phone and call."

Wells: I had one supervisor in a day care center explain to me that she was used to working with children and to communicating with adults, but when it came to teenagers, she was a little confused. It was a totally new experience for her, she needed to learn how to handle it.

Who should teach teenagers to be responsible workers?

Vail: It would be nice if all teens came from families where they see responsibility every day. I don't think you can walk up to somebody who is 15 and suddenly teach them how to go to work.

Bradford: I think most schools have some type of vocational program. That's critical and helpful.

Wells: Students have to learn to communicate and get along. Even if they don't get along with their supervisor, they have to learn how to carry out the job and set aside the feelings. That's a big thing for them to learn.

What are students' misconceptions about work?

Burd: A lot of students have their idea of a dream job, and it is hard for them to lower their expectations and find out that's not how the job is going to start out.

Yasutake: They have problems understanding how payroll works. They think that once they have worked two weeks and turned in their time sheets, they should be paid right away. They can't understand the two-week lag.

Bradford: They need instant gratification. This is one of the biggest problems. They are used to instant gratification. Jobs don't give you that. It takes a long time to get personal rewards.

How can students learn to accept their jobs?

Vail: I think going to work, doing the job, and knowing that is what has to be done is the best teacher. Students need to hear, "Even though you don't want to do groundskeeping, this is your job." A lot of times they work out their own problems.

Bradford: Children are still in the "me" stage where everything has to center around them. The routine of having to do things they

CLEANER! I WANNA BE ABLE TO **LICK** PENNIES OFF THAT DARN FLOOR.

don't want to do teaches them to mature. A job helps them realize that the world is not fair and that there are things that they are going to have to do that they don't want to do.

However, there are some employers who claim nationally that they are doing a service to teenagers by giving employment at fast-food places. In fact, they treat kids just terrible. Most of the advisers will not refer kids to those jobs which make kids close late at night. The kids get home at 3 o'clock in the morning. They must, or they will lose their jobs. That whole industry is exploiting teenagers terribly.

Because the jobs are highly visible, that is where kids go to apply. But there are a lot of companies that would take teenagers and train them. But kids don't know about them. The kids don't think of applying there.

What can be done to protect teenagers from exploitative companies?

Bradford: It has to be an internal policy of that corporation not to do that. That's not going to happen.

It would have to be a groundswell effort by parents, school people, the public going to the window and saying, "What are you doing working at 1 o'clock in the morning?" I don't think they'll ever change.

How can teenagers improve relationships with employers?

Vail: Employers need to tell teenagers, "The reason we do things that way is because we're a

profit-making venture and this is what you need to do in order to make a profit." It's really cold, but it is the main reason that teenagers have the jobs.

Bradford: A lot of teenagers don't respond to logic though.

What solutions exist for the problems?

Bradford: The studies I have read indicate that teenagers who work do more poorly in schools. I think there is a question whether it is good for high school students to work, but I think they learn other things on the job that they cannot be taught in a classroom.

The most important part of job training, resume writing, should be made part of the school curriculum.

Yasutake: When I was in high school, we had a two-week work experience. I was in the business area so we got to choose where we wanted to work for two weeks, just to see what it was like. We went to the IRS. We worked there for two weeks. That was excellent.

Compiled by Cathy Mau

Solutions

Teenagers are taken advantage of by their bosses. The bosses realize that teenagers will be moving on and there will always be more. . . . They don't have to give raises or advances. They will just get a new teenager.

Diane Ginnaty, 17
Great Falls, Montana

I have a fantastic advantage in relations with my boss in that he

generally needs me as an employee more than I need employment. . . .

I see no reason to strive for self-betterment as a cashier. . . . When I have no customers, I feel inclined to commit the abominable act of sitting on the counter and occasionally opt for just walking around.

This greatly annoys the more orthodox cashiers who practice zen tactics in becoming mentally and spiritually "one with the register". . . . I feel I can "slack off" in my work because I do not need the job and therefore the headache.

Chris Pack, 16
Little Silver, New Jersey

I take advantage of my boss by always expecting a second chance whenever I do something wrong. I had been caught doing drugs (marijuana) outside by the dumpster while taking out the garbage, which only takes five to ten minutes but had taken me thirty-three minutes.

When I returned, my boss wasn't even angry. He just gestured to me in a polite manner that what I did was wrong, and since that moment, I haven't taken advantage of the head boss.

17-year-old male
New Jersey

Employers and employees should be able to joke around but still get the work done. . . . They should both be open-minded to listen to new ideas and accept them. This can be developed by . . . opening up to one another, . . . talking freely, being friendly, and asking . . . questions.

Kristin Sanek, 15
Munster, Indiana

I would improve working conditions by making all employees eligible for health benefits. Social medicine should be available through a work program. Then I would make sure there would be no discrimination on sex, race, or color. . . .

18-year-old male
Arizona

Employers and employees must work together, not as adversaries but as friends, to improve efficiency and boost production or sales.

Employees should realize that a company is not a democracy, but employers should nonetheless pay close attention to an employee's needs, wants, and ideas.

Robert Kehoe, 17
Countryside, Illinois

If I were to become a boss, . . . I would try to install more incentives that will encourage the employees to come to work. I feel that a motivated person will create a better . . . product for the company. I would do this in . . . more profit sharing, improved working conditions, pleasant surroundings, better food in the cafeteria, and flexible hours.

Creating a feeling of partnership between boss and employee would be beneficial. . . . The boss and employee should feel equal even though the boss has more responsibilities and receives a higher salary. A feeling of equality may chase away a lot of bitter feelings every time a person hears the word boss.

Cindy Felice, 16
Wood Dale, Illinois

An ideal relationship between employers and employees is being friendly while on the job but not too friendly. Things cannot get out of hand because the problem of favoritism could arise. During the working hours, there should be a businesslike atmosphere, but there should also be some socializing.

Terry Kish, 16
Munster, Indiana

The employer should develop his relationship with his employees by taking a personal interest in the worker. . . . My boss will call in school for me so I can stay home, give me tickets to a basketball game, and ask about problems. . . . This way he brings the maximum effort, at least from me. On the other hand, the employees should be grateful for what the employer does. The employee should take interest in the boss's welfare and work for him more diligently.

17-year-old male
Illinois

If I were to become a boss, I would make sure my employees wanted to be doing what the job required them to do. I would establish a relationship where the employees felt comfortable, yet realized their position versus mine as their boss. I would hope my employees would be able to communicate with me about business as well as personal problems. I would give my employees an open voice on issues such as hours, pay and raises, working conditions, and time off.

Jill Douglas, 15
Wood Dale, Illinois

I work at a . . . quick stop store. At first, . . . I got along with everyone except the boss. He always treated me like the stupid teenage employee who didn't know any better. . . . As far as he was concerned, I could never do anything right. After this went on for six months, I decided I was going to make peace with him. Every day when I came in, I made it a point to say hi and . . . a few kind words. . . . I began to try to change my attitude because I knew he'd never change his. Now, nine months later, we still aren't best buddies, but we are better than we have ever been.

Nicole Granack, 16
Munster, Indiana

Employees and Employers   69

Chapter 4.

Teens and Law

Encounter One

The sunlight beats heavily upon your body lying still among the tall swaying grass. The slightest sound makes your heart beat faster. Your sweat cascades down your face and stains your clothes. You silently pray that the cop who was chasing you will give up his search and leave you to walk home.

You laugh silently to yourself and think about how stupid the cop is. You were only trying to amuse yourself on this sweltering day with a couple of friends. Shooting crows with a pellet gun is not a capital offense. Crows are only garbage-picking scavengers. How were you to know that it was against the law? How were you to know that some police officer was going to go after you as if you had tried to shoot the President?

You hear a helicopter. Glancing upwards, you notice the airborne vehicle gliding closer and closer to your grassy hiding place. A police helicopter on your trail? How ridiculous.

You leap to your feet. Darting over one of your accomplices in crime, you run desperately for your life. Your parents will kill you if they ever find out that you were picked up by the police.

Closing your eyes, you fervently wish that you had never gotten into this situation. You open your eyes. Nothing has changed.

Encounter Two

Fireworks light up the night sky. You gaze upwards, marveling at their kaleidoscopic beauty.

Gleefully, you grab another artillery shell. You run to the launching tube and stuff the shell into it. Listening to the sound of other booming fireworks in the distance, you strike a match and light the fuse.

You step back.

BOOM!

The shell spirals upward and explodes in a blossom of fire, light, and noise.

Detonating too close to the earth, the shell releases a shower of colorful sparks which fall like meteorites to the rooftops and yards of surrounding houses.

Heedless of the possible consequences, you can't help but gaze breathlessly at the beautiful scene.

You run back to your pile of artillery shells and grab one. About to repeat the process, you find yourself blinded by a car's headlights.

A tall figure exits the car. All you can see is the silhouette of a sturdy, arrogant figure looming in front of the car's high beams. You think to yourself that you have seen this scene in a movie somewhere. The figure moves closer to you.

"You do know that fireworks are illegal in this state, don't you?"

Despite the questioning tone of the voice, you know that the figure is accusing you. You answer with a simple shrug of the shoulders.

"Well, they are. I have every reason in the world to take you in. I want you to give me every firework that you have left."

"Over my dead body," you think knowing that your fireworks are going to end up amusing his kids if he gets them. Dropping the shell you are holding behind you, you lie and say that you have no more.

"No more? We'll see. If I see another firework, I will be back. And I'll definitely take you in."

He turns around and goes back to his car. Then, he is gone.

Hatred shakes you to the core of your being. You wish a thousand curses on his family and friends. You close your eyes and wish you could be somewhere else where you can shoot your fireworks in peace. You open your eyes. Nothing has changed.

Encounter Three

Twin lights strike your rearview mirror.

Instantly, you know that it is the police car you passed over a mile ago. Hidden in the night's blackness among dense trees, it had been waiting to catch unwary speeders.

You look at your speedometer. You are not speeding. In fact, you are running exactly two miles per hour under the speed limit. Is that cop after you? What did you do? What will you say? You did not do anything to entice this lawman into coming after you. No. You know that you have done nothing wrong, and you conclude that the cop is not going after you.

As if to prove your guess incorrect, the cop car speeds up until it is following close behind you.

Panic seizes you. This is not good. This is very bad. You do not even dare look behind you to see the driver's face. You try to calm yourself.

Quickly you run a list through your mind. Do you have your license? God, you hope so. Do you have the car's registration? You had better find it. Where did your dad put it? You can get 15 years for grand theft auto.

Other cars soon catch up with you and pass you. You think that this is your chance to escape. Or, at the very least, find out whether the cop car is following you.

You position yourself within a group of cars and hope that some fool will pass into your lane behind you. Some fool does. And then another one does. And another one does.

Calming down, you take the ultimate test. At the next intersection, you turn. You look back to see whether he follows. Except for the handful of cars that also turn, there is no cop in sight.

Triumphantly, you go along your merry way.

He is there.

Far behind you, the cop car turns on the road you are traveling. He is speeding, trying hard to catch up. He weaves between cars in his pursuit of you.

Desperately, you increase your speed. You weave between cars and try to put as much distance between him and you as possible.

Lisa Fowler LTHS

You see your chance. Climbing and descending a steep embankment, you notice that you are hidden from the cop car's view. At the next intersection, you turn. You drive deeper and deeper into a housing development. At the next intersection, you turn again. Turning five more times, you finally park and try to catch your breath.

Waiting for any sign of the cop, you notice how you are drenched in sweat. You curse and slump into your seat.

A car comes speeding out of the shadows.

You freeze.

It is a false alarm.

A stream of curses flows out of your mouth. Then you realize it. You look around. You are lost.

Your mind boils with a hatred so evil that it threatens to consume your body as well as your mind. You hate and hate and hate. How could that pig do this to you? How are you going to find your way home? It is 3 a.m. Who are you going to ask for help? You are going to ask a cop? When hell freezes over!

You close your eyes and try to soothe your rage. You desperately wish that you could be at home. You open your eyes. Nothing has changed.

Encounter Four

You are running for your life. Through alleys and city streets, you leap over garbage cans and sleeping vagrants. Familiar buildings become unfamiliar with each step you take. They are after you.

Why you? You have killed. That is the only explanation you can come up with. If you had only wounded him, they would not be hunting you down like this. You would not be in so much trouble.

The gun. The damn gun. Where did you leave it? Do they have it? Your dad's gun. A cop's gun. Where the hell is it?

You hear the sirens. You do not stop. You hear their footsteps. You do not stop. Heart beating wildly, you search for a hiding place. They are yelling at you now. You see an alley and run into it.

Too late, you see the dead end. How appropriate you think. There is nothing more you can do. You turn to face them.

"You made the biggest mistake of your life. Do you know what it means to shoot one of us?"

You pray as you have never prayed before. Your parents, your brothers and sisters, what will they think?

You are doomed.

You close your eyes and wish for a way out of this situation. You wish and wish and wish and wish. You want one thing, one simple thing.

You want a cop.

Where are they when you need them?

You open your eyes. Everything has changed.

Dave Palomares

Conflicts

If it's left up to me, I'd change one law—the one that stipulates that a person must be 18 or accompanied by a guardian to gain admittance to a bar. . . . I don't drink and have no interest in being at a bar for that purpose. There have, however, been several occasions when I had wanted to attend a concert being held in a club but was barred because I'm not 18. This seems a bit silly to me.

First, I want to know why the average 18-year-old is allowed to be in a bar that the average 16-year-old is forbidden to enter. Neither can be legally served.

*I wonder why there isn't some sort of exception made in the case of a concert. Nobody tries to keep 16-year-*olds out of theaters where the same groups play. . . . Why is it all right for . . . 16-year-olds to be in that same establishment as long as mommy . . . is brought along for the ride?*

Scott Smith, 16
Grosse Point Farms, Michigan

Curfew laws should be changed or abolished because police use that law as an excuse to harass teenagers. The law in San Francisco states that teens must be home by 11 p.m., unless they are accompanied by an adult or returning from work or a social gathering. . . .

I stay out late quite often, and I have been stopped by police. . . . A
couple of times I have even been stopped before 11 and searched because it's almost curfew time. The cop "doesn't want to take any chances on trouble." . . .*

I think the law should be changed so that only teens causing trouble, like being loud or drunk, will be picked up. I know one kid who was arrested for being out past curfew while he was waiting for a bus. The police didn't believe him, and they arrested him. The law is a farce.

Norman Lieberman, 17
San Francisco, California

There's a curfew set for teenagers, and there should be one set for adults, too. You can't drink until you're 21. They say it's because of teenage accidents, but look at all the accidents adults cause. . . . They say teens can't be trusted, but neither can some adults.

Tammy Gallant, 14
Clearwater, Florida

On a Friday night one summer eight high school juniors were driving around town in a van. Around 10: 40 p.m., a police car pulled them over without reason. The police never approached the car but called in two back-up units and forced the van to remain there until 11 p.m. At this time the police asked everyone to get out of the van because it was after curfew. They searched the van and people and found nothing wrong.

The police then informed everyone . . . that it was after curfew, but they would let the people off with a warning. One of the kids . . . was 18. As long as you are with an adult, you can be out after curfew. So the police had held the van for over twenty minutes without any reason and could have been sued for wrongful detention. . . .

When the high school lets out, the police always have a patrol car at each end of the street that the school is on and one car circling the block. This accounts for three out of the five cars on duty. It seems the police are devoting a lot more time than necessary in trying to catch high school kids doing something wrong.

John Mohan, 15
Grinnell, Iowa

I think there is a bias against teens among police. We are the troublemakers of America—the ones who grow up and steal cars, kill people, lie, and cheat. But we're also the ones who grow up to be doctors, reporters, and teachers—and even police officers just looking for a teen to bust.

Susan Stonelake, 14
Clearwater, Florida

Some teenagers can't have fun without doing something illegal. The police

realize that and are . . . a lot more careful with us, even the teens who haven't done a single wrong thing in their lives.

Jennifer Congdon, 14
Albuquerque, New Mexico

A mistake the government has made is the inconsistency in the legal age to perform certain acts. For example, the legal age to vote and get drafted is 18. Contrary to this, a person can't legally buy a drink in a bar until he's 21 but can attend an R-rated movie or get a driver's license as early as 16.

15-year-old male
Michigan

Police officers seem to look out for teens more than older people. The police must think that we constantly break the law, or at least border on it. Who are the murderers, embezzlers, thieves, and drunk drivers? The older generation.

Teens should be governed, but watch the adults, the people that feed the teens a warped and evil outlook on life. Make sure the adults don't break the law. We, the children of disruptive and destructive parents, are not the unlawful people everyone sees us as. Give us a chance. . . .

Steve Marra, 16
Bluefield, West Virginia

I want to go into a bar to dance, but it's illegal. I want to stay out until two, but it's illegal. I want to go to a party with my friends, but the cops come and send everyone home or take them to the station.

Why can adults do things that teenagers can't? Why is it illegal? Adolescence is just a twisted form of adulthood.

Heather Hopp, 16
Laramie, Wyoming

Members of any community see laws and regulations only as a minor annoyance and indulge themselves in their beloved chaos. The phrase ''innocent until proven guilty'' no longer has any meaning.

Huge corporations hire staffs of lawyers to find loopholes to protect them from prosecution. Dangerous criminals are free to run the streets because their rights have been violated. The victim's only right is to remain silent, most often from the grave.

N. Chad Caldwell, 15
Princeton, West Virginia

Raising the drinking law to 21 years of age hasn't really been a big success. You can find someone the age of 21 to buy beer and . . . anything else you

want. But it seems that if you're old enough to fight in war at 18, why not drink? . . . As long as alcohol and drugs are around, laws will never be obeyed.

Michelle Vest, 16
Bluefield, West Virginia

Our city council is trying to put an end to any form of skate boarding, such as scooters and skating. Our town is small so there isn't much to do. Every week on Wednesday night around 100 skaters and some parents go down to city hall and complain. I wish something could be done.

Jodi Contreras, 16
Woodland, California

Wearing seatbelts should not be a must because it may be uncomfortable and it may also hurt persons as much as it may save them. . . . Another law that . . . is not fair to teenagers is that when you receive your license, you are on probation. If within a certain period of time you receive three tickets or get into an accident, you have to go to classes to receive your license again. The law is not fair because no matter what age you are, you may get into an accident and may hurt or even kill a person.

Paula Latona, 18
Garfield, New Jersey

A lot of 15, 16, and 17-year-old teenagers, especially girls, find relationships with 21- (and over) year-olds. Not only is this against the law, but it is against a lot of parents' laws. I find my parents really uptight about things like this, and it stops me from doing the things I want to do. . . .

Laws cause people to lie. . . . Even police officers lie, saying that you were going 80 in a 40 mph zone, or exaggerating their reports. If the police cannot be honest, who can? After all, who is enforcing the law? Dishonest cops?

17-year-old female
West Virginia

When kids want the right to do something and the city just won't let them, that gives the kids more of an incentive to go against the law and do anything to win.

Jennifer Kreiter, 17
Woodland, California

In this proud country, criminals don't have to escape from jail. They hire a smart lawyer who will get them off because the arresting officer left out one word when reading them their rights, the warrant for their arrest had one misspelled word (therefore declared invalid), or another insignificant procedure was botched. Most of the

criminals set free because of a technicality are clearly guilty.

The people who write the warrants or read them their rights are only human and will make mistakes. Is that any reason to let drug dealers back on the streets?. . . . I ask you . . . which is worse, a misspelled word or murder?

Danay S. Neal, 15
Bluefield, West Virginia

I get kicked out of bowling alleys and restaurants when my friends and I are talking. The law officers call it loitering. As I leave the restaurant, I look back at an elderly couple who is

Ulric Davis

doing the exact same thing. Their age makes them responsible, I guess. . . .

Officers should protect not harass. By picking fights with the youth of America, they are only provoking a war. I really respect policemen, but when they are looking to bust you, that really pisses me off.

18-year-old male
West Virginia

At the ''hang out'' in Bluefield everything from drugs to alcohol is down there, yet . . . there is never police patrol. . . . Businesses are obviously supplying kids with this alcohol. The laws are there, but the enforcement is not.

Tiffany Quesenberry, 15
Bluefield, West Virginia

Discussion

Youth law expert *Washington, D.C.:* Teenagers tend to have more contact with the criminal justice system than any other age group.

Teenager *St. Petersburg, Florida:* After dealing with so many of the wrong elements of teenagers, police become hard toward teenagers.

Tucson, Arizona
A local high school

How do the police react to teenagers?

Jason: Some are mean. Some are friendly.

Sangra: They think you're doing something wrong just because you're a teenager. They see you pass by, and they keep a close eye on you, more than if you were an adult. Now, they're giving us a curfew which I don't think is fair. If you're 18, I think you should be allowed out as late as you want. But now 18-year-olds have a 12

o'clock curfew. I really think that's unfair.

We like to go riding up and down this street. It's a place where everybody just goes riding up and down. Now they're giving us a limit that we can only go through there once or twice. It gets pretty crowded on weekends when everybody's there, but now they're taking that away from us too. We're not allowed in nightclubs. What fun can we have? People think the only fun we can have is to smoke, drink, or have a party some place where nobody will find out. It's really dumb because we're not doing anything wrong riding around.

Mark: The stereotype of teenagers is bad. Even my doctor asked me how many stabbings there were at our school last week.

Are police more biased against teenagers?

Mark: Yes, they get suspicious if you hang around. It's more likely that they'll bust a teenager than his parents.

Sandra: They think we have no sense of responsibility. They don't think we're trustworthy. They have an image of a teenager always causing trouble, drinking, smoking. None of us are like that. Some of us just go out and ride around. We don't even drink or smoke. They treat us the same as those who are causing trouble and fighting. I really don't think that's fair.

What do the police do to show that they care?

Mark: They give you breaks.
Sandra: Warnings.
Mark: They'll have a good attitude about it. A lot of them don't. They should say, "Hey guys, you can't park here. You'll have to move." Just a nice friendly attitude about it instead of "Get out of here!"
Sandra: If somebody talks to you nicely, you'll listen. It's different

from someone saying, "Get off here! You're not supposed to be here, you dumb little kid." You just stay there on purpose. You'll circle around the block and come back just to get him mad.

Do the police treat minority groups differently?

Sandra: They think Mexicans cause more trouble than the whites on the east side.

Mark: On the east side they still park illegally even though the police said they stopped that practice.

Sandra: They haven't taken anything away from the east side.

Mark: But over here the policemen actually block the entrance to Jack-in-the-Box, and they don't let anybody out without giving them a ticket.

Do they treat Hispanics differently than blacks or whites?

Mark: It's pretty evident on weekends that you'll see the majority of the cops on the south side. You see more cops than you see girls.

How can teenagers help improve the relationship with police?

Mark: We could explain the situation of teens to the police. Be able to talk. Try to relate to each other.

Sandra: Communicate.

Mark: Make them respect us as growing individuals.

Tina: People are going to have their own impressions no matter what you do. Everyone believes different things and has their own prejudices. But people should remember when they were teenagers.

Boston
English High School

How do students feel about treatment by the police?

Huston Crayton *social studies*

teacher: Students in the cities have a different perception of the police than kids in the suburbs. Here, the police are the enemy. The laws of the street say take advantage of any situation. If someone gives you two bucks extra for change, you don't tell them. If something is sitting out there, you take it. The kids feel that it's your stupidity for leaving it unsecured. I'm talking about kids here who don't know where their next meal is coming from. A lot of these kids are on their own in apartments at 16.

If you are in the suburbs, your mother and father own a home. You have food, and you usually have a bike. You have transportation. These kids don't have anything like that. They have a bunch of cement basketball courts and get certificates if they win championships. For basketball, all you need is a ball—something round. That's why you have a lot of basketball. Blacks would love to play hockey, but there are no ice rinks. There is no money. Even the poor whites can't afford to play.

"Look, nobody gives a crap about us. We got to make it any kind of way that we can. Nothing's wrong with selling a few nickel bags here and there," they feel.

It is basically a Robin Hood idea. "We're victims, and we have to make it." Blue collar crime is no worse than white collar crime. Some of the kids have some morals—they believe that you shouldn't kill anyone. Some kids believe that anything goes.

What kinds of attitudes do police have?

Crayton: The police have become apathetic. I saw two of my students get shot last Christmas. I was at a gas station on my way home, and I heard shots. When I went over there, one of the kids was lying on the ground. Two kids were killed in front of the Chez-vous Skating. We had a big memorial service on Martin Luther King day.

The police didn't even get out of the car. The kids were lying in the street. One black policeman came out with his gun drawn after the shooting. After the shooting, he went up and held one of the kids. The white police didn't get out because if a policeman shoots someone, he can lose his job, especially if he is white in a black neighborhood.

It was black on black. They were fighting over a girl. A kid came out and shot two of the fellows that he was fighting with. Point blank. Right up and shot this guy twice and ran down the street and shot the other one. The white policemen did not leave the vehicle. When I got there, I looked on and saw kids lying there. Somebody walks up and punches another kid in the face. Everybody runs because it was so unstable. The situation was unstable for at least an hour. I took off. I went back to the car. It was very unstable for anyone to do anything.

I heard from mothers. I said, "Hey, these guys didn't want to risk their jobs. If they get out and there is a guy with a gun, the only way to make him drop it is to shoot him. If you shoot someone in the city, then they are going to suspend you without pay. And you have the parents and the community after you."

Does this type of violence happen in the suburbs?

Crayton: I don't think so. It's the concrete jungle type of thing. There is so much crime. I think it's a different kind of animal. It's pretty raw. People walking on top of buildings with machine guns to protect the drug selling area. You are coming home from work, and all of a sudden two guys open up on each other. One lady was shot in the cheek last summer.

The police have become like some teachers. "Hey, it's a monster here. There's nothing I'm going to be able to do with it." The teacher says, "Look, see this student over here. I will push him through because he wants to learn, and he wants it so I'll help him. These characters over here, they have no respect so to heck with them. I'll just flunk them or give them a D and let them get out of school and get a job at the car wash." They're apathetic. They won't take time with students.

The kids feel that no one cares. They don't care. I think it's the mentality of the kids. There is some Scripture that says, "This generation, the young shall be weaker and wiser.'' And there is some truth to that. Our parents could work twenty hours a day and be 85 and be strong and take it. Out in the cold, you couldn't get these kids today to do that kind of work.

Yet 6-year-old kids can hold a conversation. My 6-year-old daughter is as articulate as I was when I was 16 or 17. She sits down and talks about what is negative and what is positive. They know what sex is. They know how to be apologetic. They know everything because of the media. Kids are much further along than we were. The kids know a lot more now, and it breeds a different kind of reaction. The kids just have much more to go with.

Lombard, Illinois
Glenbard East High School

Are police biased against teenagers?

Sue: Yes. I was at the park, and this guy was in his mother's Z-28. He was spinning out in the parking lot. The car slid into a cement wall, and the tires were bent in. When the policeman comes, the first thing he says when he gets out of the car is, "How do you feel now, punk? Do you feel good about what you did?" The guy, who's standing there crying, said, "No, I feel like shit!" The officer said, "Good, I hope you do. I'll take your license away right now. Get in the truck." He didn't even ask how it happened.

But from my experiences with the police, I would say their bark is worse than their bite. They threaten you and get you all shook up. Then they say, "Oh, I'll let you go this time." I don't know how many times they've said that to me.

Kris: We were stopped for speeding on the way home from a party once. When the driver got out of the car, two empty beer cans rolled out. The policeman goes, "Okay, everybody out of the car!" He gave us a half-hour lecture in 20-below weather. We were all just standing saying, "Okay, okay, let us go." It was just bull. Nobody was even drunk. Then he let us go.

Sue: Whenever I go driving with my dad, he speeds by cops all the time. My dad will go by a cop ten or fifteen miles over the speed limit, but the cop just sits there. When I go by with a boyfriend, the cop will pull us over for going five miles over the speed limit.

Meaghan: They think we're ignorant.

Kris: They always think, "You were speeding. You had better get out of the car, suspicion of alcohol."

Sue: A lot of times I go out and don't drink. Just because I drive around doesn't mean some cop should think I've been drinking.

Cops should approach teenagers with an open mind and not say, "They've probably been drinking. Let's follow them for a while and see if we can stop them for something."

Minneapolis
Minneapolis North High School

Troy: The police are getting worse because of the gang situation. They treat most black teens like they're in a gang. You can't go downtown without being forced to keep walking. You can't even stop and talk. They treat everybody like they're bad people. I don't think it's fair. I've never been in trouble for anything. I've been a good student all my life, and I have to worry about being harassed by the police because I'm black and they think I'm in a gang.

I think teenagers should stand up to gangs more. If all teenagers stand up for their rights, then maybe the cops will see that there are some teenagers who aren't for gangs.

Police think that teenagers

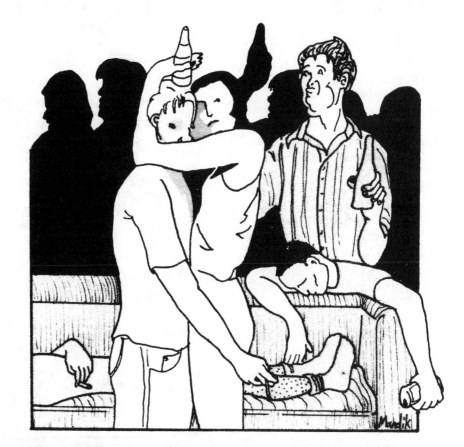

know nothing about the law and don't know if their rights are being violated or not. Adults would be able to see that their rights are being violated.

Berkeley, California
Interview with member
 of the Board of Education

How do police deal with teenagers?

Anna de Leon *attorney:* It depends on the color of their skin. In my experience black and Hispanic teenagers are treated differently from whites.

In Berkeley we have had an open-campus policy, and teenagers may wander around the city at will. Officers tend to see the white and Asian students who are high-achieving students as people on legitimate business and the black and Hispanic students as people on business they shouldn't be on.

But the merchants don't want any students around the community. They think if the teenagers are not ripping off the merchants, they are "making litter."

Are there more problems with police misconduct relating to teenagers?

de Leon: I haven't experienced that in Berkeley. In Oakland, there was a case of a police officer who grabbed a guy by the back of his head and slammed his face into a car. The guy required surgery on his face. His violation was that he was out past midnight. When they took him to jail, the jailer refused to admit him. He was 16 or 17 and had no record. The jailer said, "I'm not going to admit this man. Look at his face. He needs to go to the hospital." The cop, who refused to take him to the hospital, dumped him back where he found him. By then it was 2:30, and the teenager made his way home. His family sued the city

and won. He won $15,000, and his mother was awarded $6,000 for emotional distress. I think he should have gotten more.

What that cop did was disgusting. But I'm unaware of any discipline. I think nothing happened to that police officer.

How should police treat teenagers?

de Leon: Everybody's going to have to be involved and see what the truth is and see what's going on in a city like Oakland, which is similar to most other communities.

I think that the spirit of Miranda should apply to juveniles. In Berkeley, in fact, it does. Teenagers who are arrested should have a right not only to counsel, but also to see their parents or probation officer. My feeling is that for teens, the right to counsel is not that meaningful. They'd rather see their parents. In Berkeley, teens have the opportunity to talk to their parents before they're questioned, which I

G.E.H.S.

Mike Pistilli

feel is in the spirit of Miranda.

How should police react to teenagers?

Theresa Price *investigator:* Police should not be such a hard or cold type of individual when dealing with teenagers. They should be more responsive to the problems the teens are having.

Ted Hall *supervisor, youth and missing persons unit:* Also, the juvenile process was set up originally to help all juveniles. It was not designed to punish. Today's young person is about 17 years of age when he enters the adult criminal justice system in this country. We have to take a serious look at reconstructing the juvenile code for youthful offenders. In the past we haven't punished. It's called treatment.

We're going to have to take a look at punishing young people for some crimes. Juvenile judges need to be trained to deal with juvenile issues. A lot of the judges are unfamiliar with juvenile code. As it stands today, we are not doing a very good job of addressing the problems. When we start handling them the way they should be handled, some of the problems will go away.

Price: I think that we're taking the role of slapping them on the hand. We also provide them with counseling. We're telling them how to handle their problems. They need to recognize that they have a problem.

What kind of illegal actions do teenagers get involved in?

Price: A lot of young girls get involved in various things. They start working the streets as prostitutes. They all become street-wise. They learn how to steal. They learn about drugs and become involved in all the wrong

elements. Also, the younger kids mold themselves to the older kids. The older kids, 18-, 19-, and 20-year olds, teach the 13- and 14-year-olds how to shoplift for them.

What are the major legal issues facing teens?

Bernt A. Monsen *chief of police:* The use of alcohol and drugs is a major issue. The problem with alcohol is that it's socially accepted. Parents don't look at it as being as harmful as drugs. It's almost a relief for Mom and Dad when they find out their kid was drinking. Thank God it wasn't drugs. The problem is that underage drinking is against the law. To get the money for drugs and alcohol, a lot of kids turn to crime.

A problem for us when dealing with teenagers is that on one hand people want us to get along with them and encourage them to respect the law. On the other hand, we're called to be the bad guy and bang them over the head because they're violating the law. We'd like to get along with kids but I know a lot of teenagers grow up with a dislike for the police. We've got a job to do. We do to some extent try to be reasonable, but some teenagers don't respond to warnings.

If a kid's parents have a bias, it has a great influence on the kid. If a parent has a bad run-in with a police officer, the kid picks up the bias.

What are the major legal issues facing teens?

Nicky: School officials are able to search your belongings, your purse, your person. They only have to have probable cause, not a

warrant or a police officer present.

Sam: By the time all the teachers meet to decide on searching the locker of someone who is suspected of having drugs, Joe Blow, the campus's big drug dealer, hears the rumor and gets all of his drugs out. That wrecks the entire search and seizure.

Cynthia: A friend of mine was in the bathroom one day when the dean walked in, smelled cigarette smoke, and searched my friend. She emptied her purse, but there was nothing. There was no cigarette so the search wasn't really necessary.

DJ: There's too much left up to the officials in school—not only with search and seizure but with the new dress code they just came up with.

Nicky: You can't look distracting.

DJ: There's nothing to define distracting. It's up to the officials.

Nicky: There's nothing that says the school officials are qualified to make any of these decisions.

Sam: I disagree. I think it's essential for the safety and protection of the other students. The administration might be able to prevent crimes, prevent drug sales, and prevent violent things from happening.

Should locker searches be permitted?

Troy: I think it violates my rights. If they search my locker, all they're going to find is papers and books.

Tina: I think it's good. If there was someone around here who was sick and had a gun, then it would be good if they search that person's locker.

Troy: I think they should have a really good cause and a warrant like the cops do. So you can be there to defend yourself.

When is it right for teenagers to break the law?

Troy: It's never right for anyone to break the law. The law is put there for our protection. If people can break it, then there's no reason to have it.

Tina: I think there are some laws that are broken by teenagers all the time. Under 18 you can't smoke; under 19 you can't drink.

What laws should be changed?

Troy: I would make the drunk driving law harsher. People have to feel their mistake because it takes the lives of too many good people.

Lombard, Illinois

Are the laws against drinking and driving strict enough?

Julio: I think a lot of people still get away with drinking and driving.

Sue: If they carry through on it and take your license away, okay. But the law is so negotiable. Some people can have twelve beers and drive fine. Some people can have one beer, but they're still as wasted as the guy who had twelve beers because their blood-alcohol level is real low.

How would a lower drinking age affect teenage drinking?

Sue: I think I would drink more.

Kris: No, I think it would be less.

Sue: Just think how easily you could get it if you could go buy your own beer. I think I'd drink more. If you want to drink now, you have to get someone to buy it for you. You have to pay them extra money just to buy beer. Then you have to go somewhere and drink it because you can't drink it in front of your parents. The thrill of drinking would be lost, but it would be like drinking anything else. Have a glass of milk—have a glass of beer. I think there would be more casual

drinking. Right now you go out and say, "Okay, I'm going to get drunk. I'm going to puke." You'd have a beer at a time. You wouldn't sit down and have six.

Kris: There wouldn't be all those high school parties where the parents are gone.

Sue: It would take some of the fun out of it.

Tucson, Arizona

Are students' rights ever violated in school?

Sandra: We were given the right to use all of the front parking lot. The teachers were supposed to use the lot in back. After a while, something happened to their lot so they parked in front. Some of the students were forced to park in the fire-lane, and they all got tickets.

Maik: A lot of the teachers resent the fact that we drive to school. Some say, "Can't you walk to school?"

Sandra: Or, "Can't your parents drop you off?"

What law affects teenagers the most?

Sandra: The drinking age.

Mark: The drinking age is 21, but the people who want to drink will drink regardless of the law.

Sandra: If kids under the age want to drink, they can have their older sister or older friend go buy liquor for them. The drinking age used to be 17. Then it went up to 18. It just kept going up.

Mark: It's not only the drinking age. You can't get inside any place even if you don't drink. If you want to go dancing, you can't. Or if you want to see rock bands in clubs, you can't. You have to be 21.

Washington, D.C.
National Crime Prevention Council Headquarters

Terrence Modglin *director of youth*

programs: Teens are victimized at a higher rate than any other age group in our society. Teens, particularly between the ages of 16 and 19, also have the highest rate of violations of the law. So, the teenagers tend to have more contact with the criminal justice system than any other age group on a per capita basis. More than half of the calls that the police and sheriffs undertake in the United States involve teenagers.

When the crime practitioner, police officer, or civilian practitioner comes in to the sixth or seventh grade, the kids are relatively accepting. But when you get into junior high and senior high, the kids are more skeptical. It's much more difficult and requires more skill to run a program for teens. Consequently, we find fewer programs for that age group.

For the teen, the lifestyle is a little more adventurous. It involves the testing of parameters. It's a period of questioning what society is about: who you are as an individual and what is the impact you want to make on society.

How can police prevent juvenile crime?

Modglin: Police need to learn to work better with young people. Dealing with juveniles should be a number one issue because that age group is more likely to be involved in a call to duty more than any other age group. The other thing is stereotyping. Teens are as diverse as any other age group. Sometimes we don't think of youngsters and teenagers as citizens. They're citizens as much as adults are citizens. The key question is what teens can do together rather than what they can do apart.

Why do teens commit a crime?

Modglin: Economic opportunity is one aspect. A black kid in the ghetto is highly influenced by seeing a drug dealer or pimp making a lot of money. They're making it easily without eight years of school. You can't change the kid's values with a five-minute talk. To combat that influence, it takes a person willing to spend long hours instilling the right moral values. The number one predictor of career criminals is the track record—how many times they were arrested as a juvenile.

Compiled by Doug Addison

Solutions

Changing laws is just like humoring the people . . . that have nothing better to do than circulate petitions . . . and cause trouble. I think we should just start over. After all, the Constitution is very old. Society has grown much more complicated. Coup d'etat!

> Gregory Barton, 15
> Oklahoma City, Oklahoma

I'd like to change the law that states all San Francisco public high school dances and activities must terminate at 10:30 p.m. At dances, people are just beginning to enjoy themselves at this time. The wallflowers are beginning to dance. . . . Then the dance ends abruptly with that last song.

I know the reason for this is to prevent teens from drinking, drug abuse. . . . But those activities are timeless so why deprive the other teens of having fun?

> Helen Chu, 15
> San Francisco, California

Drop the age of drinking to about 17 and then raise the driving age to . . . 21—that would make up for the drinking and driving and most of the people that are killed each year. . . . Most every teenager drinks. . . . Since a person would start drinking at that age, . . . by the time they would be driving, they would know how to handle themselves.

> Phil Shefferly, 16
> Grosse Pointe North, Michigan

WELL, DUDES, AFTER THIS ONE I GOTTA GO. GOTTA MAKE IT HOME BEFORE CURFEW. I DON'T WANNA BREAK THE LAW OR ANYTHING.

PEASLEE

Tax laws should be changed. People should only pay a base percentage of their income. It is not fair for those who make more money to pay a greater percentage. They probably worked just as hard as the other guy to earn their money.

> Amy Erikson, 16
> Oklahoma City, Oklahoma

I do not believe that all police hate teens. I have been picked up for speeding twice, and in both incidents

the police were friendly if I was friendly. I even got off with a warning by one of them.

> Jeff Wodle, 16
> Kellogg, Iowa

When individuals . . . reach their 18th birthday, they are . . . considered legal adults. They are required to register for the draft, are eligible to vote, are tried in the higher court, and are no longer dependent on their parents. Why then, . . . are they not able to go out and have a beer with their buddies? . . .

When one is 18, . . . he should be able to freely make his own choices. Drinking is a free choice every individual chooses to make.

Kelly Shibilski, 17
Stevens Point, Wisconsin

Each year many teens die from gunshot wounds. The only possible solution for this increasing problem is gun control. . . . If gun control were in effect, some of the 800 policemen . . . killed last year might be alive today. In our society . . . nearly 3,000 murders occur in our major cities and metropolitan areas every year. . . .

Gun control must limit the sale of all guns (not just handguns) if it is to work. Under the laws of gun control, every American who would apply for a gun permit must present a probable reason for owning a gun to a judge and jury and report each time the gun is fired. If firing of the gun is not reported, those who are caught will . . . serve 90 days in jail.

Kimberly Webb, 15
Southfield, Michigan

The proposed law of mandatory AIDS testing for immigrants . . . will slow the risk of spreading AIDS. Why should the Americans, whose country this is any way, suffer because an immigrant who wishes to become a U.S. citizen has AIDS? Although the

POLICE ACADEMY REPORT CARD

PURSUIT IN CAR	C
ON FOOT	C-
TARGET RANGE	D+
SELF DEFENSE	D
TEEN SIGHTING	A

11-15-87   WW

"Hey! I might have what it takes to be a cop after all"

U.S. is known as the melting pot, there have to be some restrictions.

Maggie Leffel, 15
Bluefield, West Virginia

I would like to change the . . . draft law. This law states that all men 18 or older must sign up. . . .

My question? What about women in this age group? I feel women are equally qualified for the draft. . . . Most men are just as stupid as women when it comes to military tactics. . . .

Yes, it's true: Women do produce the babies. But without men who are off at war, females are at a dead stop in this practice.

16-year-old female
Michigan

The Constitution . . . states that Americans have the right to bear arms, but in some cities that right has been taken away. . . .

The opposition states that because of this right, crime increases. This statement is wrong. Crime increases when young kids get . . . guns and use them for their personal gain. If the law were changed, the parents of a child caught with a gun would be fined heavily. . . . If the child took the gun without his parents knowing, he would be given a warning. If caught again, the child would be put in a juvenile home.

J.P. Cormier, 16
Harper Woods, Michigan

The death penalty laws and "innocent by reason of insanity" laws . . . are letting dangerous criminals off the hook too easily. . . . If someone takes another person's life, that person should be put to death. The person . . . murdered can never come to life again or . . . be replaced. Often other lives are shattered. . . . Maybe if criminals know that they will pay for their awful crimes with their lives, it will deter their actions. . . .

The "innocent by reason of insanity" laws . . . allow criminals to get off lightly with . . . a short

sentence in a psychiatric ward until they are deemed mentally stable. . . . These people often . . . commit other crimes. If they go insane once, how do we know they won't go insane again?

Todd Harrison, 15
San Francisco, California

Today not many people respect . . . the speed limit, especially with the help of radar detectors. The speed limit was raised to 65 miles per hour, but people will drive about 75 with a greater risk of an accident. If the speed limit were lowered to about 45 miles per hour, people would still go about 10 mph over it, but it would be a bit more reasonable.

Kevin Sheehy, 17
Grosse Point Woods,
Michigan

The ideal age for the legal consumption of liquor and also . . . to possess a driver's license is 18. . . . The age of 18 would be compatible with the voting age of 18, the military draft, and . . . the age of high school seniors upon graduation. Furthermore, American society suffers from a massive drunk driving problem. This could be remedied in part . . . if the driving age were raised to 18. . . . Teenagers tend to drink anyway, even if the legal drinking age is 21. . . .

In the United States, over 75,000 accidents a year are caused by 16- to 18-year-olds. This number could be substantially reduced if this segment of the driving population were restricted.

Kevin Meek, 16
Grosse Pointe Woods,
Michigan

Many religious groups believe in the marriage of one man to several wives. . . . If someone feels the obligation to have a multi-marriage, he should be able to have one.

A lot of women would probably say that the above are sexist remarks, but . . . there is no reason why a woman should not be able to have more than one husband, provided that she is able to support them.

The change of this law would probably mean a cut in the divorce rate due to the added variety of marriages. It would also help a lot of lonely single people find companionship by giving them a wider choice of whom they could marry.

David Cohen, 16
Southfield, Michigan

Laws prevent some conflicts by setting guidelines for actions. Even though exceptions occur, they are rare, and the enforcement of laws helps create order in society. . . . Without laws society would be in a primitive, chaotic state.

Monica Pawlowski, 15
Bluefield, West Virginia

Some of our laws are totally odd. For example, our drinking age is 21. In Europe and Australia, the drinking ages are lower, and there are fewer accidents. We need to have a younger drinking age . . . like 18. If you can vote, why not drink legally?

Another problem is our current statutory rape law. It is illegal for an 18-year-old and a 16-year-old to have sex. That is just plain stupid. Let us make up our minds about sex ourselves, not the lawmakers. These sex statutes are just "blue laws" that need to be changed. We need to let teens have more rights and govern their own lives.

Paul Wherry, 17
Ellensburg, Washington

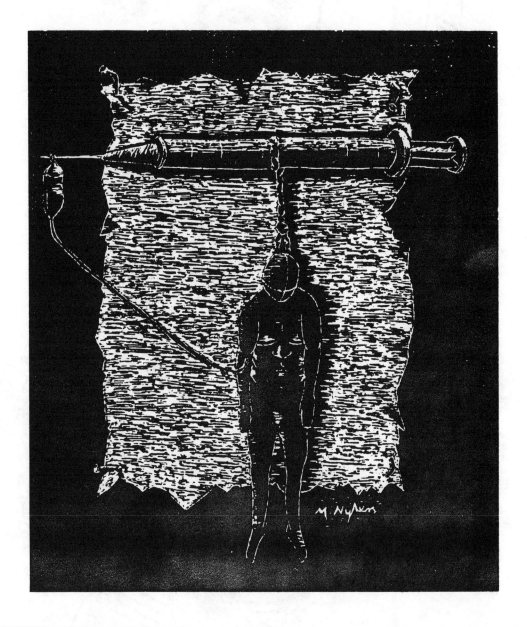

Chapter 5.

Teens and Politics

Justin Adaise came home from school hungry, thirsty, and tired, as usual. He grabbed a bottle of 7-Up and a box of Cheeze-Its, and plopped down in front of the TV to unwind from yet another tedious day at Arthur High. He grabbed the remote control and switched on the cable channels. Instead of watching Whitney Houston squirm her way through her latest musical masterpiece, however, he saw the inside of a Senate hearing room on the tube. Someone had left on C-Span, the Washington, D.C. government channel, from the night before.

"Nice walnut paneling," Justin thought as he stared at the wall behind the committee chairman's desk. Justin had often entertained the thought of becoming a public official because of the great furniture they had in their offices. All that real walnut, oak, brass, and leather would cost a fortune to buy yourself. If you were elected a representative, or a senator, or even a state comptroller, however, they just gave all that free furniture to you.

"I wonder if I could get my desk made with Tennessee ash . . . it has such a rich grain," Justin thought as he stifled a yawn. Strangely, Justin's last class of the day had been U.S. history, where they had discussed the pros and cons of the Federal Government. Or rather, where Justin's teacher, had lectured on and on about how great the United States government is.

"The U.S. government is the embodiment of greatness," Justin said with a smile imitating his teacher. "It will stand as the model for all others to follow as long as the earth revolves around the sun. . . ."

Justin's voice trailed off as he fell asleep and into a dream world. It was a world that was familiar to him from TV and newspapers but one in which he had never actually been. Now, wearing a blue pinstripe suit, a gold Rolex watch, and genuine Gucci shoes, he was seated in a cushioned leather chair behind the nicest Tennessee ash desk he could imagine. He was surrounded by ninety-nine other men and women dressed as neatly as he and seated behind similar desks.

Suddenly a booming voice snapped Justin's attention to a huge desk at the front of the chamber. There, under a giant American flag, stood a little weasel of a man in a blue pinstripe suit and glasses. He spoke loudly again into the microphone.

"Senator Adaise, how do you vote? Yea or nay?" the man asked him.

Justin stared at the man in puzzlement. "Senator Adaise?" Justin asked himself. Then he finally recognized the weasel who was questioning him. It was the Vice President, the presiding officer of the Senate.

"Senator Adaise, have you been sleeping?" the Vice President asked, to the chuckles of Justin's fellow senators.

"Well, as a matter of fact, I was sleeping, and then I had this dream," Justin began to say.

"Should the minimum wage for teenagers be lowered to $1.72 an hour?" the Veep interrupted. "Yea or nay, senator, yea or nay?"

Justin immediately realized that the bill would drastically affect his own personal income. If he were to make only $1.72 an hour, he could forget about the car stereo and the U2 concert, too.

"Nay!" Justin said. There were some gasps and stares from his fellow senators as he voted.

"Very well. The final vote is 99 yea, 1 nay. The bill passes the Senate. Next bill, please," the Vice President said.

Justin was stunned. He had been outvoted 99 to 1 on lowering the teenage minimum wage to $1.72. How could such an outrage have occurred? It must have been a slight overreaction by the senators because of the economy or something, Justin reasoned. He was sure that the next vote would be fairer.

The nightmare, though, went on. And on. With each vote, the senators oppressed the teenage citizens of America more and more. Justin took some notes on the voting results. His list looked like this:

Issue	Vote	
Eliminate federal loans to college-bound teenagers	99 yea	1 nay *Justin*
Ban the sale and distribution of contraceptives to teenagers.	99 yea	1 nay *Justin*
Institute mandatory drug testing for all teenage employees	99 yea	1 nay *Justin*
Place a health warning on chewing tobacco	1 yea *Justin*	99 nay
Lower the drinking age to match the draft age.	1 yea *Justin*	99 nay

Justin was now shocked beyond belief. Worse yet, his fellow senators had now taken notice of his dissenting vote on every issue. Every time Justin voted, catcalls, boos, and insults abounded from the other senators.

"Communist!" a senator screamed at Justin.

"Liberal," shouted another.

"Teen sympathizer!" the senator next to Justin screamed in his ear.

The brouhaha reached its climax when an outraged senator stormed the podium, grabbed the microphone from the Vice President, and bellowed into it, "Senator Adaise, you are a free-thinking bastard."

At this, Justin cowered under his desk, which was barraged by a shower of newly-confiscated teenage drivers' licenses and about-to-be-issued teenage draft cards. The Vice President, however, grabbed the microphone and calmed the angry senators.

"Ladies, gentlemen, please!" he shouted. "We have one more key vote today. Let's give Senator Adaise one more chance."

The senators quieted after giving Justin many angry glares. In his best Rodney Dangerfield manner, Justin climbed out from under his desk, loosened his tie, stared wide-eyed at the angry senators, and said, "Us teens don't get no respect, I tell ya!"

Immediately, the senator sitting next to Justin jumped up and shouted into his microphone, "Teen! A teen! Senator Adaise is a teenager!"

The senators stared at Justin in silent shock. Never before had such a peon dared to enter their hallowed chambers. A sergeant-at-arms rushed over and grabbed Justin. The man slapped handcuffs and leg irons on Justin before the teenager knew what was happening. The Vice President instructed the sergeant to take Justin's wallet and check his identification. The sergeant held up Justin's soon-to-be-confiscated driver's license and announced, "This boy is only 18 years old, sir!"

"Eighteen years old?" the Vice President replied. "Why, he belongs on the teenage chain gang that is washing and waxing my Fleetwood limo. Sergeant, give that boy some Turtle Wax, and get him out of here. Next vote."

As Justin was dragged out of the chamber, he heard a chorus of approval for the next bill, which made mandatory two weeks of annual indoctrination at a Presidential Youth Camp every year for people between the ages of 13 and 18. Justin shielded his eyes as he was dragged from the building into the bright, hot sunshine. There, at the base of the Capitol steps, he saw a 200-foot limo being washed and waxed by about 100 teenagers. They all wore T-shirts with big American flags on the front and the words "God Bless the President" on the back. They all sang a bizarre version of "God Bless America," very slowly and sadly, as if it were a funeral dirge. Justin's eyes widened in fear. He began screaming, "No! No! Washington! Jefferson! Lincoln! Help! Noooooo...."

Justin jumped awake in his easy chair. He looked up at his walls. Pure plywood, no walnut there. Then he looked at his clothes. Old polo shirt, faded Levis. No pinstripes or Guccis anywhere to be found. He glanced up at the TV, though, and shrieked in fear. C-Span was still on, and there was the Vice President himself, looking more like a weasel than ever, about to cast a deciding vote on some unknown issue. Justin grabbed the remote control and quickly switched back to MTV. It was a Twisted Sister video, where some teens were making life miserable for an annoying parent. Justin relaxed, smiled, and took a swig of 7-Up as he watched the video.

"Aaah...," he sighed. "Just what I need. A heavy dose of reality."

Erik Landahl

Conflicts

The Divine One stepped forth and proclaimed, "Let there be government."

So stepped out the uncouthest of the uncouth, the corrupt, and cantankerous. And He said, "You shall be the leaders of our pseudo world of reality." . . .

The world was overwhelmed by government's ineffectiveness. Government brought to its people the depression of 1929, two world wars, terrorism, and today an outburst in Nicaragua.

Then judgment was passed upon the hamlets and villages throughout our world, and the people were found guilty of the charges of following the feign leaders.

Our punishment is Reagan.

Tom Lees, 18
Newark, Ohio

Our government is obsessed with power. The President of the United States chooses to bomb a country, not only killing innocent children but also hitting the embassy of our allies, the French. The Libyans told us that we could not cross an imaginary line. We had no reason to cross that line, but we did it anyway to make a point.

Ronald Reagan said we were stopping the Libyans' fight for worldwide power. But when you examine our own country's government, what do you see? You see a President who's trying to give aid to the contras so that they might overthrow the Nicaraguan government. He wants power over more than just our own country. . . .

Worldwide control is what it's called, and the government has no right to attain it.

Kathryn Graham, 15
River Forest, Illinois

Every day after school, dozens of hungry, thirsty students migrate to a nearby convenience store where they are met by the sign: "only three students in store at one time."

This is discrimination worse than anything in the '50s and '60s because it is condoned. If the sign read "only three blacks" or "only three cripples," the authorities would remedy the situation immediately. And yet they sit idly by and let convenience stores everywhere practice their legal alienation of youth.

Although I love my country, my state, my town, all three practice discrimination against teenagers and other youths. Perhaps someday we will be emancipated. Maybe the Martin Luther King, Jr. of children will rise to fame and freedom so that one day "little black boys and black girls will be able to join hands with little white boys and white girls and walk together as sisters and brothers"—but without a chaperone to watch them.

John E. Trainer, 17
Hickory, North Carolina

I don't feel I owe the government anything beyond what is required by law.

17-year-old male
Ohio

Teens don't think highly of the political games played by government officials. It is hard for them to be encouraged when the government cuts such programs as student aid and uses that money to develop a bigger and better way to blow the commies half way to Saturn.

A lot of people do not recognize anybody under 18 as being significant because they cannot vote. With political trash like this being thrown around, and the minor being the

victim, how can we be encouraged?

Bill Everett, 16
North Plainfield, New Jersey

When a person is a teenager, he or she is going through a difficult time—the transition from childhood to adulthood. Becoming aware of the political scene is part of this transition. But for the most part, teenagers have many other things to worry about that are more important to them than politics. While I think a teen should at least know the candidates for president, I don't believe teens need a great knowledge of politics.

Lisa Detert, 16
St. Charles, Illinois

I owe the government nothing. They owe me what I paid for with my tax money. They owe better roads, more teachers' wages, and many other things.

Stephen Thurston, 15
Red Oak, Texas

A nation's government represents the country and . . . promotes a strong, confident image. Unfortunately, these efforts are usually channeled into the building of arms rather than building the well-being of its people. . . . We have become too militaristic.

Perhaps this is a result of our defeat in the Vietnam War. Judging from people's positive reactions to our escapades in Granada and Central America, the bombings of Libya, and even the recent slew of ''revenge'' movies, there is a desire to make America a winner again. It saddens and worries me that our warlike actions are seen as positive. . . .

Violence only serves to spread violence, and revenge is a vicious cycle. We always feel we must strike back lest we appear cowardly. Yet we rarely have the courage to lose face by taking a step backward and refusing to perpetuate the violence. This would be a truly courageous act.

Amy Norton, 18
Oak Park, Illinois

On the state level, the government has both disappointed and encouraged me. During the summer of 1986, I was a page in the House of Representatives for Austin Allran. The time spent with Representative Allran and my experiences in session proved to me that the delegates work hard to uphold their constituents' wishes.

On the other hand, I was

disillusioned when our state submitted to blackmail by the national government . . . when President Reagan demanded all states to raise the drinking age to 21 or else their road funds would be cancelled. . . . This act betrays what our forefathers fought hard to achieve and that is freedom from absolute monarchy.

The road-act, however, only begins the disappointment. . . . Now, the discouraging news comes with the Iran-Contra scandal. By breaking an international pact and selling arms to Iran, the government has deceived its people along with other nations.

Snow Ashley, 18
Hickory, North Carolina

Discussion

Washington, D.C.
Youth News Service

What is politics?

Jason *Summer intern from Berkeley High School, California:* Politics is what keeps the country going. It's a group of people who are trying to make the laws of the country and make sure they're obeyed. They're supposedly trying to make it equal for everybody.

But to the kids I know, politics means backroom deals, a lot of corruption, a really shady image.

Before I came here, I had that image, too. But when I saw the Senate and House in session, I felt they were really trying to work for you. The more you see government in action, the more you feel that they're working on your behalf.

There's bound to be some corruption, but I don't think it's any worse in politics and government than in anything else. I believe that the government is trying to work on our behalf, but it's not as easy as people think it is.

What ethics should a politician uphold?

Jason: You would hope a politician would be honest. He should do what he told the people he was

going to do when he was running for office. Obviously, he may not be able to do that, but he should be able to uphold whatever he's pledged to do.

What characterizes the typical politician?

Jason: The typical politician is about 50 years old, balding, looks very busy. He is trying to do what he promised to do with varying degrees of success.

For instance, when I call a senator's office, I find out that the senator is always busy. Politicians don't spend their time kicking back in the Bahamas. They work hard, and it's not just an image.

But my image is very atypical because most teenagers haven't had the chance I've had to see government. The attitude back home is that government is for the rich and against the poor. People think that politicians are trying to make sure that they can have their

nice houses and that they're not really working that hard.

Back in the early '60s, a lot of people had a good image of government because of Kennedy. Nixon and Watergate really shattered that image and wrecked a lot of people's hopes. People lost their faith in government, and that's not an easy thing to regain.

What keeps our politicians from abusing their power is the fact that they want to get re-elected. As long as they want to get re-elected, they're not going to do anything to upset their constituents. What leads to an abuse of power is unlimited reign. If politicians don't have to worry about getting re-elected, or even getting impeached, they don't

have to worry about abusing power.

How much political power do teens have?

Jason: Very little because we can't vote. But we can write or call our senators. We can lobby, and we can come and help out. Basically, though, we don't have that much power. Everything's won through the vote. If we don't have a vote, we can't really make a difference. I don't believe I have any political power until I'm 18 years old. But I think teenagers can make a difference by influencing other people. The only way to do that is through persistent hard work.

I think that the government should at least listen to us because we are the future government. So, basically, by ignoring us now, they're killing us, and they're killing themselves later. We're not going to be prepared to do the things we have to do. I think they should make sure that we have a good grasp of the fundamentals of government.

Should the voting age be changed?

Jason: I don't think so because 18 is pushing it right now. A lot of teenagers could make an informed decision, but too many couldn't. They would not have any idea what they were voting on. I hear criticisms of the President all the time. I don't like him either, but the people who criticize him really don't know why. They say, "Well, he just wants to get us into a nuclear war." That's just not true, but that's what a lot of people believe. Too many teenagers are too uninformed to be allowed to vote.

I don't know how you could force teenagers to read the newspaper, but that would help. Kids just jump to the sports page, which I do, too, sometimes. It's not easy to make an effort every day to pick up the front page and read the political stories. A lot of it's very depressing.

Better education would help. The way to get more people interested in government is to make it interesting to them. For instance, in our school, there's one class called Politics and Power in which there is a model U.S. Senate and House. Every kid in class plays a senator or representative. Each student actually has to act out the role and vote. Everyone comes out of that class very interested.

What is the most important political issue facing teens today?

Jason: The most important political issues facing teens today are the most important issues facing anybody. I could say the drinking age, or child abuse, but that's very limited because in five or ten years we're going to be the adults. Nuclear war is the most important issue facing everybody.

Teenagers should join together to fight the things that are affecting us now, like politicians' restrictions of our rights. For instance, what they're doing with our driver's licenses in California. You're restricted to a provisional license until you're 18. If you screw up before you're 18, you're in a lot more trouble than if you screw up when you're older.

Boston
English High School

How do teenagers view politicians?

Vicki: Cold, plastic.

Weena: Snobbish.

Juan: People full of problems. They don't know what to do next.

Louis: Confused.

Weena: I say they are greedy. As soon as they get one power, they want to rule the whole world.

Vicki: My uncle is a politician so I kind of get that from him. He doesn't come over to visit his

mother. But when he needs money for a campaign, he's there.

Weena: Politicians forget about the little people. They forget about everyone else. They should get involved more with people. Mostly, they get involved with people of their own class.

Why should teens be interested in politics?

Juan: Well, to tell you the truth, we don't even discuss politics. We don't even think about it.

Michelle: My friends and I don't discuss it. It's just not one of the typical questions that pops up.

Vicki: What can you do about the government? You can't do anything. You can't change it.

Weena: What is the sense in talking about it?

Juan: When I think of political things, I think of boring stuff. I think of other people's problems. I've got my own problems. We don't hear nothing. We don't see nothing. We don't feel nothing. So we don't get involved.

Vicki: Even if you do get involved, the police come along and put you in jail. My friends don't like the way it's going, but they don't want to get involved because they don't want to come off like politicians themselves.

Angel: My friends don't really care. All they do is drink.

Weena: I care. I think some kids do, some don't.

Juan: We don't care because we don't have the right education.

Weena: Not too many teenagers care to get organized. But if all the teenagers got together, then the politicians' ears would be opened and they'd hear us. Also, politicians need to get involved with teenagers. That's the only way they can communicate with us—can hear what we feel.

Juan: They should poll the schools, ask questions. All the

schools could send the replies to the government, and the politicians can do what we want.

Weena: They're not going to read them. They're going to go play golf.

Vicki: They don't live our lives so they shouldn't make rules for us. Politicians don't even recognize us. They don't care because we're not old enough to vote. We make no difference to them.

Weena: If I were a politician and I had a lot of power, I'd let teenagers vote when they're 16. Teenagers do have minds of their own. Politicians feel as though we're just kids and we don't know anything. But if they really look at it, teenagers know more than politicians think. We watch TV. We watch the news. We're not dumb.

Vicki: I think they should let 12-year-olds vote.

Angel: Right now the voting age is 18. What's the difference between 18 or 17 or 16? If you're 50, you can still be thinking like an 18- or 16-year-old guy or girl.

What is the ideal politician?

Angel: I wouldn't be as greedy as the other politicians. I'd keep living how I do, help poor people, and help everyone out.

Juan: I'd get everybody—the poor people, the rich, the middle class, Chinese, white. I'd get them all together and try to work something out.

Weena: To me, there would be no such thing as poor people because I would lower prices.

Vicki: I'd vote for you.

Silver Spring, Maryland
Forcey Memorial Church

What characterizes a politician?

John: I see a person who wants to win at all costs. An individual who has a desire and drive to get where he wants to be and not let things like truth get in his way. Politicians are people trying to bend the rules to get where they want to be.

Tom: I see people who care about their surroundings, their community, or their state. They want to do something that is better. I think it's a good image.

Kathy: Just the word politics is kind of negative. I get that from school when we're studying all the scandals. When politicians do something wrong, it's in the news. If you say, "I'm going to be a politician," people say, "Oh, corrupt."

Tom: But I think politicians care. They have good intentions.

John: But they care only about the people who are voting for them. They care about the people who can put them in office or take them out of office, but teenagers don't have that luxury.

Kathy: Teenagers don't have much control at this point. But I think politicians care a little. They realize that we're the next ones who are going to be voting.

John: No, I don't think so. They're passing regulations about the drinking age and driving age, and they don't seem to consider the teenager's point of view.

How can teens protect their rights?

John: Well, we can show our views. In the '60s, those who were about to be drafted and didn't want to be drafted burned draft cards to demonstrate their views against the military. Some people demonstrate in sit-ins to show their views to politicians.

Tom: My parents would go nuts if I started demonstrating.

John: But I think writing your congressman is a good idea. You can keep up with the issues. You can know what you're talking about. You can sound off, but it certainly isn't consequential if you don't know what you're talking about.

Tom: How are you going to get in contact with them? How are you going to let them know what you feel?

Kathy: Writing petitions, protests.

Tom: Lobbying.

Kathy: They're all good ways. It's a responsibility that we have because they can't represent us if they don't know what we want. You can choose how much political power you have. You can choose to write to your congressman, or you can choose not to. So you have the power to change a congressman's views. But whether you use it or not is up to you.

John: You have access to power. After all, you do have parents. If you can influence their vote— bring them to agree with you— then you can influence the politicians' views in turn.

Kathy: If we don't get involved, we can't complain about what's going on in the government.

John: While we have the responsibility to tell the government what we think, officials have the responsibility to listen.

Kathy: Not only to listen but also to seriously consider what we're saying.

Tom: To listen, to care. I think they should try to be aggressive about finding out what we want. I don't see anybody doing that.

Are teenagers interested in politics?

John: Many people are interested in politics. They don't seem to say, "I don't care."

Kathy: Where we're at, people don't really talk about it. There's always something else to talk about.

Tom: I don't feel the calling to get involved.

Kathy: Neither do I. I don't feel that I really need to get involved at this point. Even though it's against what I'm doing now, I think teenagers should be involved. We've got to be aware of what is going on in the world. We've got to be aware of what our President is doing. When it's our turn, we've got to know what we're doing. We can't say, "Well, I don't know."

John: We can't suddenly have an information explosion and suddenly we're very enlightened. We have to gradually grow into knowing about politics.

What ethics should a politician have?

John: They shouldn't believe that they can get personal gain from their office.

Tom: Well, I wouldn't particularly like a homosexual. I think married. I'd like a Christian. That's really important.

Kathy: I don't want somebody representing me who's doing something that's wrong. It's like you don't want a thief to represent you.

What part should religion play in politics?

Tom: If politicians are religious, they'll have God looking out for them. He'll guide them in their decisions. I think their decisions will more likely be the right ones if they have God with them.

Kathy: And I think you're more likely to do the right thing if you know that God's above you. If you don't have God above you, you think, "I can get away with anything," which isn't true.

Duncanville, Texas
Duncanville High School

"A depressing part of government is that people created it and people made it. It's like a product of humanity, but now it's almost out of our hands."

94

What are politicians like?

James: Fat, lazy.

Jennifer: Protestant.

Todd: They're wimps. They don't have any guts.

David: Typical politicians get into politics because they think that they have something they can give to society. The more they get into it, the more they realize that you really can't do that much. You have to do so much bullshit to stay in office.

Kelly: They're more worried about staying in than about helping anyone.

Todd: And once they get in, they're worried about having to vote their party line. They're trying not to offend everybody.

Why aren't teens involved in politics?

Todd: Because they don't know anything. It's abstract to them. It's too far away.

David: They're ignorant.

Kelly: When there's a big ball game Friday night, who cares?

Todd: It's not that the teachers aren't teaching government. It's that the kids aren't willing to get involved in it.

James: Well, most of the kids here should care because if they go to a war, they're going to get drafted. I don't think we can get them interested as kids. If I went up to some thug in a Judas Priest T-shirt and said, "Let's go to the school board meeting," he'd tell me, "Get out of my face."

Jennifer: If it's something that directly affects them, they might get interested. It's hard to get them interested in something they don't see any relationship to, like the Libyan crisis. You have to find a way to make them directly relate to it.

James: Start a junior political party.

Jeannie: It's hard to keep going. It will start going great. Then they'll get bored, and it will fall apart.

Jennifer: And once they get started, it will be, "Oh, gee, I can't go to the meeting tonight. I have to go to a football game." You're not supposed to worry about things like this when you're a teenager.

What is the most important political issue affecting teenagers?

Richard: "No-pass, no-play."

Kelly: I'm more worried about a nuclear holocaust myself.

Todd: Like Kelly said, I couldn't care less whether I pass or play. I'm worried about whether our army is good enough.

What does the government owe teenagers?

Jennifer: I guess protection, security, peace of mind that the world is not going to blow up in the next three seconds.

Jeannie: Financial funding for colleges and for those who can't afford to eat.

Jennifer: Give us every opportunity to be successful as adults so that we can go in and run the country well.

What do teenagers owe the government?

Kelly: I don't owe them anything, except to defend my country.

Todd: Your time and your thoughts.

James: If you feel you may have a chance to hold some sort of political office and you think you can do a better job than the person who's already in there, you should try and run for it. You should try to make things a little better.

Richard: What if you don't want the responsibility?

Todd: Then back someone who will.

Jennifer: Everyone complains, but does anyone want to get out there and do something?

Does it matter if teens are politically ignorant when they turn 18?

Todd: If they're politically ignorant, they won't go out and vote.

Jeannie: That's not true. They'll follow their parents' vote.

Todd: When they turn 18, half the people don't give a damn. They don't vote.

Jennifer: I think that the biggest problem with teenagers voting is that they don't look into the issue. They just say, "Well, this guy sounds good." That's the problem with everyone in America. They don't look to the issues. They look to the people.

Washington, D.C.
With the press secretary
to Oklahoma Senator Don Nickles

How do politicians regard teenagers?

Paul Lee *press secretary for U.S. Senator:* Republicans used to look at teenagers as a threat because they thought that teenagers held very liberal views about all political issues. Now that's different. Recent studies show conservative trends among American teens today. At the high school level, we've seen political groups formed which are conservative—I mean very right-wing. It's exciting that at least they're starting to think a little bit more about the issues rather than just deciding that liberalism is the only way.

The kids don't think in terms of group thinking. They think of what's best for themselves. They're thinking about their own personal gain rather than what's good for the country.

What are the most important political issues facing teenagers?

Lee: Maybe this is revealing, but it's not an issue we give much time to. And it's not because they don't vote. It's not because we don't consider them. When you are a teenager, you're thinking, "I don't want government to do anything." And how do you contact teenagers? They're not in any organized block except for school. They're a difficult group to reach.

They're not organized, but they're very important. My boss would give anything to be able to speak before a graduating class—not only because he reaches the kids but also because the parents are there, too. The power teenagers have is through their parents. It's going to be the parents who can vote and who can influence things.

Now if they're 18 or older, that's when they get involved in issues. I didn't personally become involved in issues until I had the right to vote. It wasn't that I didn't care. There were more important things in my life.

There are a lot of issues that affect teenagers specifically—everything from the nuclear freeze issue to birth control to drug laws to religious freedom. They should voice their opinions about these issues through their parents and the PTAs. It's possible that teenagers can affect the media agenda somewhat if they use their collective will to influence the media.

How do teenagers view politicians?

Lee: There's a general feeling that politics is a dirty business—"I'm not going to get involved in it. It's not worth my time because they're only looking out for themselves."

96

And so they become disenchanted with the whole process.

Power is easily abused because usually you're abusing it, but you don't know it. You come to a point where having a position is as important as doing the will of the electorate. Keeping your position of power becomes as important as the issues themselves. You have the voice of authority so maintaining that voice, getting re-elected, becomes an issue of paramount importance.

It can be argued that trying to stay elected helps the democratic society because you're going to be trying to do more of what the people want. You're trying to reflect your constituency that much more. At the same time, it hampers responsible decision-making. You may decide that it's not in your own best interest to pursue a particular issue because it's not going to help you get re-elected though you know you should be pursuing those things.

Everybody wants to be considered a statesman. Nobody wants to be considered a politician, but there are more politicians than there are statesmen.

A statesman is someone who puts his own political future on the line because he has evaluated the information and disagrees with the majority of his electorate, who are responding to emotional, rather than sensible, courses of action.

It's like giving a kid candy. You know he wants it. It's going to feel good for a while, but he's going to get so many cavities. There are going to be some long-term consequences. So you have two choices. You can give the electorate what they want, or you can give them the hard medicine that they need to take. The statesman gives them the hard medicine. The politician gives them the candy.

Chicago
Executive House Hotel

How much political power do teenagers have?

Senator Paul Simon *U.S. Senator from Illinois:* The question has to be reversed to "How much political work are teenagers willing to do?" If people want to have impact and not do work, they're asking for something that is not possible. Every politician pays attention to letters to the editor in newspapers. Teenagers can write a letter to the editor of the Tribune or the Sun-Times as well as anyone else. The other two ways of getting involved are finding a candidate you believe in and volunteering to help that candidate. The third way is finding an issue you're interested in and getting involved in that issue.

Teenagers are not just interested in the latest record or the latest cars. Those of us in politics ought to do a better job of reaching out and trying to tap those other interests.

What is the most important political issue facing teenagers?

Simon: Any issue that is important to senior citizens or anyone else is also important to teenagers. The issues that have to be considered the most important are simply the survival of humanity. Arms control. Teenagers have to help build a world where we understand each other more, fear each other less, and spend our resources not on arms, and do more about helping other people. A second issue that has to be of concern to teenagers is education—making sure they have a quality education, making sure that higher education is available. A third one is how we put America back to work.

How can teenagers address these problems?

Simon: Writing letters is effective.

Second is town meetings. I did one just the other night, and there were two teenagers there. Unfortunately, there is not the interest on the part of teenagers that there once was. When we were involved in Vietnam, there was a very practical reason for paying attention.

Teenagers ought to be asking themselves not, "How much money can I make?" but "How can I contribute?" If they start asking that, then they can reach people who have power and influence. As soon as you start digging into an issue, you're going to start rubbing shoulders with the people who make decisions.

Tucson, Arizona
City office

How do politicians view teenagers?

Rudolfo Bejarano *city councilman:* The word that comes to mind is apathy. There is a lack of desire to participate in the process until an issue directly affects their lifestyle. I think that their generation doesn't want to grow. It's more important to be in school or to go to that party or to the prom. I usually find that very few have a good grasp of the effect official decisions have on their lives.

How can teenagers get involved in politics?

Bejarano: The most important way to get involved is by actually working on someone's campaign. That experience is eye-opening because any issue that may be controversial will develop during a campaign. If their sacred cow is being gored, they're going to be more involved than if the issue doesn't affect them in the least. In the schools, I'd train them on an ongoing basis and encourage the students to be aware of what is happening to them now. And of what might happen to them if they're not willing to get involved.

should work on education and on the issues. When their time comes, they can do a much better job than we have.

Do politicians care about teenagers' problems?

Redd: I guess that the squeaky wheel syndrome applies. When teenagers create problems for government, the government becomes aware of them. When teenagers are not creating problems, we kind of overlook them.

Berkeley, California
With the Vice Mayor

Veronika Fuksen *vice mayor:* Berkeley has a commission that advises us on youth problems. The Berkeley Youth Commission forces the city council and the school board to work together, and it has a majority of young people working on it. So, young people are very involved in this city.

One problem is that they're very resistant to having adults tell them what's best for them. So it's very important for us to listen to their perspectives about what's best for the city. I happen to think that teenagers are very valuable.

The way we treat our young people is the way we're going to be treated when we're older because we're conditioning them. So I suggested to my colleagues that we fund a professional to talk to a group of young people about what they think our downtown should reflect for young people. And the young people came up with very good suggestions about what is good about Berkeley and what they want to change. In addition, the young people gained experience in surveying, in graphics, and in other planning skills. They are now using the skills in another project in a different part of the city.

How much influence can teenagers have?

Bejarano: I doubt that they can have influence collectively and individually. They're skeptical about having the power to influence the future. Perhaps the parents have not inculcated the idea that teenagers can control their future.

If teenagers have a concern, politicians have to give them the courtesy of listening to them and of responding to them in some reasonable manner—even if it means, "I'm sorry I can't do anything for you."

Are teenagers ready to lead the country?

Bejarano: The reality is that any generation will have a few individuals who don't care, a few who will care only when an issue affects them, and a few individuals who are aware and care about everything. Hopefully, the leadership will come from those who are aware, who care about everything, and who will be involved.

Newark, Delaware
City Hall

How politically aware are teenagers?

William Redd, Jr. *mayor:* Most teenagers are barely aware of politics, particularly at the local level. I think they are primarily aware of the media coverage of Presidential politics.

I would very much like them to be aware of us. Since Delaware went from an 18 to a 21 drinking age, and we've been enforcing that, suddenly 18- and 19- and 20-year-olds are becoming very aware of us. But I don't think teenagers have very much political power. That involves the vote, and they don't have the vote.

But even if teenagers themselves don't vote, their parents do. When my kids were teenagers, they had a definite impact on their parents. So indirectly they have clout.

The best way for teenagers to become involved would be to prepare themselves to play intelligent roles in the future. They

It is important for teenagers to let us know what the problems are. It's also important for them to help us find solutions and to let us know when they think that we're going on the wrong path.

If they have the sense that they're talking to an adult and there's going to be an age trip laid on them, then they're not going to be willing to talk. Teenagers have to have the sense that they're being treated with respect. That's a hard one because a lot of people in government are very intimidating.

Are teenagers ignored by government officials?

Fuksen: Sure. I think it happens all over. Government has a tendency to ignore the powerless.

And the poor are powerless. Teenagers are powerless, and a lot of senior citizens are powerless, and the disabled are powerless. That's four groups, and "poor" covers a lot of that.

Teenagers are not a voting block. They're not organized so it's easy to put them aside, sometimes unintentionally.

Are teens willing to work in government?

Fuksen: Absolutely. Part of the problem is they don't know how to get involved. They don't know where to go so they give up.

I think we have to work through the schools. We have to try and make the connection between the city's needs and their school curriculum. Internships help a lot. Employing young people in city hall helps a lot.

I think that we can make it possible for young people to assemble peacefully. We can help them by making programs and speakers available to them so that they can empower themselves. But we can't hold their hands. We have to provide the experiences, but we have to let them draw their own conclusions. We cannot

throw too much propaganda at them. I don't want to brainwash anybody.

You don't really learn about your convictions until you're challenged. And you're not challenged if the other side is absent.

How have politics changed since the '60s?

Fuksen: Well, we had a quiet period, but it's happening again around South Africa and Central America. The pro-divestment campaign is growing. There are rallies on the high school campus. The involvement of young people about foreign policy in Central America is growing all the time, and I find it very exciting.

I don't think there's any better way to get to parents than through young people. And I don't mean that you prompt young people to go home and tell their parents what to do. But parents can't relax when their young people are sitting there telling them how terrible it is. I mean, talk to kids about something and they don't stop. They get on a crusade.

Youth have to demand to their parents that they participate and that parents fight for teenagers' rights.

Teens have to ask their parents to join them, and they have to ask their church leaders. Look at all those church youth groups. Those church leaders should be standing up, and those youth groups should be doing more than saying their prayers and singing their hymns and talking about the good life. Those youth groups should go out and talk about the real problems that are facing youth. And the real problem is that young people don't have the inclination to finish high school because high school is irrelevant to them. They don't think they're going to get a job because there's no money for the kinds of

programs that a lot of those young people need.

What are the major problems facing teenagers?

Fuksen: Unemployment is the most serious, not only the unemployment of young people but also of their parents. And that sense of hopelessness. I've spent a lot of time talking to young people who are involved in anti-nuclear work. That is more cosmic. Unemployment is the most serious, but there is also the lack of money for education.

Compiled by Cathy Mau

Solutions

A teenager should become serious about politics before he or she reaches voting age. The sooner the teen becomes involved, the better off he is. Once a teen becomes aware of modern governmental practices, he can make up his own mind about what should be done to solve the current problems in the world.

> *John Lindenberg, 16*
> *St. Charles, Illinois*

"Ask not what your country can do for you. Ask what you can do for your country." President John F. Kennedy expresses much wisdom in these words. Citizens in the United States, especially young people, tend to take their freedom for granted. They don't heed the age-old advice, "Count your blessings."

Instead, they complain about things that they could help change . . . like poverty, hunger, and bad politicians. Everyone has the right to vote, and voting is the best way to change government for the better.

Young people often complain about the threat of being drafted, but the chance to serve one's country is a small price to pay for free education and the right to speak, write, and think as one pleases.

John Coyle, 17
Arlington, Texas

When President Reagan okayed an air raid on Libya, many of my classmates thought another war was about to happen. . . . Armed with facts, teenagers can form opinions of their own about national affairs.

This is so important because future elections and political decisions depend on teenagers today. Apathy makes bad politics. Teenagers should inform themselves about the current political scene, for the experience will help them when they involve themselves in the politics of tomorrow.

Lori Ludington, 14
Wayne, Illinois

I am a minority, and I am hurt by the treatment of the government. President Reagan argues against the ERA and the special treatment of minority workers. How am I and my minority friends supposed to overcome covert racism when it seems like our federal government doesn't care?

Mia Piggee, 15
North Plainfield, New Jersey

A teenager should become active in politics as soon as he or she . . . has an opinion. . . . There are no laws that restrict a person from participating in the democratic process.

Although one has to be 18 years old to vote, a teenager can still participate in politics. He can watch the news on TV, read the newspaper, or listen to the radio. From these he can develop an opinion on politics. . . .

Why should a teenager become involved so quickly in politics? To dismiss any notions that teenagers cannot think for themselves.

Eric Feddern, 16
St. Charles, Illinois

A teenager should get serious about politics right now. Get into the punk movement. Stop all war; stop Ronnie Reagan and his corrupt deceiving pigs.

John Blakenship, 16
Auburn, Washington

Our responsibility to our government is to vote, pay our taxes, and take an active part in the decisions made by the government. . . .

The government's job is to take care of the people, to care for the poor and the sick, and to protect the groups that are treated unfairly. Another job of the government is to keep us out of conflicts. The only way they can do what I ask is if I take an active part in the government.

Dan Fitzgerald, 17
Arlington, Texas

The leaders in our country portray images of always knowing what they're doing and that they always do the right things even though many others disagree with their policies. Our leaders think they have such a tough image to other countries because we are one of the most powerful nations. . . .

Have you ever seen a nation admit that it's wrong? It seems like it's unthinkable . . . to reduce our power and strength and give it to other countries. However, the real strength comes in admitting one's faults. . . . Someone has to set the example, though. With our status, the U.S. could try to do it.

Jenny Toendly, 15
St. Charles, Illinois

In my small town my local government has totally disappointed me. Recently one of our star basketball players broke into one of the elementary schools. He was caught in the act. . . . His coach along with members of our "loving" community helped him get off with just a fine.

In our small community I know that basketball brings a lot of money. It even brings students who need scholarships or just students who want to be part of our high school.

But despite all that we still know right from wrong. He should have been punished just like anyone else, not given special privileges. It seemed like our own citizens forgot what they were doing because they enjoyed basketball and/or the money it brought our community.

16-year-old female
Washington

It's easy to get discouraged with our government today. Nationally . . . it is really discouraging that our President (at least for as long as I've been in high school) is so incompetent. But in some ways his actions sort of backhandedly encourage me to get into government and change things.

Josh Geller, 18
Aptos, California

While the government has strived to encourage young people to be responsible adults, they have failed in several aspects. Because it belongs to the Bible Belt, the local government is extremely conservative. The dress code for our school district was redesigned to hamper the distractions at school, but the new restrictions have stirred up more controversy.

The rules against wearing shorts and mini-skirts have been put into effect, but the townspeople have voted against installing air conditioners in the schools. The opinions of the students have not been heard by our government officials. The heat in the classroom becomes unbearable, and the heat, not the bared legs, becomes the real distraction.

The school board needs to concentrate more on our education instead of worrying about boys wearing earrings, students having unusual hair styles, or students wearing slippers to school. . . .

The national government has the responsibility to set good examples for its people. In the Iran arms crisis, government officials were incompetent in their decision making. Primarily, the government . . . needed to be straight-forward and let the truth be known. . . .

Honesty at convenience is not a good example.

Dawn Wiley, 16
Lubbock, Texas

I don't completely understand why the government would keep supplying many types of nuclear weapons and armaments. I thought the chief reason was protection of our young to build a better future generation. We, at this point, could blow up our country approximately 100 times over. Some day the people in our country will understand that in such an uncivilized land today, how can we grow to become our future leaders?

Louis Danyus, 15
North Plainfield, New Jersey

I believe that government has disappointed young people, especially girls, with the treatment it gave Geraldine Ferraro. She was criticized for many of the things she stood for and believed in simply because she's a woman. This aspect, criticism, has deterred me from thinking about a public office because some of the male members of government will not support a female candidate.

Heidi Crall, 17
Perrysburg, Ohio

Politics today have become a shambles, between the indictments in New York City and the Iranian scandals. How can the President not know what's going on with something so big? When they found out the President did not know what was going on, they thought that was good. That is just as bad as if he had known.

Doug Speeney, 17
Watchung, New Jersey

The leaders of our country have blatantly been caught in scandalous activities, most involving money. These leaders, role models for young people, should have been setting good

examples, not teaching us how to bribe another human being.

In North Plainfield, there is a vicious war between the Democrats and the Republicans. Council people in our town have had their position relinquished because they were not voting their straight party line because they did not agree with what their party had to say. What ever happened to freedom of speech and opinion without punishment or ridicule?

Karen Serpineto, 17
North Plainfield, New Jersey

Federal government has disappointed young people by lessening its commitment to education mainly in higher learning. What used to be a multibillion dollar student aid program now only ranks in the millions.

State government, at least in New Jersey, has strengthened its commitment to education. This year New Jersey provided full funding asked for by public education. This has shown to the young people that the

state truly is concerned about their welfare and our country's future.

Matthew Holz, 15
North Plainfield, New Jersey

Our government has been pushed around just too much lately by Lebanon, Iran, Libya, and all the other Third World countries. They have taken our people hostage, burned our flag, and killed some of our people . . . through terrorist acts in the past six years. The time we bombed Libya just wasn't enough. We need to teach these people how strong America really is. . . . We need to fight back.

Keith Mann, 16
Lubbock, Texas

MICHAEL MARBURGER L.T.H.S. 88

Chapter 6.

Teens and Media

I decide the elections. I force the politicians into action and drive the criminals underground. My editorial page influences everyone. Or does it?

I can't reach the teenagers. They treat me as a source of coupons for acne medicine, not as a source of insights. For example, the Smith kids just finished ripping apart my Lifestyle section. The front page was left untouched.

It's like this every morning. Mr. and Mrs. Smith separate my sections carefully. Mr. Smith hides behind the business section as he eats his breakfast. Mrs. Smith claims the metro section to catch a familiar name in the local news. Eventually, they work their way through me. Granted, Mrs. Smith doesn't pay as close attention to the sports as her husband does, but they both seem to respect me as a complete newspaper.

But their kids, that's another story. They rip into me to find the comics or the movie ads. Those teenagers care only about entertainment. When my editors forgot "Cathy" one morning, the Smith kids hurled obscenities at me.

They gripe if a concert is not reviewed. They moan and groan if the list of the top ten songs is hard to find. If Dear Abby is missing from her usual page, they think the world is coming to an end.

If the world really were coming to an end, those kids would never know. They pick up the front page only when they need an article for current events. "It's boring," they complain. "Who cares about Libya?" they ask. They forget that if the United States goes to war, the teenagers are the first ones on the plane to the Mideast.

My editors and I try to appeal to them. We run stories on the problems of teenage years, such as a four-part series on the pressure to drink and to take drugs. In a Sunday issue, we devoted a Lifestyle spread to teenage pregnancy.

But do the Smith kids appreciate it? Of course not.

They simply complain that we are too negative. "That damn newspaper only shows the bad side of teenagers," they say. "Where are the stories about all the good things teenagers do?" they ask.

In the sports pages, we report on teenage wonders. My editors work long hours on a page about the high school volleyball teams and on a preview series about the upcoming football season. During the season we run every high school score. But that doesn't count. The Smith kids are not into sports.

Because they want stories about the academic achievers, we run a list of the National Merit Scholars in the front section. Maybe we should print the list on the comics pages where the Smith kids might see it. Even when we did a feature on the top scholars of the area, the kids complained about the paper devoting so much space to a bunch of "goody-goodies." What the hell do they want, a page one headline that screams, "Debbie Smith got an A on her Spanish test"?

I have heard the Smith kids suggest that we run a teenage section. But like other major metropolitan newspapers, I exist to make money. I rarely see a teenager reading a newspaper. In fact, I never see a teenager buying a paper.

Television newscasts have the same problem. "Kids are ignored by the network news," the Smith kids complain. But the President gets only thirty seconds, if he's lucky. Compared to him, the high school science fair is pretty insignificant.

The networks aim to please everybody. They have tried different formats for teenage news shows. But so far all the shows have died painful deaths in the ratings war because teenagers like those damn Smith kids watched reruns of "Gilligan's Island" instead.

The networks try to put teenage viewpoints in the news. But how do you ask teenagers how they feel about the state of the economy when they don't even know what GNP stands for? It's a vicious circle.

Oh God, here comes that Smith kid again. I thought he finished with the comics.

Diana Slyfield

Conflicts

One troubling aspect of local news . . . is the excessive devotion to sports and to the weather. While both of these topics certainly are important, devoting one third of local news time to them is clearly a poor investment. The great irony in this, however, is that these two aspects of the news are probably the most-watched. Why else would such time be expended covering them?

It seems that on network television, at least, too much time is devoted to limited, relatively simple issues such as natural disasters, and accidents, such as airplane crashes.

John Bernard, 17
Philadelphia, Pennsylvania

In the present times, newspapers and TV newscasts have become too powerful. They no longer just influence the people; they practically control them. Most people believe what the media say for the absolute truth.

However, what most people don't realize is that the media overglamorize

and exaggerate their stories to further influence their viewers.

There are many reasons the media may do this. One may be to impress their public. Another may be to compete with their competitors. The most important reason, though, is to increase their ratings and thus earn more profits.

Holly Barnett, 17
Salem, Virginia

I . . . am getting sick of hearing about an elderly lady getting stabbed forty-seven times or of a hostage crisis. Why can't they ever report something good like some nobody who gets a scholarship for doing good work or someone getting a reward for being a good citizen. . . . It's getting to be where I don't even want to turn on the television anymore.

Tim Ahrens, 16
North Plainfield, New Jersey

When people have just experienced a personal loss or tragedy, . . . within

minutes some guy with a microphone and camera crew is on the porch asking, "How do you feel?" . . .

The reason seems to be an effort above and beyond scooping the competition. I don't sit at home with TVs or newspapers side by side thinking, "Gee, that's KOMO's third scoop today. KIRO has one, but they won't catch KING today. Thirteen scoops, hard to believe."

Jim Riggers, 15
Seattle, Washington

I know the President is important, but I don't think he is so important that all the channels have to have him on. When we shot at Libya, it wasn't on the TV news until the next day. But when Reagan goes and gets a physical, they put it on all three channels and don't stop until they get the doctor's report.

Brad Evenson, 15
Albert Lea, Minnesota

I think that newspapers relay news the worst because by the time you read it,

you have already heard the news on radio or television. Also, it takes less time to listen to the radio or watch TV.

For example, the other day I was reading about the bomb that killed four people on a jet. It was a long article. . . . It said that officials were looking for a man who was sitting in seat 10-F of the plane.

When I finished reading the story, I turned on the TV. There was a report on saying that they had just arrested a woman for suspicion of placing the bomb. . . .

I was much more informed about the incident after watching the report on TV.

Mike Jameson, 15
Dubuque, Iowa

In the morning I listen to the radio but depend on the newspaper for the news. Throughout the day, while listening to the radio for music, I also listen to the news segments.

If I hear of something important happening during the day, I may turn on the TV (usually CNN-24 hour news program on cable).

I like the newspaper for its variety

and in-depth quality, but I don't like the untimeliness. I like the TV because it seems to be more personal, and I can find out more in a shorter amount of time.

Lisa Fromm, 16
Grosse Pointe Farms,
Michigan

Fairness is not only tactfully showing things as they actually happened but also giving both sides voice and importance. . . .

The reporter should let the reader make up his own mind on the subject. They should in no way try to change anyone's opinion. . . .

Almost all forms of media seem to favor one side of an issue, especially those of national concern. . . . This can only be expected and will probably remain that way.

Jon Rich, 15
Bakersfield, California

I think newspapers are the best source to find the news. . . . They give pictures and can tell you more about incidents that go on. . . . In newspapers you not only get the city's

news, but foreign news, advice columns, weather, almanacs, horoscopes, and comics. . . . I like newspapers the best because then I only have to read the article I want to read.

Karen Houelog, 14
Dubuque, Iowa

When it comes to an important news story, like the explosion of the Challenger, the TV stations are the best in covering it. The TV was able to keep you up-to-date, and they showed videotapes of the explosion. . . .

When it comes to everyday news, the radio only spends about five to ten minutes, and they only choose about three stories to tell you. . . .

My personal favorite is the newspaper. A newspaper can do more in-depth reporting. . . . With the newspaper, you can choose what news you want to read, and you get the added bonus of reading the comics, which is something I do every day.

Patricia Duffy, 18
Grosse Pointe Park, Michigan

Many in the media today are not at all fair or scrupulous in their dealings with the general public. It is the media that produce the news, and it should be the media that ensure that the news is fair and accurate. . . .

If it becomes evident that the media cannot keep themselves respectable and fair, the . . . public should get involved. The public should instruct the media in what they consider fair and right.

If the media choose not to listen, the public is then left with the option of boycotting various aspects of the media which do not cooperate.

Jeff Maberry, 17
Bakersfield, California

The radio only carries the news at a national level and not too much that happens at a local or statewide level. I feel that most people are mainly interested in this type of news.

The news on the television and in the newspapers is pretty much the same. In newspapers, though, people have a chance to read and re-read the articles that interest them most. . . .

Also, newspapers have comics and cartoons . . . which give the reader a chance to get his mind off all the tragic stories he has been reading. . . .

Steve Ricke, 15
East Dubuque, Illinois

It is very difficult for any newspaper to relay the inner thoughts and emotions of any journalist. The radio also lacks in this area. What the radio gains in presenting the reporter's voice, it loses in not being able to present any visual material.

My preference is the TV. While hearing the information, I can see the reporter's thoughts and opinions in his facial expressions and tone of voice.

This is almost as important to me as the news itself, for I respect the opinions of others. Their opinions help me form an opinion of my own.

Jeffrey Pfaendtner, 19
Grosse Pointe Park, Michigan

It is . . . our responsibility to ensure fairness in the media. I think that there should be more conservatives reporting. There seems to be an awful lot of liberals.

I know that your own opinion will show through when you're reporting— through your tone of voice and facial expressions, but people should try to monitor that. I think it is the conservatives' fault so many liberals are in the media. Now that we realize it, maybe we'll do something about it.

Kelly Ewalt, 14
Galesburg, Illinois

Discussion

Media Bias

New York City—NBC executive: The media have inherited a negative view of kids. It's symptomatic of the normal discrimination against kids that you've always had—"Don't bother me, kid."

New York City—teenager: The media are no good. Either they exaggerate, or they report on things that are no good.

Cleveland
National Scholastic Press Association convention—with teenage delegates

Kris *Watertown, South Dakota:* Whenever teenagers are represented in the media, it's for something bad. We could do all the good things that we could possibly do, and I don't think anybody is going to pay attention. If we do something bad, we get attention quicker. It's always "Teenagers choose drugs. Teenagers choose alcohol. Teenagers are getting pregnant." They never have anything good to say about us.

Wendy *Lakewood, Ohio:* Unless something controversial is going on, they don't pay that much attention to us. I don't think that we will ever get as much recognition in the media as we want.

Mike *Sioux Falls, South Dakota:* I would say just the opposite. Just recently they did a story on a Cambodian refugee who goes to my school. They're always doing something with the teenagers. It goes all the way up to the national level, such as those who have received awards like the Presidential award for courage. They try and give teenagers as much coverage as possible.

Kris: National media are not concerned about us. It's like we're a separate race. It's like we don't directly affect the government, politics, or our community. I don't think the media really consider us to be a part of anything that

happens. But when you're an adult, all of a sudden it's different. That's probably why we don't get that much coverage.

Wendy: People are so wrapped up with the negative side of things. Sometimes newspapers and news programs sensationalize the negative side of things. They can't just say, "Hey, the SAT scores are up. Our students are learning more."

Kris: The United States has a big problem with its media—everything centers around our people. For example, you listen to something about a plane crash in Nicaragua. If there weren't any Americans on board, they don't make a big deal about it. But if Americans are involved, it's a big story.

Wendy: My main interest is South Africa. Half the time you can't even find it in the newspaper because you only hear about the local stuff. It's really hard to find broader stuff because we are so centralized on America even though there are more important things going on in the world.

How can the media influence opinions?

Kris: A well-written editorial, column, or political cartoon can sway your opinion.

Mike: They can sensationalize a certain subject. For example, during the AIDS conference, experts were saying that the media have skyrocketed that problem and that the epidemic isn't that

bad. There were more than two stories a week in all papers on AIDS so people became more aware of that problem.

Kris: The media can have a great effect on people. Think back to the Vietnam War and all the problems there. I'm not going to say the media were the cause of the protest, but they helped it along. They informed teenagers, and that's why teens were so outraged.

Tucson, Arizona
Journalism Education Association convention—with teenagers from Santa Rita High School

Shaw: The media will always think of teenagers as rebels and as bad.

Scott: According to the media, teenagers can't do anything that would be good for anyone else. We just think of ourselves and do what we want to do. We're really irresponsible. That's not true. That's just a cliche that adults have about teenagers.

Shaw: Adults almost always think of us as rebels. They rebelled against their parents when they were young so it's only natural that their kids rebel.

TJ: They get this view from the media because that's what the media mostly write about—things that teenagers do that are bad.

Amy: Most of the articles in the newspapers that are about teens are about teenage pregnancy, suicide, drugs, or alcohol. You don't hear about how well teenagers do at school or how they participate in their community.

Billy: In sports, you have the athlete of the week.

Amy: Yeah, but that's just athletes. What about the other ones who aren't athletes, like your scholars at school?

Shaw: The only way they get recognized is through the school newspaper and not even that sometimes. It's mostly sports and that sort of thing. The sports section is the only section where they deal with teens. You never see things like local scholars in the newspaper.

Washington, D.C.
National Public Radio

Ted Clark *executive producer, "All Things Considered"*: The media takes teens' parents very seriously. The whole approach of the media to teens is from the eyes of the parents. How do we deal with our children's drugs, with sex? Rarely do the media see it through the eyes of a teenager.

Nina Totenberg *legal affairs*

correspondent, "All Things Considered": I'd like to see the breakdown of who listens to us or who watches the nightly news as far as the teens. I don't think that would change dramatically if we had ten minutes of teen notes every night. I don't think of my audience as teens. We think of our audience as including teens.

Who decides what goes on the news?

Clark: There's just so much information that somebody has to say, "This we will put on the program." If the news director or program producer starts making too many wrong decisions, he'll hear about it very quickly from listeners and from reporters. It really is a consensus process. Every idea that is going on the air is brought up before the entire staff. If the staff thinks it's a boring idea, then it probably won't get on the air. The staff represents the public at large. That makes it important that our staff be a diverse group of people.

New York
Children's Express office
  in Greenwich Village

Roger Clampitt *director:* The media need to cover things responsibly. They love a story like the day-care abuse story. They've spread hysteria all over America so everybody is hysterical about their kids in day-care centers. It has not been responsible coverage because the abuse that's taken place is really incredibly limited and small compared to the number of day-care facilities across America and the number of terrific adult human beings who are pouring their lives into taking care of little kids. They sensationalize something like that instead of dealing with it responsibly. They scream. They holler. They're like the members of a lynch mob.

Other times they will do brilliantly. The Gannett newspaper chain did a year-long series on child abuse in Oklahoma institutions. They hit us both with television and press coverage, and they changed the state. They got the legislation changed. They got the guy fired who ran the system. They almost cost the governor his job. The press has enormous power.

Plano, Texas
Administration office
  of Plano Independent School District

Larry Guinn *director of student service:* To me, national news media people literally border on being animals. They fly in from New York or Los Angeles and do their stories, but they don't have to worry about anything.

Too much media news coverage can plant seeds in people's minds. I was interviewed by every major newspaper in the United States, every major television network in the United States, as well as London and everybody else. And there were some of them who were very sensitive and did a good job. And there were some who did a very poor job and took things out of context and tried to get into areas that were detrimental to the families involved. And it hurt.

I had people come in and interview me for TV. After the TV camera went off, they would leave the recorder on and ask me some questions hoping that I might say something controversial. Not everybody was bad. The closer we got to home, the more sensitive people became. But the farther you got away from home, the less sensitive they became.

A good example is when I was interviewed by "Good Morning America." A guy came down, and I gave him a tour of our school. Without any warning at all, they turned the cameras on. He was

almost a Dr. Jekyll/Mr. Hyde person. When they turned the cameras on, he stuck a microphone in my face and said, "Mr. Guinn, I talked to a young man last night who had attempted suicide. He said that you personally and nobody in this school cared about him. Is that true?" Now that's how I started my interview on Good Morning America. Almost every one of them had a zinger question like that, especially in the TV area.

The media wanted to disrupt the school and to get into classrooms. Our students got so sick of the media that it was almost a riot everywhere when someone came on our campus. They felt like they had been dealt with unfairly. They were tired of it, and it was a very negative experience for our students.

San Francisco
Pacific News Service

Alvin: Some of the media portray kids as people who jump and run away at the slightest whim. Personally, I do not think that is the way teenagers are. There are quite a few teenagers who have their own businesses or who are writers and reporters. Many have achieved a lot. Sure, there are runaways, but nobody wants to help the ones who have the problems.

The public and media just portray teens as bad people and say we are tomorrow's future. If these are going to be tomorrow's future, we are going to be in pretty bad shape.

Carol: I think the coverage is pretty well-balanced. I seem to hear bad things once in a while. Other times I hear features about the teenagers who are really involved.

Louis Freedberg *senior correspondent:* It is hard to generalize. I have been involved with youth in the media now for many years. The media do not really know what to make of teenagers. There are certain issues that the media have kind of latched on to. One is latchkey kids. Suicide is another one. Child abuse, runaways, and teenage pregnancy are other hot issues.

What concerns me is that the media do not understand what is going on underneath. There is a crisis mentality, as if the problem kind of emerged from nowhere. All these problems have to do with the fact that we do not know what to do with teenagers in society. They are in this peculiar state halfway between being kids and adults. On the one hand, we expect them to toe the line and be kids. On the other hand, we expect them to assume adult responsibilities. We expect them to be independent rather than giving them any real responsibilities. If we were very clear about the role of kids in our society, we would not have these kinds of problems.

Media Appeal

San Francisco teenager: How many kids actually sit down in the morning before school and pick up a newspaper? More kids listen to the radio. Everybody can listen. Not everybody can read. It's easier to be told something than to read it for yourself.

Tucson, Arizona

TJ: The media still does not write for us. They're thinking about the adult world, not ours.

Billy: But the adults buy the paper, and the adults do everything.

TJ: Well, don't teenagers buy papers?

Billy: Do you buy a paper?

TJ: I don't have to.

Billy: Your dad buys it.

Shaw: If the newspaper wrote more things that interest teens, more teens would read the paper.

Scott: Like, we don't care about Libya.

TJ: Yeah, but that stuff in Libya affects us.

Amy: It's important, but it depresses people. If they don't have anyone really near who is going to be sent away, then they don't want to listen to it. They say, "Well, it's not going to affect me. I don't want to listen to all this bad news."

TJ: People want to read things besides the comic page that would make their day a little brighter. Why would people pick up a newspaper just to read bad things?

Cleveland

Kris: The news was never important to me before, but now I realize that people want to know what's going on. If you know what's going on, you're more in tune with things. If you don't know what's going on in your own school, then you're not part of that school. I've realized that a lot more since I've worked on the school newspaper.

Wendy: We have a broader grasp of the media because we've written news stories and know how hard it is to write them. You get a better feel of what they're trying to say.

A lot of my friends aren't that affected by the news. I'm not saying I read the papers every day, but I usually read them two or three times a week. But it's just you're so worried: "Oh, I've got my English Lit test and this report is due and this term paper to do, or I've got to work tonight."

Kris: If you didn't have media, people would be in the dark most of the time. People wouldn't know what's going on.

Which type of media is most important?

Wendy: I don't think televised news will ever take the place of printed news because the TV news is only that little blurb on the front page to get the readers to turn to the complete story. You don't get the rest of the story on the news. You've only got 30 seconds to say the story and say it with a smile. "Well, 30,000 people have been killed, but have a nice day."

But the paper gives you the real story. They give you the full coverage, or at least they try. And on the news they really don't have time. The only restriction in the newspaper is the space, but usually you can work around that. People who only watch TV are not really misinformed, but not completely informed.

Kris: I don't think television can take the place of newspapers because we're such a time-squeezed society. We have our jobs. We have our family. We really don't have the time for extra things. A newspaper you can pick up any time of the day and read any time you feel like it. You don't have to turn the news on at 6 o'clock to catch it.

Wendy: The newscasters on TV have to have the ratings—that's how they stay on the air. You have to say everything with a smile. You have to have the gorgeous girl up there or the good-looking guy. It all has to be picture perfect, and they all have to wear these plastic smiles. They're up there to entertain you and give you a vague look at the news.

They always put the smile in at the end. "And we'll be right back with this," they say with such a big, broad smile after they've just told you how many people have died in a car accident. It just seems so fake to me.

Mike: When TV news does major stories, they're not smiling about them. News gives the perspective but doesn't go in depth with quotes from other people telling the story. They just say what's been happening. It's all surface.

Kris: People care more about the entertainment value than the news value because the news is so depressing. You watch the news, and there's nothing on there you want to hear anyway. That's a terrible thing to say, but it's all these people died and this person raped here, murder there, crash here—you can only listen to so much of that in one day. Then you

just about go nuts. If you really sat down and thought about the news every day, people would probably go out of their minds because the news hardly ever has any good things to say. That's why people have entertainment. That's why people watch TV.

Washington, D.C.

Clark: We have an obligation to inform people and give them useful information, but what makes people tune in to your competitors is the entertainment value.

If you only concentrate on the educational value, then what you do on the air might be very important but begins to sound predictable. People know, "Oh here comes another civics lesson," or "Here comes more information that I should listen to, but I'm tired. I'd just like a little something that will put me to

sleep." So you want to avoid that. On the other hand, if you do only entertainment, people start to hunger for useful information and will stop listening because they're only getting fluff.

Lombard, Illinois
Glenbard East High School

Brad: I have tried to avoid media ever since I realized how depressing it was to sit around and listen to how many people get killed. I wish newscasters would put something a little bit more entertaining on the screen. They don't have to be so boring. I hate their lack of emotion.

Sue: Do you get most of your information during a crisis from the TV and radio? Don't you feel they give you a shortened, capsulary version?

Brad: No doubt about it. I just don't feel like spending the time to find out more about it. It depends whether it is something that affects me or something I'm interested in.

Tucson, Arizona
Offices of Tucson Newspapers, Inc.

Edith Sayre Auslander *human resources director:* We have a responsibility to be as accurate and as thorough as possible since people tend to be highly critical of the media and greatly influenced by it. If we do a bad job, we have a negative influence. I don't know why people trust what they read in the news columns as gospel, but they do.

Readers need to read lots. If you read only one paper, you are going to get a certain tone. We need to be better educated about how the media make decisions about what stories to run. But the media folks need to put out the good and the bad.

There is a love-hate relationship with the media. People read it, listen, and watch, but they're very critical. They can't do without it. We tell everyone else's stories but not our own. I guess there's some sort of power in our secretiveness. We need to get the public more involved with our medium by inviting letters, bringing community leaders in, and listening to their criticisms and ideas. There have to be people in media companies who go out to the community and get their ideas and know what people are thinking.

I have yet to see an effective way to reach the young teen or adult only with entertainment. I'd like to see more news. Things don't have to be played down for teens. There are a lot of topics that interest them, and there could be better ways of covering them. The coverage of teen events is very hit and miss. They're sort of an ignored population.

Washington, D.C.
With the press secretary
for Oklahoma Senator Don Nickles

Paul Lee *press secretary for U.S. Senator:* Last week I took out a few of our college interns in advertising and public relations, and I said, "How do you get your information?"

"Well, we don't have time to be informed. There are too many things going on in school. We've got papers to do." I said, "Wait a minute. You're all going into public relations. You guys are saying you want your life to be advertising communication. Information is a key ingredient there."

That's pretty dangerous. What are teachers telling them—that it's not important to know what's going on in the world? Every day I read the *New York Times*, the *Wall Street Journal*, and the *Washington Post*. I subscribe to *U.S. News and World Report*. In my office, Cable News Network is on all day. I'm on the phone all day with people who can tell me things I can't get out of the media. But I still don't know it all. Yet these kids were saying, "I don't read." That's a problem.

Scholastic Media

South Dakota teenager: If you want to know anything about yourself, your school, or your peers, your school newspaper is the best source of information.

San Francisco
Youth News office

Damir: What we hope to do is to provide an opportunity for kids to have a forum. We also hope that the kids will get a different perspective of reporting.

Adrienne: We do stories that kids doing print journalism probably wouldn't do.

George: It's more believable on the radio. If you read something about teen prostitution and you use someone else's name, how many people would believe that you really talked to a teen prostitute? But on radio, you can tell that you're really talking to this person.

Adrienne: There is greater impact when somebody says, "Yeah, I've gone out and killed somebody." You don't get that impact when you're reading.

Damir: I cannot see the guy who killed someone talking to an adult reporter the way he talked to Holly. An adult reporter would not have gotten that radio tape because the kid who was talking would have been afraid and felt inhibited talking to an adult.

Adrienne: We're non-threatening. We're not going to turn kids in. Kids pick up on things that adults don't simply because we're overlooked.

Holly: It's an adult world. For a kid to survive in the world, you have to be observant. You have to see the things that a lot of adults don't.

Damir: Holly and another one of our reporters got to spend a day on the set of "Fame" in LA and talk to the stars of the television show. Those are some of the best interviews I've heard because they talked kid-to-kid. I don't think an adult would get the same answers or ask the same questions.

Adrienne: There are certain questions that we'll ask that adults won't ask because a lot of adults want to be polite. In the eyes of a lot of adults, we're cute. We're adorable. We're doing what they've always wished. We're living out our dreams, and they see us a lot differently than we see ourselves.

When we went to this thing called Comedy Day in the Park, there were a lot of really important

reporters there. I was in the middle of an interview when a well-known commentator grabbed my microphone and said, "Here, I'm going to show you how to do a decent interview."

But I'm giving the interviewee good questions. We're getting good tape. But this guy thinks he knows more about this than I do. Older reporters look at us as rookies who don't know what we're doing.

Allen: When kids are interviewing adults, sometimes kids just get the basic PR hype. A former sheriff of Marin County came over here to be interviewed, and we didn't have anybody here except one of our kids who was a brand new reporter. She went in and got a lot of the PR hype.

When it came time to edit, the PR hype hit the floor. I know he went out of here satisfied because I overheard him make a phone call to his assistant saying, "Well, that went great. We got 'em, boy! They bought it all."

Damir: What got on the air was the revealing stuff that we wanted to get. He felt very easy—"I just

went in and really blew this kid away." When he heard the final tape, he would not have felt that way at all, believe me.

_____

Cleveland

Dorothy McPhillips *president, Journalism Education Association:* The scholastic press plays the same role that the professional press has in society. Their responsibility is to communicate— to deal with information, issues, and problems that would be of interest to the audience.

John Wheeler *chairman, JEA Commission on Journalism in Secondary Education:* In addition, it provides a forum for the exchange of viewpoints, both on opinion pages and in articles themselves. The scholastic press has all of the standard functions that the press has always claimed that it had and rightly so—to inform, to entertain, to create a forum for opinions.

My school board president once said that she appreciated that the newspaper was an excellent example of a pure education. She felt that it was a way that

teenagers could talk to other teenagers. She also said that it was somewhat irrelevant if adults disagreed with specific articles because it was important that the board support teens talking to teens.

What are the successes of the scholastic press?

McPhillips: One of the sure signs of success as far as I'm concerned is the number of high school papers that are dealing with issues that are of prime importance to high school students. Ten or fifteen years ago, you wouldn't have found suicide, drugs, or sex on the front page of school newspapers.

Craig Trystad *director, Youth Communication:* Adults can't handle young people facing so many of these tough issues so early because they never had to. Ten or fifteen years ago kids would not even have thought they could have covered or should have covered some of those issues. One thing that is most impressive is the sense that they should be doing that. I know there are not enough publications doing that, but there are some that are quite extraordinary.

Wheeler: There's a danger of jumping on the bandwagon. One of the real difficulties right now for student newspapers is to find a way of legitimately covering the AIDS situation. What can the student press do that hasn't already been covered better in the New York Times or Newsweek? There's that danger of simply jumping on because it is a hot topic. Instead, they need to give attention to what needs to be communicated to their readers that they can't get from some other sources.

McPhillips: Is it possible that some of them think that their peers will read their paper but they might not read the New York Times? That might be one of the reasons. Also, I think we can't ignore the trend that students are becoming more conservative and in a sense censoring themselves.

Trygstad: I think teenagers are probably the most conservative of all age groups, contrary to what people believe. Maybe there are fewer outspoken students than what I would like to see.

Why is journalism important in high school?

McPhillips: Journalism gives the students the most realistic experience they can have in high school. People say, "Well, high school isn't real, and the kids know that." But the kind of experiences they have in high school with publications are the same kind of experiences they can have after they're out of high school when they have a mayor who hates the paper and a community that dislikes what they do. They have to answer to readers if they make a mistake.

Trygstad: A free press is a pretty precious commodity in this country. There is no way to learn it any better or any earlier than when you're actually in control of a publication. That's what a free press is. It just drives me crazy that kids learn one thing in a social studies class about the Bill of Rights and the First Amendment, but when they try to practice their rights, they are shut down.

What elements are necessary to produce an ideal paper?

Wheeler: First, there has to be administrative support. Second, that support has to extend to granting an individual time and money to develop a program. Third, there has to be an educational atmosphere in which people are willing to accept their publications, their strengths, and their weaknesses. Supportive parents are also essential.

McPhillips: Good physical surroundings are important. There are a lot of papers that are produced in a classroom, but it sure helps to have a journalism lab.

Trygstad: Since journalism, at its best, means giving information to an audience, the process often requires that you have to work when nobody else is working. That's when you can get the information. So that's why you need supportive parents because you're going to be late getting home. You also need supportive boyfriends and girlfriends because your social life is going to be messed up.

Also, it helps to have a faculty that's willing to let the paper be a paper—to accept it the way the mayor of Chicago accepts the *Chicago Tribune.* He knows it's going to be there every day, and he must deal with it. I don't think I would care if the principal hated the paper as long as he/she didn't mess with it.

Media response

New York—NBC executive: I don't think the burden of change is on the teenagers. I think the burden is on the media.

Cleveland

Kris: If all the kids in our school did something bad, we'd get attention. But if we did something good, nobody would care. I really don't think there's any solution.

Mike: Teens have to make the news. For example, Sioux Falls has been having problems with fighting between schools at football games. Even homecoming got out of hand. Students are being taken to court for egging some parents and some cars. Letters were written from students and faculty members telling people not to look at the negative side. The community's attitude was changed within a week.

Wendy: Last year we had a big thing with shorts. Girls can wear super-short mini-skirts, but the guys can't wear shorts. The paper sent a reporter down. The kids were able to express their opinions.

Mike: Letters to the editor are written all the time. I wrote one about government red tape. We had about seven people killed in an accident on a road the government was supposed to have fixed that year, but they were waiting for the lowest bid. Because of the government red tape, some people lost their lives. I asked what's more important, the money saved by the taxpayers or the lives? After the newspaper printed my letter, it was surprising that some people then realized that teenagers are trying to fit in and trying to be a part of the community.

Who should regulate the media?

Wendy: If anybody other than the media regulates the media, it's censorship. Individuals can watch the news if they want to. If they don't want to, that's how they're regulating themselves.

Mike: It's both the people's and the media's job to regulate. The media have the job of deciding the most important stories and how they should be dealt with in an unbiased way. The people then have the choice to believe it or not. The government really doesn't have anything to do with it unless it gets too slanderous and libelous. Then the public, through the government, should be able to take action.

HAND IT OVER, YOU LITTLE RUFFIAN.

WALT GUTHRIE 87

Wendy: If the media sensationalize something, it's the editors' responsibility to do something. It's their responsibility as well as the owners of the paper.

San Francisco

Freedberg: The adult press should pay more attention to the issues that are being covered in the high school press. You can get a sense of what is going on in youth culture. The high school press is kind of the ignored strata of media in the society.

It does require adults to work with teenagers and give them the skills to be spokespeople for the youth culture. You always have the articulate kids. But I do not think young people have the objectivity by themselves. The mass media have to bring young people into the media, and I am afraid that very few are willing to do so.

Reporters have a tough time tracking down kids. That is why we get calls a lot from television stations that want to interview our kids, as if these are the only twelve teenagers.

A lot of adult reporters do not have contact with kids. Part of the problem is that a lot of reporters tend to be in their twenties and thirties and do not have kids.

Also, getting into the schools is a big pain. The schools are one of the most conservative institutions in society. They set up all sorts of roadblocks to prevent the media from talking with the kids about the important issues.

Tucson, Arizona

Amy: The media should go to the high schools and sit around for a day and find out exactly what teenagers do in their spare time. Then they would understand that we're really not all that bad.

We have an organization at school called SADD (Students Against Drunken Driving). They work to improve things because you hear about teenagers driving drunk and killing themselves.

Shaw: Inform the media when you're going to have a SADD meeting. Just say, "We're doing this. Maybe you want to cover it. Maybe you want to come out and say something about it."

Amy: The problem is that it's the older people whom they talk to because they're not interested in us. We're not important.

TJ: We have to be important because we're their future generation.

Compiled by Kim Peirce

Solutions

The press is responsible for maintaining the highest legal and ethical standards to protect and administer First Amendment rights but not to abuse them.

The public, I think, must aid the press but not let them "get away" with too much. . . .

The media have responsibilities . . . for telling the whole truth fairly, honestly, and without bias. The public must then judge, criticize, accept, and correct the media's methods and outcome.

I suppose people could look at media/public relations the same way they could view student/teacher relations—what one does, the other evaluates, corrects, and teaches.

> *Stacy Green, 16*
> *Wheeling, Illinois*

I would add more information on what is currently happening in many foreign countries. . . . The developments going on outside the U.S. could eventually affect us. . . .

Another important reason for this is so that the public could . . . help in

other countries. . . . Millions of people were dying of hunger in Ethiopia, and not many people knew about this. Then a station in England showed the Ethopian crisis to the public. Since then, millions of dollars have been raised to aid the starving in Africa. Although many are still dying of hunger, many others are alive today because the media showed the situation to the public.

> *Marcos Medina, 16*
> *North Plainfield, New Jersey*

The responsibility to ensure fairness in the media is held by the editor and the writer. . . .

The editor should make limits of what can be written and what can't. . . . Freedom of the press should not be taken lightly or stretched beyond certain limits just to make a story.

> *Denise Hutton, 17*
> *Eagle, Nebraska*

Fairness in the media should start with the journalists themselves. I don't know what they try to do when they blow somebody's quotes out of proportion or make them look bad.

However, if the journalists are going to keep writing things unfairly, then the publishers should look for stories that are unfair and censor them.

> *Reid Spears, 15*
> *Prospect Heights, Illinois*

If I had the power to change newspapers, I would be a lot stricter on the false and hidden truths of stories and articles. There are many newspapers and magazines that are so-called gossip magazines that put out false stories to catch the people's eye. They are leaving out one thing—the truth.

> *John Lanya, 18*
> *North Plainfield, New Jersey*

If I controlled the newspapers, . . . I would change the wording around so

PRINT IT. CAN IT!

that when someone would read the paper, it would be true.

Ronnie Powell, 17
Rosman, North Carolina

If I had my own news channel, the first thing I would say in opening is, "This is channel 67, the good news channel." I would report on things like people helping other people and how the poor are begging to get jobs and improve their lives.

On the set and behind the set, I would have pleasant pictures so the viewers would have peace of mind. Then comes the weather. If it wasn't going to be a sunny and pleasant day, I wouldn't let there be a weather report at all.

Franky Mastroianni, 16
North Plainfield, New Jersey

Newscasts today seem far too concerned with their ratings. Instead of concentrating on important news that could affect everyone, they try to bring in extra viewers with cheap gimmicks.

An example of this is the incredible amount of time spent on the personal lives of stars. Another gimmick for increasing ratings is the interviewing of relatives of either missing or tragically killed people. This may satisfy some people's morbid curiosity, but it is hardly ethical or necessary.

Finally, if there is a slow newsday, and there's not enough important news to last for the whole hour, the network should just put on some music videos or something of that sort to fill up the time instead of digging up junk to bore viewers with.

Josh Willwerth, 16
North Plainfield, New Jersey

Newspapers and newscasts always report bad news and rarely report good. They give the bad side of the story. . . . They also constantly degrade our President. Our President is the leader of our country, and the press should give him a just report.

If I had the power, news would be fair and accurate to all, including our President. I would report good news, such as people's accomplishments and

acts of heroics. I would report terrorist bombings, political scandals, but I wouldn't magnify the truth. It would be a fair report.

Douglass Kropelnichi, 16
Lake Toxaway, North Carolina

TV journalists are often one-sided in their coverage of even the most noncontroversial topics concerning the President. . . .

When correspondents give a viewpoint, they should very simply state, "I feel" or "In my opinion" instead of "He obviously" or "This is." If such opinions are given, an opposing one should also be provided for the American public so they may draw their own conclusions. Journalists should make every effort to keep their own viewpoints out of their stories. In that way, the true purpose of the media is achieved—informing the American public.

Tom Finan, 17
Little Silver, New Jersey

The media is obsessed with "dirty laundry." What makes the mangled, decapitated victims of a serial killer good six o'clock news footage?

A recent race car accident in South America serves as an example. Along the course of a road race a car spun out of control and crashed into a crowd of spectators, hurling tens of bodies into the air. . . . The first newscast I saw just showed all the people dying.

Newspapers and newscasts can change by first rethinking what news is and the impact of news. The purpose of news is to communicate important current events to benefit society through the information.

Political elections and successful heart transplants are news. Dead bodies . . . are not.

Caren McNelly, 18
Lubbock, Texas

Chapter 7.

Teens and Entertainment

Channel 2 Truth or Consequences (R)
Channel 4 The Young and the Chestless
Channel 13 Movie—"Media on the Entertainment Express" B/W, Elisha Cook jr., Nancy Davis (1986)—A bunch of teenage media stereotypes share a train in this low-budget fantasy.

"Roy, cut it already with the pentangles! Our train's here." Roy, who served as official vandal for the Satanic Pranksters, sheepishly capped the red spray can and followed the fearless leader, Fabian, onto the platform. Pinned under a headset, Fabian's outsized ears flapped like bat wings to the pounding beat of "Subaru to Hades."

The Pranksters were going on their first field trip. Originally founded by a group of impressionable teenagers who happened to listen to a Shaun Cassidy Christmas album backward, the group had become restless with the routine cross burnings, run-of-the-mill Blistered Gristle concerts, and ritual pet slaughters that each weekend brought. With his young mind shipwrecked on the shores of Satanic rock music and the attendant alcoholism and drug abuse, Fabian could dream up nothing more adventuresome than a trip to a Cub's game.

After starting a small fire and levitating around it to the lurid strains of a Demon Toasties song, the Pranksters were joined at the next stop by a young couple.

Sixteen-year-old Chuck, who was on his fourth profitable sequel, had been mortified by the enduring nature of his virginity. Though he had installed a zoom lens on the girls' locker room light fixture, flooded his high school with mayonnaise on prom night, and accidentally bombed the Soviets out of Afghanistan with his computer modem, he still hadn't gotten down anyone's pants. He and his affably disgusting pal, Jinks, made a pact that Chuck would "score" this summer or die trying.

So after an astonishingly funny series of misadventures concerning a bordello, a stolen Delorean, and a sociopathic drug dealer, here Chuck was on a hot date with the cutest girl at Nixon High.

And she wanted to do it on a train! Chuck's fears about legality and lack of flexibility were swept away by the smoldering fire in Glenda's eyes. If only those unkempt-looking characters with the pitchforks weren't gulping heroin Slurpees in the next seat. But what the heck, it was just another wild day in the wildest summer in teenage cinematic history.

The Zenith family probably wouldn't have boarded the train if they had seen what was happening behind the steamed-up window hiding Chuck and Glenda. God-like Rob, Supermom Laura, 17-year-old boy-crazy Sarah, and her rascally semi-pubescent little brother Gary were embarking on a half hour situation. Big brother Maury was left behind due to a C he had received on a math exam last Tuesday at 8, 7 o'clock Central and Pacific.

Mr. Zenith's wacky facial contortions showed his discomfiture with the barbiturate-swilling musical satanists and the interlocked nerd and cheerleader. After trading a few wittily banal non sequiturs with his wife, Mr. Zenith used the entire mess to illustrate the folly of sexuality to his raptly attentive, yet titillated, offspring. If they were ever to get involved in sex, drugs, rock music, or any combination thereof, Rob intoned gravely, they were to come to him and communicate honestly so he could ground them for the next show.

"And so, kids, I guess what I'm trying to say is 'Just say no,' " Zenith concluded neatly.

"Gee, sure Daddy," Sarah grinned.

"Dad, I gotta go to the john again," Gary chirped, and the entire family departed the train chuckling.

Chuck and Glenda wound down and got off two stops later, walking hand in zipper into the sunset. Dragging their Oldsmobile-sized boom box behind them, the Satanic Pranksters exited at the stadium. And the train car rolled off, disgorged of unreality. The Cubs won 4-3.

Eric Kammerer

Conflicts

The helicopter flew in, shooting rockets and bullets everywhere. Suddenly Rambo *ended; the audience still left in awe. I walked out of the theater, my mouth hanging open. I felt a certain rush in my body. The good guys had won.*

Two days after that I was awakened from my sleep by strange sounds. . . . I looked out the window to see . . . two kids in my front yard.

They were clutching plastic machine guns and shooting at each other in mock battles. One of them yelled something that I remembered hearing from the movie. I smiled to myself, thinking that "boys will be boys. . . ."

It hadn't hit me then, but soon I started to notice all of the things that you could buy bearing the Rambo name. Plastic guns, action figures, bubblegum cards . . . everything. . . .

One day I turned on the radio and heard that we were inches away from being at war with Libya. That scared me. I didn't want war. The news was

never clear. I couldn't tell who the aggressor was. Could it have been us?

More days passed, and that situation cooled down. . . . I overheard the two kids talking before they started their daily war. "You be Libya," one of them said. "I'll be the U.S."

Off they went. The United States fighting Libya, both with Rambo-brand weapons. Were boys still being only boys? I didn't know anymore.

I think that movies are a good thing, but like everything, is there too much? Are the producers trying to make money by selling toys, and in the process, pushing violence all over kids? . . . Is it a big deal that we were almost at war? Not to the kids. I think that they think that war is just another game. . . .

What will these kids be like when they're older and not holding plastic guns anymore?

Scott Clark, 16
Western Springs, Illinois

My mother grew up with "The Beave," and I'm growing up with "Miami Vice." Very different values—my mother and I, and the shows.

Jennifer Vargo, 17
Pinckney, Michigan

Movies see teenagers as massive party animals who get drunk and have constant sex. They also see us as dirtballs, grubby, or just in a gang. We're just a bunch of hippies who don't give a damn. . . .

The reason we are stereotyped as disruptive, carefree, don't-give-a-damn kids is that producers base it on a few individuals, not the whole society of kids.

Stereotypes cause problems because the parents see us all as meatheads or inconsiderate jerks.

David Junker, 16
Winona, Minnesota

Movie stars and rock stars . . . represent a part of

ourselves, a something that we secretly want to do. We all dream of playing to a sell-out crowd in Madison Square Garden, and we all dream of being followed by photographers, going to large parties, interviews, wearing glamorous clothes and hair and make up.

We all dream of it, but we can't all do it. So . . . we live vicariously through those people.

Christine Jarnick, 16
Troy, Michigan

I've been to rock concerts where people . . . grabbed at the singer. People seem to really think that rock stars are above humanity.

Lara Lockard, 17
Lee's Summit, Missouri

I personally believe that a song is just a song. . . . I feel the biggest influence comes from the singer himself. A person has a vision of how he would look or seem to other people if he was as cool as a popular person, such as Prince. . . . The adults seem to believe that the lyrics of the music or the subject of the song title have changed their sons or daughters. Actually it is probably how the singer dresses or acts that has changed the person, not the music itself.

Hopefully most people are not so unsure about themselves that they would try to pattern themselves after someone else.

Brian Beach, 15
Hillsdale, Michigan

Today many movie and music stars are regarded as modern-day heroes. . . . An example of heroism is the infamous Rambo. Children also look up to Sylvester Stallone. He is very strong and can handle weapons with no problem at all.

In the movie First Blood, Rambo manages to wipe out an entire town in a matter of a few days. Rambo is so popular they now have Rambo plastic guns, knives, hats, and even Rambo plastic figures. Many children are playing with these toys.

Most of today's heroes are not very good influences on children. Many of them represent violence and unpleasant things that children really don't need to see.

Kelley Congleton, 16
Ludlow, Massachusetts

Movie stars are seen as heroes because they are so . . . publicized. . . . They are surrounded by beautiful people and costly objects. We see in them what we dream of getting out of life.

Stephanie Renshaw, 18
Blue Springs, Missouri

Some teenagers' lives revolve around rock music as if it's the only thing that exists in the world. They seem to be so obsessed with the music that they forget about everything else, such as parents, school, social activities, and everyday life.

I feel teenagers who are in this type of situation are mentally deprived in some way. Some may have had psychological problems

beforehand. . . . It's almost like they put themselves in another world.

Sara Munsell, 18
Hillsdale, Michigan

If kids want to listen to rock, it isn't any worse than what they will hear in school. I hear worse in school than in music. Besides, if you don't want to listen to it, don't.

As far as kids go, parents are not going to stop them from doing some things they want to do. Parents go up to their kids and say, "I don't ever want to catch you listening to that trash. If I do, you'll be in deep trouble."

So what's the kid going to do? He's going to go out and blast his eardrums out. Parents don't have half the control they think they do.

Jeff Traughber, 16
Irwin, Idaho

A lot of the movies today portray teenagers as nymphomaniacs and alcoholics. They do this because they think that is what the public wants to see. As a result, adults don't trust us.

They feel we are good-for-nothing, lazy bums. And if they act negative

121

towards us, we're not going to have a lot of respect for them. Stereotypes put up walls between people.

Aimee Vessel, 16
Dakota, Minnesota

If a person is crude and likes disgusting things, many times the music they listen to is the same way. Music doesn't form this person's personality. It just expresses it.

When I'm in a good mood and full of energy, I like to listen to loud, fast moving music. This doesn't mean I'm wild or destructive. I just enjoy that kind of music.

Penny Sue Stuart, 17
Idaho Falls, Idaho

Adults are the ones that make the movies, direct, and produce them. They don't want to make themselves look bad, so . . . they put down the younger generation.

Adults know very little about teenagers. They don't understand them even though they were teenagers once themselves.

Annette Drenckhahn, 15
Minneiska, Minnesota

Recently I attended a dance in Boise with a group of friends. One of the guys was quite hyper in the beginning of the dance. After about an hour his mood changed. He became violent and kept telling me he wanted to hit someone or something.

I was quite alarmed at his sudden mood change. But after observing the dance for about an hour without dancing, I noticed this change in behavior in several people. . . . The music . . . had become like a dangerous gun ready to go off.

17-year-old female
Idaho

Rock music influences teenagers to be crazy and high strung because of the fast pace of the music, but I don't feel this music has anything to do with

teenagers turning to Satanism or drugs.

Teenagers . . . just like the sound of the instruments and the rhythm of the beat.

Adults feel that kids become corrupted by this music and that the record companies should put a warning on any album containing swearing, use of drugs, or the worship of the devil. . . .

Adults were teenagers when rock and roll music came about. They liked it, but the adults did not. I think it is just a trend each generation goes through.

Aaron Freese, 18
Hillsdale, Michigan

When I hear a younger child using bad language, I usually ask them where they hear that kind of language. Sometimes the answer is "at home." But it's usually, "On television."

Bret Nicholaus, 16
LaGrange Park, Illinois

Movies are constantly stereotyping teenagers. Either they are stoned, drunk, flunking school, or a combination of these. This is very far removed from the truth. Teenagers are

one of the nation's hardest working age groups.

How many parents could go to school eight hours every day, be involved in extracurricular activities, and hold down a job part-time? Not many. . . .

Parents see these movies and automatically assume that their son or daughter is doing what the kids in the movies did.

Jeff Kosidowski, 16
Winona, Minnesota

Movie and music stars are regarded as modern heroes because they lead the life everyone wants to live. . . .

They can basically do, buy, say whatever they want, and even marry whoever they want. Some of them don't even have high school diplomas. The problem is that because of the freedom they have and because they are celebrities, these people have no morals.

Everyone sleeps with everyone else's wife. They party all week, and they can afford whatever drugs they want. These people are dying left and right: John Belushi, Jimmy Hendrix, Keith Moon, John Bonham, Janis Joplin, Marilyn Monroe, and Judy Garland. . . .

Being a celebrity, they have a passport to do things that they aren't necessarily qualified for . . . Ronald Reagan becomes President, and . . . Clint Eastwood ran for mayor. Why can these people be our idols when they live the life of scum?

Tim Almstedt, 17
Hinsdale, Illinois

Movies stereotype teenagers as alcoholics, drug addicts, criminals, or sex fiends. They do this because the only time you hear about teenagers, it is negative. You never hear, "Well Johnny was at a party, and he didn't drink at all."

Dina Wyss, 17
Pekin, Illinois

Discussion

Movies

Wilmington, Delaware
Eye Magazine office

Becky: Movies are becoming a little more realistic thanks to directors like John Hughes, who did the *Breakfast Club* and *Sixteen Candles*. He gives viewers a stereotype of each teenager but lets the character step out of the stereotype that everyone else sees.

Patty: The movie's message is true. We're all a little of everything—jock, brain, and the beauty queen.

Becky: There were movies of the *Porky's* genre that were good, like *Fast Times at Ridgemont High*. The person who wrote the screenplay went to high school in California as a teenager for a few months. He wrote the movie based on what he saw. But other people didn't do the research so they couldn't portray teenagers as realistically. They had to rely on things like sex to make it exciting.

Dallas
A private home—with teenagers from
  Hillcrest High School

Rebecca: *The Breakfast Club* had characters who were semi-realistic so you can relate to them. But in *Fast Times at Ridgemont High* you had your stereotype—Spicoli, a drugged-out guy. The teenagers aren't responsible. You don't see the other side of things.

Tara: They can't deal with teenagers without a classification. *The Breakfast Club* was a good representation, but it was classified.

Kenneth: That's because teenagers tend to classify things a lot more than other people. We look at things and make instant judgments. I think the movies are trying to move away from the teeny-bopper image and show teenagers as real people, but they are trying too hard.

Laurie: At school, you do break down people into certain stereotypes. But *The Breakfast Club* was a breakthrough because of

what they had before—like *Fast Times at Ridgemont High* or *Cheeleaders Make Love*.

Kenneth: The only realistic part of *The Breakfast Club* is at the end where they say that they are not the stereotype and that they are all like everybody else.

If people want to make movies like *Fast Times at Ridgemont High* and we pay to see that, then let them. I don't always go to a movie because I want to derive a meaning for my life. I want to be entertained. I'm not offended by the fact that they're stereotyping teens because there's stereotyping everywhere you go. To present something in a two-hour block of time, directors are going to have to do some classification.

Directors make it seem that teens should be happy-go-lucky and just live a life of fun and frolic. It's not like that.

Laurie: I tend to find a lot of the Marcia Brady syndrome. I read that this girl said that she had grown up watching the "Brady Bunch." When she got into high school, she thought that she was supposed to have dates every weekend and was supposed to make cheerleading. When these things didn't happen, she was really upset.

When John Travolta was in *Saturday Night Fever*, disco became the craze. Then *Urban Cowboy* and all the wild stuff. If people are stupid enough to shape their lives by the movies, then they deserve what they get. But pre-teens think that all the teenagers are like the ones in the movies.

Kenneth: When I was 10 or 11, I was actually mortified about the prospect of being a teenager. I saw movies of these 16-year-olds going out, getting smashed, and wrecking cars. That really turned me off. I didn't want to go through that phase. I was really relieved that I wasn't about to be like that when I got to be 16.

Do movies also stereotype other people?

Rebecca: The thing that bothered me about *Rocky 4* and *Rambo* is that a lot of mindless people see these movies. The movies stir up a lot of anti-Russian and anti-communist feelings that otherwise wouldn't be there.

This is a lot of propaganda. The USA and USSR are on a big screen with lots of emotions involved. A lot of people come see it, and they get real excited. They're like, "Kill the commies" without even realizing what they're saying. It's not that easy. It involves a world war.

What bothers me is not that a bunch of intellectuals will see it, but that people who don't know any better will see this and think that the USA and USSR can't co-exist peacefully.

San Franciso
A private home

Jackie White *independent film maker:* It's hard for me to consider most commercial film as art. So much has to be compromised in the film making industry to make the ones who are paying for it happy. The lawyers are making the major decisions by what's going to make money. I think that is limiting.

The compromise causes films to be muddled and not directed in terms of one vision. Directors are making films to please a group of people rather than making a film to make yourself happy.

I'm producing for myself. There's no market and no money.

It's similar to a painter who paints what she likes. If a painter tries to paint what she thinks is going to sell, the painting won't because it's not coming from the artist.

I think that movies really stereotype teens. They make it seem that teens can't take anything seriously and that they can't handle true emotions. I think they are underselling the complexity of teenagers. There's

bound to be all levels of teenagers.

Television

Wilmington, Delaware

Becky: Teens are portrayed on TV as gum-chewing mini-nothings. My least favorite show in the world is "Gimme a Break." You have three stereotypical teenagers on that show. The oldest teenager is the pretty blonde who knows

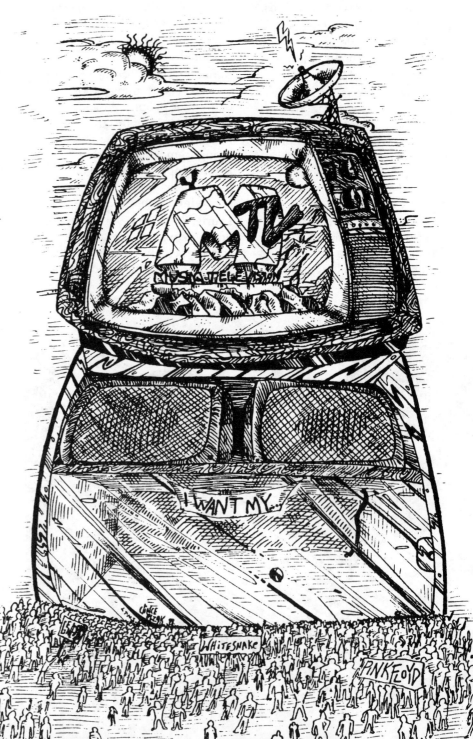

nothing and flits around the house. Then you've got a middle child who is the smart one. She wears glasses, and her hair is cut in a real dumpy way. Then you've got the youngest child who is a tomboy. They have ultra-stereotypes all in the same show. I couldn't believe it.

Lynetta: In cop shows, you'll see young black teenagers in a bad neighborhood. They are always into dope or getting arrested. They will be on the streets their whole lives. They'll be shot in gangs.

Patty: They portray teens to the extreme. They either show really bad teenagers or really good teenagers. They forget that most of us are somewhere in the middle.

Becky: The "Cosby Show" has the most believable teenagers on television. They don't even make them look stupid. When they do a show, they express a teenager's point of view without making them seem self-centered or narrow-minded.

Patty: But with things like the "Cosby Show," people are capitalizing on teenagers. The shows are with teenagers, but they're not about real teenagers. They're just using them as scapegoats.

Sarah: You can't say there is one accurate view of teenagers because there are so many different teens. The "Cosby Show" is good for down-to-earth kids, but there are people out there whose parents beat them, who drink, and who have other problems.

Becky: It's a lot easier for a TV producer, if he's on a schedule and under pressure, to throw a stereotype on the screen. It's too much work to really capture the intelligence of teenagers no matter what setting they are in.

Patty: People don't want to see real teenagers. People don't want to see kids whose parents beat them and kids who are parents

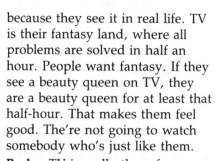

Kelly Mitchell
LTHS

because they see it in real life. TV is their fantasy land, where all problems are solved in half an hour. People want fantasy. If they see a beauty queen on TV, they are a beauty queen for at least that half-hour. That makes them feel good. The're not going to watch somebody who's just like them.

Becky: TV is really there for escapism. You don't want to be serious. If you want to be serious, just experience your own life. It's hard to overcome prejudices and realistically portray a minority group. They just want to take the easy way out because it will sell and because it's acceptable to people.

Sarah: I haven't seen many minorities on TV, and it's really disappointing. There's more than just white people in this world. The only time you do see minorities, they are thieves or hookers or something like that. They don't get any good roles.

Hollywood
KNBC-NBC studios

How does the public perceive the entertainment industry?

Fritz Coleman *Weatherman/ comedian*: People who don't know much about the entertainment

world believe it is wild parties and beautiful women. They think there is a lot of drug abuse and craziness. I think that the people who do that aren't going to have careers. Soap opera actors and actresses have to be on the set 20 hours a day in peak form. There's no way you could abuse drugs and do that every day.

What responsibility do stars have to the public?

Coleman: People pay attention to people in the limelight even if the people in the limelight don't deserve it. Rock stars set examples. Kids are committing suicide while listening to satanic messages in heavy metal rock music.

Entertainers have to be careful because they set an example. The majority of Americans are easily influenced. The guys in the limelight don't realize that there are 8-year-old kids who have their posters hanging in the bedrooms. They have a responsibility to set an example—not to be reckless with their morals in a public area.

But the *National Enquirer* and Rona Barrett will take just one little sliver of the entertainment community, such as the drugs or loose sexual morals, and make it front page news. They take an insignificant part compared to all the lifestyle of commitment.

How does television influence American values?

Coleman: I'm really scared about the subject matter on some shows. Violence is glamorized. "Miami Vice" is a great show with attractive actors, great music, and murders. The victim wears clothes that complement the color of the wall paper. It makes it look like a romantic environment.

Does the network television cater to the already established tastes of Americans, or do they establish the tastes of Americans? Networks argue that this is what America likes. But when you look at TV, it looks as if they are guiding the moral tastes of America. That can be dangerous when large corportations begin to dictate the personal tastes of Americans.

Mediocrity is what seems to sell. "The Dukes of Hazzard" was on television for eight years. Is it the network's fault for putting it on or for keeping it on after it proved to be successful?

New York City
People magazine office

How are teens portrayed on TV?

Jeff Jarvis *television critic:* A couple of seasons ago, we saw smart-assed kids whom viewers wanted to slap around a little bit. It was unrealistic. Recently it switched because of "The Cosby Show." We saw a slightly idealized but realistic view of teenagers. That was a good influence for other shows. The kids could still be funny and smart, but they are not so hard to take. "Cosby" made teens into real people.

Now we are switching back to the smart-assed view. You see it in "Growing Pains." Out of the 24 new shows for the 1986 fall season, there were 13 "nuked" families—eight widowed mates,

five divorces, and nine orphans, which does not include split homes. On TV, kids are presented with two reactions—smart mouthed or whining. For either case, you want to slap them around. That's a disservice to teenagers. That's not realistic or flattering. It's a cliche and two dimensional.

Why haven't realistic portrayals of people survived on TV?

Jarvis: There is a limited amount of writing and producing talent in Hollywood. What's really changed is that in the top ten shows, we see good shows. In the bottom ten shows, there are bad shows. That encourages good stuff to come out.

The other problem is the demographic bit—saying, "We want teens this hour. What do we give them?" These middle-aged white men don't know so they guess and go for the cliches and the obvious. A few seasons ago, "A-Team" was a top-ten show. That was seen by moguls as what teens and men liked. "Let's give a lot of action."

Enlightened desperation caused the good shows like "Cosby," "Golden Girls," and "Hill Street Blues." Cosby went to all the networks before he went to the most desperate network, NBC. They said, "We'd tried everything else. We are desperate. What the hell, let's put on something good. Also, we can't afford to put on ten different shows in ten weeks so let's stick with it." That's how Cosby succeeded.

How can people affect what is on TV?

Jarvis: I honestly think writing letters does help. That doesn't mean just to the networks but to magazines so the letters are seen. Watch and talk about the shows. It is like a new restaurant. If you see quality, support it.

What responsibility do actors have to the public?

Jarvis: I think an actor has a responsibility to turn down irresponsible scripts—things that are violent, bigoted, sexist, or have vigilante ethics. If actors are on that kind of show, they have lowered themselves to that level. If you work at IBM and see someone price fixing, you are morally bound to do something. The same is true of an actor. If they are in a bad show, it is their fault.

Cleveland
The Cleveland Playhouse

William Rys *artistic director:* I know that theater is an odd experience, but not only for teenagers. It has to do with the ease of where we get our information—from radio, from TV, from movies—and that allows us to isolate ourselves.

Theater demands you to make a direct personal response. It demands that you laugh aloud, that you cry. It demands that you get involved. You have to commit yourself to the audience around you and to the actors on stage. That's hard to do, but I'm willing to offer a very vulnerable position to you. I'm live in front of you, and I could look like a fool. I think that's a pretty good step on my part toward another person. Once people realize that the emotional, immediate response in theater is an important one and is one we don't get by watching television or by going to the movies, then I think people will begin to come into the theater.

It's the difference between going to a football game and watching it on TV. On television you get all the instant replays. We then begin to believe that's football, that the experience is being able to watch it, to be able to relive it, to find the mistakes. But the true experience is to sit

EXPLOIT

VIOLATE

Mardik

there and be forced to watch it.

Think about a rock concert. People spend so much money to go to a concert though they can't hear the music and sit miles away. Why bother? Because it's happening. Relish it, enjoy it. Enjoy being alive and dealing with someone.

I think we have to use a lot of new techniques. Good rock musicians use extraordinary threatrical techniques. They're up there questioning your beliefs in your sexuality, questioning your beliefs in government, and your beliefs in yourself. They're playing like crazy with your emotions. I'm saying that the theater can do that as well.

It behooves us to use some of the techniques that rock does. We mustn't be afraid of creating riots, of creating that type of frenzied excitement. It is a little more difficult for theater, but the intent has to be the same.

Videos

Wilmington, Delaware

Becky: MTV and videos became popular because they are so expressive. Listening to music on the radio is such a passive thing. But on MTV, we see it. We hear it. It's like we become a part of it.

Patty: The videos gave us something on which to base our interpretations of the music. It gave us new angles and approaches.

Lynetta: It also gave us a chance to see a performer sing and see how he feels.

Becky: One negative aspect of videos is that the artists' appearance is becoming more important than their talent. Madonna self-admittedly can't sing, but then we see her rolling around on the floor baring her midriff on MTV. She's really based more on appearance than on musical value. Sometimes the video can help the song, and sometimes it helps the musicians. But if they are good enough, they stand by themselves.

I can take artists more seriously when I know they aren't overly concerned about their appearance. I picture Simon LeBon running off stage every five minutes to fix his mascara. I can't take him seriously.

Patty: Videos bring groups that otherwise wouldn't be popular into the limelight. It can bring the minor stars up but not all the way up. Duran Duran is a super group, but I don't think they are in the same league with Genesis or Bruce Springsteen.

Becky: I don't see videos propelling a small band into major success, but they can give them a nudge in the right direction.

But right now they are getting into a rut. They are regurgitating the same things over and over. Cars and women, that's it. If artists and directors don't use what they have, videos are going to die out.

Patty: I don't think videos are going to die out. They are still going to continue to be important, but I don't think video is going to become a major thing on its own.

Lombard, Ilinois
Glenbard East High School

Gerri Long *parent:* Rock videos can be a bad influence on teens because the videos give them the idea that some of the things the musicians are doing are good and acceptable—this is the normal way to behave—when it isn't. I don't let my children watch MTV.

Sue: I've seen in my head what a song means. Then the video is totally different. I don't see where that would influence me.

Long: Some of the rock videos degrade women. Video says it's

okay to treat women like that. But teens haven't had the experience to know that it isn't. For a young teen, a 12- or 13-year-old who's beginning to feel feelings of sexuality, videos say it is okay to treat someone like this. Then they try it.

Pat Meyer *teacher:* I object not only to the treatment of women as inferior but to the acceptance of violence as a way to relate to other human beings. I don't think that's a good value to pass on.

Sue: I watch MTV strictly as entertainment. You said you don't let your kids watch MTV. My mom didn't let me watch the "Three Stooges."

Meyer: If I had children, I'm not sure if I would let them watch the "Three Stooges" either. They're extremely sadistic. I didn't even think they were very funny.

Sue: I'm very resentful that my mom didn't let me watch it.

Xuong: My parents didn't stop me

from watching the "Three Stooges," and I don't go around hitting people.

Nashville
Scene 3 Video office

Debbie Pfaelzer *producer:* Scene 3 Video does primarily country-western videos and a good deal of the contemporary Christian videos. Our videos tend to be clean and PG-rated. We don't do anything that is explicit in any shape or form.

But I disagree very strongly with the idea that music should be rated. First, it would hurt the record and the video industries. The record industry is floundering, and we don't need to make it any more difficult to boost sales. If they started a music-television channel of all the explicit or R-rated videos, everyone would watch it because they know it would be wilder and more fun.

Like anything you watch,

videos are going to have some kind of subliminal effect. If you're looking for ways to kill your mother and see a video that explicitly shows it, it's going to have a profound effect. But people are going to be influenced by anything, whether it's the headlines in the newspaper or a music video.

Without a doubt, there are values portrayed in music. Bruce Springsteen and John Cougar talk about America. There is a sense of pride generated in the music. But then you have someone like Prince, who is talking about God and sex. He has one of the most mixed-up messages I've ever heard in my life.

How do you know who to take seriously? Teenagers seem to get confused because they're trying to find their own values. Who am I to tell somebody what they should feel or think or say or do? I think our only responsibility is to keep things in good taste. There certainly is a responsibility to society to not talk about killing your mother in a song.

How influential is the entertainment industry?

Pfaelzer: Any kind of an entertainer is looked at as larger than life. It's frightening and sobering to people who have patterned their lives after people like Elvis Presley or John Belushi, who died of drugs. I think entertainers do have the power to stand on a stage in front of 60,000 people and say, "You know, kids, drugs are bad for you," and out of that group, ten people may need that message and listen.

But overall, I think stars are the worst people to have as role models because they generally lead messed-up lives. They have the same problems you and I do, but the problems are tenfold because they're in the limelight.

Music

Dallas

Tara: Music, more than movies, starts fads. It's the aura of the music, the presentation of it. The folk singers gave the '60s a peacefulness, a purpose. Hard rock gives us reason to think we're really stupid and that life is stupid. Music give us direction. It pulls you together and gives you a common love.

Kenneth: The reason music has such an impact on the culture is because it is such a strong, emotional force. Movies are a lot more cerebral. Music is a lot more emotional. You listen to music and become wrapped in it and absorb it.

Shannon: For a lot of people, music represents rebellion. It's representative of something that they have that is nobody else's.

Kenneth: A couple of years ago, a lot of the songs I remember hearing were doom and gloom—"I hate everything, life stinks, and I want to die." Now there's a lot of music coming out that's saying, "Hey, all that's behind us now. Let's pick up the pieces. Let's believe in what we do, in what we say, and let's try to live life with integrity and dignity to the utmost of our abilities."

Tara: Today music presents more of an outlook on life rather than a message. What I would consider positive music is something that presents a need to correct the ills of society and move forward. The Live Aid concert is a great example of what the new music is doing today.

Is labeling records a good move?

Rebbeca: It's ridiculous. Kids are going to buy albums no matter what kind of label companies put on them. Are kids going to have to get fake IDs to prove that they are 12? They say they want to

label so the mothers will know, but how many mothers buy records for their children?

Laurie: If anything, a kid who is 13 and wants to rebel is going to say, "Hey, I'm going to the record store, and I'm going to buy the first album I see with a sticker on it." It's a chance for them to rebel.

Rebecca: It has a lot to do with the individual. I know there was a period in my life when I used to listen to the Doors and get this strange feeling inside that made me want to rebel. A lot of the hard-core and punk kids get riled up. It's really powerful stuff that is non-stop. If you have the potential to begin with, the music is going to have an effect.

Wilmington, Delaware

Sarah: The real reason I listen to music is for entertainment. I don't really get into the values.

Patty: Some Prince songs are pretty explicit and sexually oriented. There is such a difference between that and Simon and Garfunkel from the '60s.

Becky: People cry out loud that Prince is so blatantly sexually explicit, but in the '50s people were screaming at Elvis Presley. Times have changed so the music changes. As people's views change, then the values that are expressed in music change.

Lynetta: But they talk about sex and drugs, and our parents don't want us to hear it.

Patty: Prince's "Darling Nikki" reflects society, but it reflects a part of society that we don't want to acknowledge. "White Lies" talks about cocaine and drugs.

Becky: Nothing in the songs is new. People have always been doing cocaine. There has always been teenage sex. But now the musicians are becoming more expressive, and they're not afraid to say it anymore. People don't want to hear about it on the radio so that's why they cry out. They are suddenly being confronted everywhere, and they have to deal with it.

Patty: Parents are afraid that hearing songs like "Nikki" by Prince or "White Lies" will miraculously make you aware that the stuff exists and that you are going to run right out and do it.

MUSICIAN GANG WARS

Sarah: But it's the person, his self-expression, whether it be good or bad. Who has the right to say they are right or wrong? They are trying to express themselves—it's a free country.

Patty: Music is a consumer market. If people think the music is too offensive, they won't buy it and then it won't get any radio play. Soon it will just quietly die.

Stardom

Dallas

Kenneth: Recently, a friend of mine went to the Academy Awards show, where all these ordinarily mature grown men and women were hanging on trees trying to touch these even minor movie stars and producers.

Tara: We've begun to view work not as a personal, emotional experience but as something you have to do automatically. We can't just view people who do work as heroes anymore because we don't have any respect for that. We now have to view the people who make us feel and who make us complete as our heroes.

Paul: Last Sunday a friend called and told me that the whole Duke University basketball team had trumped into Friday's. We drove all the way there, got a table right by them, and got all their autographs. It was really cool to see them doing things that we do. That's the point—they're human too.

Laurie: I think getting autographs is silly. But then I look at my room, and I have Jesse Owens all over because I met him at a party. Everytime I look at the autograph and read it, it's special to me. I don't think I'd feel the same way about an actor's or actress's autograph. It's someone who goes out and accomplishes something that makes me feel good.

Wilmington, Delaware

Patty: The main factor that makes a star is talent. You can't hide the fact that you stink. You also can't hide the fact that you're really good. It shows through.

Becky: People who are stars should be aware of how much influence they have on the public and use good judgment. But they should not change their lives just so they look good.

Becky: They do owe the public, though. It really irritates me when an entertainer says, "I need my privacy. I deserve my privacy because I'm just a regular person." But they wouldn't be a star if it weren't for the record buyers or the movie goers or the TV watchers. If you want your private life and you regret it so much that you're in the public eye, then don't do it. Get out.

Patty: I don't think they have to be on call to the public 24 hours a day. It's their life.

Sarah: They're human like the rest of us, and they deserve the same things we do.

Nashville
Welk Music Group

Bob McGill *songwriter:*
Traditionally, rock and roll is the teenagers' statement about the frustrations of trying to adjust to being an adult.

When I was a teen, my parents detested the records I listened to. To them, Little Richard was a gay black man dressed in drag. Parents hated Elvis Presley and all the acts from the South because of the black influence and because the lyrics were dirty. It's like what we have now except today's lyrics are even dirtier and more suggestive.

I think the music business needs to do some policing. I don't blame the people representing the PTA and the mothers who are complaining about rock lyrics. A lot of people in music who blame people who are campaigning to censor rock lyrics are missing the point. The point is there are always people who hide behind the First Amendment as an excuse for greed. The real problem is that the record executives are too

Hollywood
The Comedy Store

Louie Anderson *actor/comedian:* I think everybody needs entertainment as a way of tuning out all of their problems. I think a lot of entertainers were kids who weren't really accepted. I was small as a kid so I got picked on a lot. I was looking for acceptance. Now I get acceptance from things like the "Tonight Show" when 400 million people are watching.

I don't think there's any higher feeling than a live audience. You could take all the drugs, but there is nothing compared to the live applause.

greedy to tell Prince that one of his lyrics is too risque. I prefer to teach my children about ethics, sex, and morality. I really resent Prince inadvertently teaching my children his viewpoints.

When you're a teenager, it's your nature to want to rebel. Nothing is sacred. Everything is old and serious. When you're a teenager, you don't realize that it has taken society thousands of years to create a structure of ethics, morals, language, and laws that hold us together. When you get older, you want to strengthen it because you see how fragile it is.

How can entertainers be good role models?

Anderson: I think it's important not to paint a picture that isn't real. They do that a lot on TV. Not every day turns out like "Miami Vice." Police don't look like Don Johnson. They don't stumble on a big dope deal. Life is more like getting the hair out of the drain while you're trying to take a shower. Life is not having milk when you want to have cereal. Life is not real glamorous. Life is real hard. Entertainment is such a fantasy.

But entertainment could teach

teens to take chances with their lives and not stay in the set 9-to-5 job that everyone has mapped out for teens. I think teens should go from high school and take a couple of years to try things they want to try. Experience life because that's when they are alive and free. I encourage people to take chances. That's the only way you can make it.

Los Angeles
An office in Watts

Clarence Drayton *songwriter/ musician:* I believe that music carries what we think and what we believe. Whatever I believe comes across in my music. I'm a Christian so what I say is going to help kids and lift them up.

Before I was a Christian, my songs induced people to do some things that their parents would not agree with. Society has become a great garbage can willing to accept anything. If a person were to say the things that were in lyrics, you would reject it. But put it to music, and a baby will sing it. I am really dependent on Christians to stay in the entertainment industry so we can have moral concepts and values being portrayed not only in music but also on stage.

I think that putting labels on records is a necessity because morals have gone. Everything is out there. Many groups are trying to get kids into Satanism. Some parents are trying to sue Ozzy Osburne because they believe his lyric content led to their son's committing suicide. Entertainers definitely influence people. The parents should listen to what is being said. What the kids learn now is what our nation will become tomorrow. Entertainers have the responsibility to send out ideas that bring positive results. The music becomes a vehicle to carry a message.

For a time, I left the industry and became a minister. I just closed my ears to everything. But seeing and hearing all that is going on, I know that we've got to get out there and put out our best music—songs that say some of the best things about love and relationships, not the worst.

I'd write the songs that would encourage people because I believe that many people in the world today are very discouraged. That's why the suicide rate has climbed tremendously. People see no way out, except a window or a bridge. I'd write a song that would hopefully fill the void. I would like them to know that God really loves them and that He will always be there.

Charles Walker *actor:* Entertainers influence countless numbers of people. But, unfortunately, people do not separate the real person from the roles. A lot of people try to imitate the false, and as a consequence, there are problems.

Entertainers must make a living. Therefore, they make compromises. If the role that the actor is offered has some morally decadent parts in it, he will play that to make a living. The songwriter wants to make a living in this era of punk rock, acid rock and hard metal so he makes compromises. So there is a tremendous demand made between "Do you want to make a living?" or "Do you want to please God?"

Skip Scarborough *songwriter:* I feel like some of the entertainers don't think they have any responsibilities. The bottom line out there is the dollar.

Alton McClain Scarborough *singer:* When you watch television, you see adultery and fornication. "You can get high. Anything that you want to do." As far as young people can see, everything is okay.

That's how they grow up unless they have different role models.

Walker: I just did "Hardcastle and McCormick" Monday, and I like having a camera on me. And if I didn't have the Lord on my side, I would go crazy because God gives me a balance.

There are certain parts I cannot play. I cannot play a homosexual. I cannot play a person who goes around killing unless at the end of the movie the character is punished or ideally accepts Christ.

The ego is a very real animal. Unless God controls your ego, it will be uncontrollable.

A. Scarborough: If your self-esteem is not wrapped up in God, you can become so bombed-out by the rejection. You're able to really be real because you're not trying to impress anyone except Christ. You want people to see Him, and being an entertainer is really a good way to do it because of the attention that you get. If Prince was to become a Christian, think of the influence it would have on the young kids who listen to his music and who dress, act, and talk like him.

Compiled by Michelle Jao

Solutions

Rock music has good and bad effects on teenagers. The ones that tell you to go out and get stoned and drunk are bad because they try to tell you that it is right and that drugs will make your problems go away.

There are also songs that tell you to go out and find someone you don't even know and have "wild, crazy" sex. . . .

The songs that are good are the ones that tell me that I am attractive and that I am important and that even when I am down low, it all works out in the end.

Deidre Farnam, 16
Idaho Falls, Idaho

Rock music has an influence on teenagers. There's no denying that. . . .

If the lead singer of a group went out and told all of his fans that it was cool to shave their heads bald because he did, most of them probably would. . . .

I think rock music gives kids something to do. If they didn't have idols, most of them would be knee-deep in trouble. . . .

I was reading the other day where Dee Snider of Twisted Sister said that he believed when kids go to a concert and they're yelling and screaming, they're letting out their frustrations the safe way. I agree.

14-year-old female
Missouri

I think that films like The Color Purple and Cry Freedom are good because they show people striving to change in an environment that won't let them. I think films should educate people. Cry Freedom will educate people about Stephen Biko, a black freedom fighter in South Africa, who died in the custody of his government. The Color Purple educated people about blacks in the rural South. . . .

Movies should educate people, let them know what's going on, what has happened and why. Maybe we can avoid repeating our mistakes if we use the entertainment industry to educate people.

Christine Jarnick, 16
Troy, Michigan

Rock music now is mostly about drugs, sex, and suicide. I think that it is a bad influence on kids. . . .

Singers are just out to get money. If you play songs backwards, they tell you to worship the devil and do drugs, even commit suicide. . . .

I believe that if you truly believe in God, the songs will not affect you. Most kids like the beat and do not listen to the words. I heard some Christian singers have the same beat but tell you to love God. . . .

I sometimes listen with my friends to some "bad" music, but I know the devil cannot possess me as long as I have the love of God. . . . I used to like some songs, but I found out what they really meant. Now I feel sick every time I hear them. . . .

I think if parents didn't make such a big deal about it, then most kids would stop listening to it.

Jennifer Sessa, 14
Independence, Missouri

Sure, when we listen to rock, we usually just think of going out and partying, but it doesn't make us turn into devil worshippers. . . .

Parents think that it turns their children away from them and makes their children do awful things, but it's about time that they realize that the music doesn't really have much to do with it. Overall, it's the whole environment itself.

Kaylyane Carter, 17
Idaho Falls, Idaho

If I was to change TV programming, I would start by getting rid of or changing the format of many shows like "A-Team." For some reason . . . nobody gets killed. . . .

The shows really lose a lot of impact. . . . Kids will now have imbedded in their minds that they can be shot at and roll cars off cliffs and walk away. Show the people what can really happen.

Kurt Vanderhoef, 18
Iowa City, Iowa

The entertainment industry can only improve if people ask for it. . . . It's easy to say cut the violence, sex, and bad language, but how many people still watch "The Waltons"?

Lara Lockard, 17
Lee's Summit, Missouri

Rock music can greatly change your feelings. For example, if you listen to a song when you are already in an angry state of mind, and this song has a very bold and brassy sound, it can cause you to go from an angry state of mind to a very hostile and rebellious state of mind.

On the other hand, if you are feeling very depressed, rock music can sometimes cheer you up. . . .

Most adults feel that all rock music is harmful, disgraceful, and all of its influence is bad. I don't think that this is a fair assumption to make without taking time to study the music. . . . and to understand the teenagers' feelings. Some teenagers find rock music as a way to escape reality for a while. . . .

Adults should respect a teenager's right to listen to whatever type of music they may choose.

Holli Blatchley, 17
Hillsdale, Michigan

Frank Egan LTHS

Jennifer Sironi LTHS

Chapter 8.

Teens and Technology

Program: Teens and Technology

    Menu: Case study . . .
    Menu: Case study . . .
    Menu: Case study 15

Data:

3:01 p.m. His nose stuffed in Electronic World, Tom Terminal stumbles out of school toward home where his IBM System 38 beckons him. He passes teens playing football and suntanning. Tom deftly deprograms the burglar alarm and enters his prefabricated suburban home. After pushing a Howard Jones compact disc into his stereo and letting the synthesized ear candy fill the room, he sits down at the console. The glare from the monitor shades his face metallic blue as Tom masterminds another program.

    The door opens. Tom's father, Dim Terminal, saunters in.

    "Have you done your homework?" his dad barks.

    "Scroll up, Dad. It's the '80s. I did all my homework on the computer."

    "How can a mess of plastic that I can't even turn on do your homework? Hit the books, son."

5:13 p.m. After transferring his homework to a floppy disc and printing up hard copy, Tom activates his modem, which connects him to a worldwide network of computers. For the past three nights Tom has been battling a Chinese girl in a game of three-dimensional computer chess.

8:30 p.m. Two moves short of checkmate, Tom hears the pulsing bleep of the cordless phone sitting next to him. Lifting it from its cradle, he stretches out the antenna, flips a switch, and prepares to receive the transmission.

    "Hello, son. You aren't still working on your computer, are you?"

    "Not anymore," he sighs, turning it off.

    "I'm at the bank. I need you to help me with the automatic teller machine."

    "But, Dad, it's a 2.1 kilometer walk."

    "I'm sorry, son, but you're the only one who knows how to work it."

    Tom often receives calls of technological duty. After last week's episode with the automatic teller, he recorded the operation instructions on a cassette tape and gave his father a mini-cassette player.

    "Why don't you use the instructions on the tape I made for you?"

"I don't know how to play the tape," his father confesses. "Sorry, son."

"I'll be there in 17.3 minutes."

9:08 p.m.   Tom switches on his imaginative side. Operating his remote control VCR and 50-inch projection TV, which has computer-enhanced stereo, he screens old episodes of "Star Trek" and "Dr. Who." Tom dreams of time-ships, laser guns, and space travel as he watches silver robots glide through wire-covered corridors. Amid piles of copies of Popular Mechanics and Science Digest, he plans designs for space craft.

10:49 p.m.   Planning a late snack before bed, Tom deftly programs the automatic microwave and heats a TV dinner. Tom feels sorry for the microwave, which usually lies dormant because his parents can't operate it.

"Tom, you're not using the microwave, are you?" Tom's mother calls. "You know those things are dangerous. There's too much irradation."

"That's radiation, and microwave ovens aren't dangerous unless you crawl inside them."

"I still don't want you to use it anymore."

Tom, realizing that logic will get him nowhere, stops arguing. Dismissing his mom's orders, he takes the dinner out of the microwave and begins to eat.

11:30 p.m.   Awakened by his mother's shrill cries for help, Tom rushes to the entertainment center in the den to investigate.

"Tom, Tom, what do I do?" yells his mom, staring at the VCR.

"Press 'play,'" Tom repeats for the fifth time that week. He smiles benignly at his mother, who is paralyzed with fear.

"Which one is that?" she asks, still dismayed.

"It's the one marked 'play.'" Tom smiles again and shuffles off to bed.

In the eerie blue light of the TV screen, Tom's mother scans the row of buttons with her finger, saying, "P-u-llay."

6:00 a.m.   A shrill bleeping from Tom's digital clock signals the start of his day. He performs his usual morning routine while listening to announcements of another Voyager space probe on the shower-radio.

While eating his Powerhouse cereal, his mind drifts off to dreams of the future. He commands a space flight from behind a wall of flashing lights, screens, and dials. Ignition. Shuddering, the craft leaps into space. Stars fly by as the spaceship eventually lands on an alien city hovering above a distant planet. Tom leaps out of the ship. In reality, however, he merely descends from the school bus onto a familiar campus.

Although immersed in computers and science, Tom does not, as the myth says, wear thick glasses with taped nose bridges nor does he have messy, greasy hair. He merely suffers from a mild mental ache that blinds his social consciousness. As he nears his locker, two girls approach him.

"Hi, Tom," the first girl says, with a grin so wide it looks as though her chin is about to fall off. Tom ignores her.

"Earth to Tom, come in Major Tom," the second girl says. She turns to her friend and giggles. Tom, his brain in orbit, does not reply.

2:00 p.m.   Computer class. The teacher is absent so Tom lectures. After a short description of axial terminal time-sharing by the method of simultaneous polling, the class begins to work on the machines. His hands dancing across the keyboard as naturally as maggots

on a dead fish, Tom lovingly strokes the computer with logic. The day is almost over, and the cycle will soon repeat.

Diagnosis: Technorrhea

Tom's disease is common. Many people suffer from acute or chronic technorrhea. In some cases it can be fatal to a teen's social existence.

Technorrhea has many symptoms. Sufferers often have glazed eyes that appear to stare into infinity. They actually are programming computers in their minds. They infrequently communicate, or interface as they call it, with outsiders, but they usually simply respond with "Syntax error" when they do.

Although they appear socially inept, the symptom is more myth than reality. Actually, sufferers of technorrhea are quite gregarious and often congregate in herds of their own kind. They adopt nicknames like "Wire," "Leads," or "Space Ace." Many of them are what would be considered cool dudes. Smoking and drinking are not strictly forbidden, except near the terminal.

Starting as a simple interest in computers or electronics, technorrhea soon takes hold in susceptible students. Technology becomes their primary interest in life. Left untreated, the disease results in isolation—a condition Tom succumbed to due to his inability to talk with girls—and in parental conflict—another symptom Tom must endure due to his father's inability to operate the computer or automatic teller.

If allowed to proceed to the final stage, technorrhea causes the victim to lose all concern for appearance. Hair becomes unwashed and unkempt, and dress sense degenerates. The victim begins to wear green, orange, and dark brown polyester. The victim also acquires thick glasses due to staring at computer screens. He becomes what society calls, to use the colloquial term, a "geek."

Fortunately, technorrhea may be cured by increased social and physical activities. Computer use can be continued but should be limited to class assignments. In case of relapse, technorrhea can be controlled with the prescription of two beers and a fuzzy puppy.

Dave Seng

Conflicts

Technology is constantly being used for sick distortions of some society-created military psycho. . . . We can already kill everyone, poison the ocean, and destroy everything. . . .

> Gregory Lance Barton, 15
> Oklahoma City, Oklahoma

I would like to see myself leading a simple life ten years from now. Right now my life is too complex and very exhausting. . . . It's difficult these days to lead a simple life because of the rapid advancement in technology.

> Tamara Wainer, 16
> Galesburg, Illinois

I think that teens welcome new technology much more than parents. Parents seem to want things to stay the way they were instead of moving forward. . . . Teens want to see technology develop further so that we can have more gadgets to play with.

Parents . . . want life to stay frozen the way it was when they were young. This might be their way of remembering a time long gone by and maybe pretending that they're not aging.

I can think of many times when my mother has been unable to figure out how to use a new piece of equipment.

She therefore didn't like the equipment because I knew how to use it, and she didn't.

A specific example that comes to mind is our video cassette recorder. You just need to press a few buttons to use it, but my mother won't because she . . . is afraid she might break the machine.

> 15-year-old male
> Connecticut

When I am confronted with something technological—say programming the VCR to tape a show . . . I will . . . fool around with it until it's figured out.

My mom will . . . maybe get out the instruction booklet for a while, but when she doesn't get it right away, she says, "Forget it! It's not important!"

I think because kids . . . have been in school since they were five, they're used to being given a problem and told to solve it. They're accustomed to being faced with new ideas. Parents . . . aren't learning new things anymore. Their brains don't immediately set out to solve problems anymore.

Theresa Tenpas, 17
Whitmore Lake, Michigan

Nowadays, kids seem . . . attached to television, computers, and videos. When one of my friend's family went to Michigan, her brother watched the portable TV in the car rather than looking at the beautiful scenery.

Stephanie Renshaw, 18
Blue Springs, Missouri

I don't think teenagers are involved in technology because they are so tied down with their schooling.

Lisa Goheen, 17
Kansas City, Kansas

Nuclear arms scares us all. We can be wiped out in seconds by the push of a button. We the young people should protest against the government's . . . spending millions of dollars on nuclear arms.

Even Russian teenagers realize the mistakes of their government. . . . I think they should revolt against the destruction of humanity. In a flash of light, we can disappear forever.

Steve Cook, 15
North Plainfield, New Jersey

Researchers care too much about moving forward fast—they try to lighten the load by dropping their waste along the way.

Stacy Weed, 16
Round Rock, Texas

I'm all for advancement if it has a positive effect—destroying our surroundings is not pleasant nor positive. Money is being thrown away

daily for the construction of materials to destroy our surroundings. . . .

I feel we're biting the hand that feeds us. I feel we'll be very sorry one day that happiness was not enough.

Lisa Okray, 17
Stevens Point, Wisconsin

When we got a microwave and VCR several years ago, I was able to figure out . . . each of them in a couple of days. My parents, on the other hand, still don't really know how to work either one.

It may be that they aren't interested in the new gadgets, or they are too complicated.

Ron Nagy, 18
Blue Island, Illinois

Genetic engineering . . . Human life is conceived by God himself and should not be changed by humans to fit or uphold the standards that we believe . . . With genetic changes, we will not be the creation but the creator.

Michael Willard, 17
Oklahoma City, Oklahoma

When a new breakthrough in scientific technology is made, parents gasp and children cheer. The older generations feel that these new inventions are ruining the goodness of people by making them lazy.

Jim Anderson, 15
Brookfield Center,
Connecticut

I think that people abuse the amount of resources we have in order to cut our work in half but not learn anything from the experience. For example, calculators make people's work easier, but if you ask someone what nine times seven is, their actions are delayed for a second. In this way, computers do more damage than good.

Kelli Frans, 17
Oklahoma City, Oklahoma

The government . . . has no respect for the opinions of the younger generation and blatantly destroys our

surroundings and causes situations that we may not be able to solve in the future—for example, nuclear waste and nuclear arms.

They are stockpiling . . . these weapons which can leak out and cause horrible defects in people and which, at present, we have no way of controlling. Also, they have to take serious steps to solve the problem with the ozone layer and pollution. Otherwise, there may be no tomorrow for us.

The government lacks consideration for the world of tomorrow, our world, and only concentrates on what they

DAN PADILLA

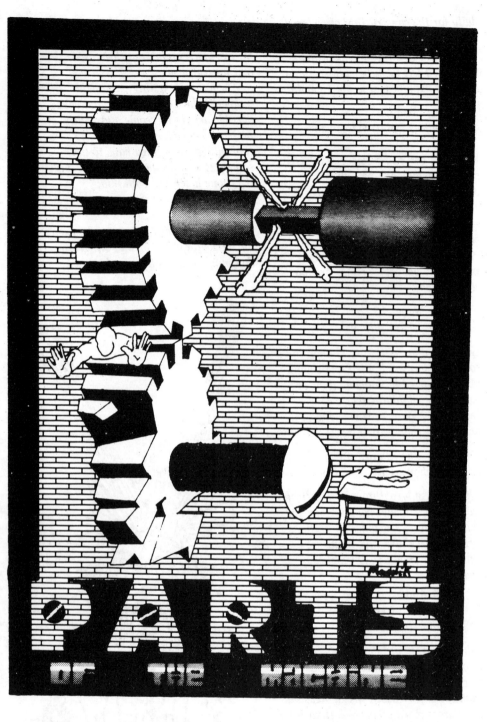

Effect of Technology

Decatur, Georgia
Mt. Carmel High School

Are computers and technology worth the cost?

Chuck: Computers can't tell anything about your personality, but I'd rather use computers because they provide a quicker and more methodical way of doing things.

Wayne: It's a matter of necessity. As the population increases, we need more advanced methods of production even though it may knock out some of the personality.

Robert: If technology was suddenly taken away, we probably couldn't function because we're not learning how to function without technology.

Chuck: Technology is getting the necessary things done quickly so we can have more spare time. It's not lazy. People still go out and exercise and do things all the time.

Wayne: Technology is going so fast that you can buy the most advanced stereo, but it's soon outdated. We're jealous because we feel we had the best one available when we bought our microwave oven. Now it's nothing.

Angela: People want things to stay the same. They stay away from technology because it's changing too fast. Our house is so underadvanced it's not funny. We don't have anything. We have electricity but very few digitals and no microwaves. We have a car, but it's about eight years old. We won't buy another one for several years.

Wayne: Older people feel like the times are changing so fast that they won't be able to catch up with it. It is important to older people, just as much as younger

want immediately. Their methods are too insignificant and will be too late unless there is a drastic change of priorities.

Leslie Bishop, 15
North Plainfield, New Jersey

I think that technology is outgrowing the need for teachers. . . . I already have classes in school where video cameras are used for teaching—not only for our school, but they also connect us to schools in our area. I also have several classes where computers teach me and the teacher is just there to babysit.

Renu Ingersoll, 16
Buffalo, Minnesota

142

people, to be a part of things and understanding what's going on.

Chuck: Young people are always jumping in and learning about technology. The older people feel like they're not needed, and they're going to be pushed behind with their old technology when new technology comes in. They're not going to be respected as much for knowing what they've learned.

Bart: My dad blames me for things not working right. We got a Betamax, and he tried fooling around with it. He could never get it to work so it was my fault. Something so simple to me, like a digital watch, my dad doesn't understand. Adults don't care to learn. They just figure, "Well, that's for the younger people." They figure they've learned all they need to learn.

Cleveland
Jane Addams Business Career Center

Michelle: Everyone is working with computers now. Typewriters are going to become obsolete pretty soon. People are using computers in the medical field and in electronics. We're using them more in the homes, with microwaves, new typewriters, vacuum cleaners, dishwashers. Soon you're going to have your own robot to wash the floor. They have robots that play with kids now.

Schools are bringing computers in because children can learn at their own rate. With computers, students are working one-on-one so they can get more out of it.

Michael: Computers are taking away our way of life and our jobs.

Michelle: The factories are where you're losing jobs, but in business you are getting jobs. You need more people to work with computers, more people to program them. People losing jobs

makes you feel bad, but it's happening—you have to step up with the times.

How do people react toward the computer?

Michelle: My friends just look at the computer. When I'm playing with the keyboard, they just sit in amazement like, "Where did you get that stuff from? How do you get stuff done like that?"

Cheryle: My friends are afraid to touch anything that might take something out of the computer. They don't want to touch it unless they have read the full 500-page instruction manual.

My mother doesn't touch mine. She doesn't even go into the room where it is. I do most of my homework on it. I explained to her, "Don't touch anything because you might knock my program out." She's scared of it.

Michelle: I have a friend who tapped into the phone system of his school, and he put a bill on their phone system. He tapped into different businesses. He never had to do his reports for school. He just typed the idea into the computer, and it would write it for him. It scared me because he wasn't learning as much as he should have. You give him a test or an essay, and he wouldn't know what to do because his computer did it all for him. I never want to rely on a computer that much.

Wilmington, Delaware
Eye Magazine office

Bob: Right now technology is just a luxury, but the environment is always going to be necessary. People could survive without technology, but they wouldn't enjoy themselves. They're spoiled. It's going to get to the point where people totally depend on modern technology.

How does technology affect teenagers?

Duane: It provides entertainment—stereos, ghetto boxes, Walkmans, compact disc players. You can see things on TV that you didn't see years ago.

Tony: Technology is a different form of evolution. As this generation goes toward computers, it will be a way of life. It is like the survival of the fittest.

Duane: It makes things easier. It is an advantage in that there are certain things that can be done for you that you just don't have time to do.

Do you think this is negative or positive?

Duane: Socially, technology is negative because you are not communicating with people. Your computer is communicating with someone else's computer.

Tony: Technology makes things more impersonal. In the Eye Magazine, we speak with other computers across the United States and use a mail service. We don't know where the base is in the United States, but they are able to read whatever we have on the lines. It should be confidential, but there always is that myth that someone would read what goes across the news service.

Bob: Computers are taking people out of jobs. Machines can make something just as good as people can, but they won't put the effort into it. If you put material into a machine and it comes out wrong, the machine doesn't know about it. But with a human, if it comes out wrong, the human would stop and say, "This is wrong," and would do it right.

People are talking about how students are starting to become less skilled in grammar and spelling and writing.

Jeff: Some people resent

technology because they can't cope with it. The older generation is having doubts because they never had the comforts of today and are afraid they'll be left out.

What are the dangers of technology?

Bob: Nuclear power puts a lot of people's lives on the line. If you make one little mistake, you could have all these nuclear bombs going off, and the whole world would be destroyed. When you work with energy and stuff, you have to know what you're doing because a mistake could destroy the environment.

Wilmington, Delaware
Du Pont Headquarters

John McAllister *executive assistant; corporate safety, health, and environmental affairs:* Look back at the changes in transportation and communications, which have been the enormous revolutions of the century. The effects of technology are profound. The car and what it's been able to do for people personally. Communications. The concept of a global village. You can have a hostage crisis and simulcast it worldwide.

It's only been in recent times that nature has been viewed as benign. If you go back in history, nature was thought to be all powerful and capricious. Primitive man worshiped nature. Nature is amoral. Mankind is moral, trying to improve nature, trying to alter nature for the benefit of mankind. That's what mankind is capable of doing.

Alan McClelland *assistant to vice president, central research and development department:* For many people, too much time in science classes is spent on abstract, esoteric, scientific concepts. This is the real challenge to education. Teaching needs to be related to the student. The kind of teaching today's student has, the

mathematical way of doing things, is wonderful, but it turns an awful lot of people off. It's not fair to say everybody has to take the same sort of science course. There ought to be a course for the people who don't like to approach things mathematically.

Everything involves a certain amount of risk—for example, nuclear power. Actually, the record is very good. It's a very safe form of power. Yet radioactivity is unfamiliar to people. Someone says "radioactive," and they're scared. That's where science education has to come in. Give students a feeling of familiarity so that they can make rational decisions.

The whole question of the use of animals in experimentation is becoming a hot issue. No one is in favor of cruelty to animals. We try to do it with full consideration of the animals, but don't we need animal experimentation on new drugs before we start putting them into humans? We have to make decisions about how we draw the line.

Our lives are science. Science is here for everybody. Scientists have made science sound like it's something different. That's one of the terrible dangers. Scientists keep inventing these big words for things. They scare people off just by the words they use.

Science is just the explanation of how the world works. People talk about chemicals. Are you going to be afraid of chemicals? Well, everything is a chemical. Wood is a chemical; paper is a chemical; skin is a chemical. Every material substance is a chemical. Chemistry is not something odd that's done in labs by people in white coats. It's just the way the world works.

Donald Dinsel *principal consultant, employee relations department:* Any technological breakthrough is looked at with fear. People were afraid of the Industrial Revolution,

but now most people would agree that it was the best way to go.

One should look at technology with joy: "What is this going to do for my life?" and "How is this going to make my existence better?" If people are informed, they're going to be able to make better decisions. If fire were invented today, we probably wouldn't allow it because it has the potential for burning, for killing people, and we can't control that.

Berkeley, California
University of California

Laura Nader *professor of anthropology:* High-tech industrialization satisfies us materially, but it doesn't satisfy us emotionally. In many ways we are a psychologically depressed country because we have all the things we ever aspired to have. But somehow there is something missing. There is not enough vision of a happy future, of an alternative way of living.

We're caught in a system that's operating for its own sake. We have depersonalized our work lives so we can't connect the action with the consequences. For example, if we have a nuclear accident, it's not so bad because we lose only two percent of the populaton. Why do they use percentages to refer to people? How many people is two percent of 200 million-plus? People are too insulated.

You know about Love Canal? It was horrible—contamination of that area and the people. People were talking about Love Canal who never felt what it was like to live there. It would be nice to send the people from those companies to live there for a month or two. You would bring them closer to the consequences so that they can see what they're doing.

We have to look at important issues that are coming up. In my

144

generation it was the nuclear issue. We worked through that. We understand it very well. We understand the minds of the people who were pushing the policy. Now we've got genetic engineering. This is going to make nuclear look like nothing. They're in the process of trying to get experiments going like "Ice Minus" that could result in changes of the weather and releasing microbes that they can't control.

The thing teenagers have that experts don't have are questions. By the time people get

"educated," they don't know what the question was. In a way people have to keep a certain naiveté to be able to ask questions. "It's true we don't know anything about genetic engineering, but we'd like to ask some questions." They can never deny you an answer by telling you, "You don't know very much. You're a teenager."

If high school students are almost old enough to go to war, they're old enough to ask any question they want to ask.

Washington, D.C.
National Science Foundation

Why do people resist learning about technology?

W. F. (Fred) Oettle *Program director:* Part of it is fear, and part of it is resentment. Fear of technology comes from the public picture of what scientists do. If you look at the movies, scientists are a weird bunch. "They're going to invent new monsters and new bugs that are going to kill us all."

Nature is doing a wonderful job of inventing new bugs to kill us. AIDS suddenly appeared. Nobody had ever heard of that before. They're just now beginning to get

some ideas of where that virus originated, but that was a natural thing. It didn't escape from somebody's lab. There is an image in the public mind that nature is good and that things that happen in a lab are probably dangerous.

Acceptance of Technology

Cleveland

How can people learn more about computers and technology?

Michael: There's a program on TV to introduce the computer to people, show them how to work it, and what everything means.

Michelle: Certain computers give you the step-by-step instructions, how to use the computer. All you have to do is to put the disk in, turn it on, and it will take you step-by-step through the instructions on how the computer works.

Cheryl: I know of a set of two-year-old twins. They are very well-educated. They are learning to

read at the age of two with the help of the computer.

Michelle: Kids between the ages of two and six are the most advanced, and they learn everything. If you give them a computer, they'll be more apt to step up in society. Because they know how to operate it, they won't be afraid of it.

Wayne: Early education will destroy the fear because people will know what computers are about and won't be afraid to use them. They'll just think it's something they're supposed to do, work with computers.

What is the minimum computer education students should have?

Michelle: It depends on what they wish to do with it. If they want to go into business, they have to go all the way up. If they're just going to use it in the home, they can use BASIC.

Cheryl: It is important to know something about languages. Teens going into any job using computers are going to use one of three languages: RPG, COBOL, or FORTRAN. Also, they should know the keyboard. The keyboard is important because it is so different from a typewriter.

Portland, Oregon
Office of Forelaws on Board

Lloyd Marvett *environmentalist advocate:* One reason we have the problem with nuclear energy is because we have never been involved in the decision-making as to whether that technology was to be implemented. It was foisted upon us by the people who sit in the closed rooms and towers of the corporate world.

The question teenagers face is whether technology is going to be a servant for their hearts and minds or whether their hearts and minds will be servants to technology. Are teenagers going to dictate our future, or is their future going to be dictated by a minority of people who control the resources and the technologies on the face of the Earth?

As far as energy alternatives go, it's clear that we have reached a point where we have a significant decision: Are we going to proliferate without consciousness, essentially acting as a cancer on the face of the Earth? Or do we use intelligence to put us in a position where we can find a balance and a harmony in our relationship with the Earth, its resources, and the people with whom we share the planet? We should seek more renewable resources. We should use our technologies to develop the various solar alternatives. And use our ingenuity in the way we design the structures we live in, the communities we live in, and the work we do.

If we don't find a path by which we embody a reverence for life, then we are doomed to disappear as an example of another species that lived on this planet.

Portland, Oregon
Handford Clearinghouse Information Center

David Newhouse *staff assistant:* We have a lot of questions about technology. The Challenger disaster is an example of blind faith in technology. We were led to believe that we were safely putting Americans in space. We found out that there is a one in 50 chance that a catastrophe could happen because of the solid rocket boosters.

There are a lot of questions about whether we should be going into outer space. Everytime we launch a rocket, it blasts a ten-mile hole in the ozone layer. Perhaps if it were not such a race with the Soviets or Europeans, there would be a lot more consideration of the impact of technology.

Wilmington, Delaware

How good is science and math education in the United States?

McClelland: In science, it is not enough to educate only the people who are going to do science. In music education, you teach the performers and the audience. What I think we have done in science very well is to educate the

performers. What we have done very poorly, because we have a single-minded concentration on the performers, is to educate the audience.

We see a lot of situations where people's inability to put the applications of science in a rational context is making it more and more difficult for the benefits of scientific research to reach society.

We need to get kids in kindergarten to recognize that science explains how the world works. It isn't something exotic that is done off in Fermilab.

Science is about continually coming up with new information and using it along the way.

Science is around us all the time. Everybody needs to learn to live comfortably with it. Everybody needs to know a little bit about how electricity works because we use it all the time. Everybody ought to be able to go over to the wall and know how to take a defective wall switch out and replace it with a new wall switch. That's just everyday living.

In addition to training good scientists and engineers, we need to teach all those other people who aren't going to be scientists and engineers the kind of understanding of science they need in order to live successfully in today's world.

Science is a wonderful thing to teach because you can let students do things. Don't sit down and lecture them. Let them try things. Let them take an automoblie engine apart to see how it works.

Washington, D.C.

How effective is math and science education?

Oettle: Science education in the United States is an odd creature. In terms of producing engineers and scientists, it works very well. Unfortunately, in terms of producing a population that understands technology, it doesn't work at all.

People are trying to deal with this problem by legislating and requiring more classes, but I'm not sure that really solves the problem. If the basic way the subject is approached is not meeting the need, then doing more of it isn't necessarily going to be better. Studies have shown that minorities get turned off by about the fourth grade. Usually by early high school, women tend to drop out of the advanced math and science courses. Studies suggest

that it's the way individuals are treated. You see those kinds of attitudes coming through. "I think it's important that you all understand this, but Johnny, why don't you come up and do the demonstration, and Paulette, you watch."

Another problem is that a lot of primary teachers themselves don't have a strong background in science. There are lots of things that industry can contribute—summer internships for teachers, visiting scientists and engineers who go into the school and work with the teacher.

A lot of the projects we support

are things like workshops in which the teachers will spend four to six weeks in the summer at a university campus, usually working with a scientist in the field. Then during the school year there's a follow-up session in which the teachers talk about how they've been able to use the material in the classroom—what worked, what didn't, and what problems they had.

We want to encourage better preparation of teachers. Scientists have to take a lot of the blame if teachers aren't well prepared because our attitude has been, "We don't want to be bothered. If we can't teach chemists or physicists, we're not interested in running the course for people who are going to be elementary school teachers." As a result, often an elementary school teacher may never have taken a science course since high school.

Let people in school experience what scientists do by meeting them. Scientists also need to be more up-front and outgoing about what they're doing and why. We have a tendency to sit in a lab and think wonderful thoughts and do wonderful things. Then we're very shocked when someone shows up at our door to protest what we're doing.

Batavia, Illinois
Fermi National Laboratory

What is the responsibility of scientists to the public?

Leon Lederman *director:* There's a responsibility to make your science socially redeeming, to make it beneficial, although scientists generally don't work that way. Often they're just curious about how nature works. Scientists should try to expose young people to the virtues of the scientific life. Insight. Challenge. Traditions that go back thousands of years—to understand how the universe works.

What is the importance of research for the sake of research?

Lederman: It is cultural. It began when people first evinced curiosity about something so it is deeply cultural. In that sense, it is not different from music, art, and literature. History has shown that science, while contributing to our culture, contributes to our means for life, to our civilization. So the average person now can push a button and flood his house with glorious news that the kings of old couldn't acquire.

People come to our lectures, take our tours, and see the enthusiastic scientists pursuing their work with a great deal of zest and excitement. Perhaps if people listen to one, two, or three lectures, they'll capture some of the excitement. Kids come to our Saturday morning physics class and jump up and down and say, "This is good stuff." Probably in the long run, they'll benefit from some of the inventions that will find their way into society.

Can technology and the environment co-exist?

Lederman: There's no fundamental reason they can't co-exist if we understand technology. We have to assess technology, see what effect it has on the environment. Ever since the industrial revolution, we've had technology that has fouled the environment, crummied it up. We never watched what we were doing.

The ecology of the planet is rather delicate. There are all kinds of dangers that were brought about by old technology dangers that now require new technology, but we have to make sure that new technology itself is benign.

How good is today's science education?

Lederman: It's bloody awful in this country. In the past three or four years, there have been some healthy movements to improve teacher salaries and to raise consciousness about education in general and about science education in particular. It's hard to improve science education without improving all education.

You can improve education by improving teachers and by making sure that parents take responsibility, too. Parents, society, the media, and everyone else has to convince young people that they can't make it in the world, in the workplace, without greater technical knowledge.

Not having technical knowledge is like being in a country in which papers and all politicians are talking in some other language. How do you vote? How do you choose what's good for you unless you have some technical knowledge?

Take things that hit the paper. Chernobyl. What's Chernobyl? What is a nuclear reactor? Why is it dangerous? Can this happen here? What are we doing about nuclear safety? What are we doing about nuclear waste disposal? What about nuclear weapons? What about arms control? What about strategic defense initiatives? Are they good things? Are they bad things? Are they dangerous? Should we put fluorides in the water to protect ourselves from cavities? Should we allow certain experiments to go on which might tamper with DNA material? These are issues where science makes an impact on society.

What's your opinion? What should you tell your congressman? He's going to listen to you, especially if you jump up and down and make noise. Nowadays, you go to sleep at night and wake up in the morning, and the world has changed. Change is characteristic of our times. Change is produced not by science but by applications of science, by technology. One has to know the difference between science and technology, how one depends on the other. Science is the quest for knowledge. Technology is the application of knowledge and things that are useful.

What are the benefits of an educated generation?

Lederman: Enormous. Our laws will be better. Our policies will be better. Our industries will be better, more competitive with the outside world. Everywhere you look, you find potential for improvement—political, social, economic, and cultural. It's a pity, really one of the great tragedies, that not enough people can read *Discover* magazine, not to mention *Scientific American*. And the joy, the possibilities—it's like people putting in ear plugs and not listening to any music. The voice of science is lyrical and beautiful. People should make the effort to learn about it so they can enjoy it. It's not that hard. A good lecture by a great scientist can be a very moving experience.

Compiled by Robert Hester

Solutions

It would be very easy for any . . . person to get a grasp on the flood of technology. . . . There are classes which any person could attend and learn more about the technology around them.

Jason Sherman, 16
Livermore, California

The abuse of technology has increased through the years. Man started advancing in technology to better himself by improving the things he made and the way he made those things. But as the years rolled on, man used technology to become more powerful than his neighbors. . . .

Perhaps this abuse can only be controlled by each man relinquishing his quest for power. But for this to happen would require a lot of faith in the Lord.

Kathryn Cupp, 17
Oklahoma City, Oklahoma

Technology is being abused in the environment by planes dumping chemicals that destroy the food chain, Brazil cutting down the rain forest and in effect raising the planet's temperature, the New York Times alone cutting down thousands of trees a day, helping the fact that soon there will be a species of tree dying every . . . day, and the ozone layer being destroyed knowingly by people who don't care.

It can be controlled by every government enforcing tougher laws on dumpage, an environmentalist group raising money to buy some of the rain forest, newspapers writing on some other kind of material and recycling it, and science developing chemicals that will not affect the ozone layer.

Erin McDonald, 15
Round Rock, Texas

If we weren't building missiles, we could be curing AIDS and cancer. If we (USA & USSR) combined our technology, we could do a lot more.

Craig Rooney, 17
Jefferson City, Missouri

I believe in the theory of moderation, and I think that computers and nuclear energy are being used to the extreme. Modern technology is great, but computers are taking away people's jobs.

Nuclear energy is far too dangerous right now because we're using so much of it while knowing little about it.

Michele Chesser, 16
Oklahoma City, Oklahoma

My mom had an operation a few years ago. She needed to know exactly what would happen, and then she put her life in the doctor's hands. She trusted the technology. Teens do the same thing. I have to understand technology before I trust it.

Barbara Molini, 17
Carawissa, Missouri

Many people today experience what is known as future shock . . . a fear of rapidly advancing technology. . . .

To overcome this fear, all the future shock victims have to do is learn . . . by taking courses for them. This is what I did. I went into high school not knowing a thing about technology, and I am coming out with two years of electronics and computers. . . . I combated and beat future shock. . . .

Eric Ziller, 17
Livermore, California

Just because something has a double-edge is no reason to remove it. If society were to go around removing all such items, the world wouldn't be left with as much as a speck of sand.

Scott Countryman, 18
Oklahoma City, Oklahoma

Conflict with Values

As pressure increases from peers and authority figures, teens retreat into their one remaining haven: the self. Once they've locked themselves inside this shelter, they feel the walls begin to constrict.

Some teenagers throw down money for a bed of comfort within these narrow confines. But material luxuries do not alleviate the pressure.

Teens then desperately search for some absolute with which to brace the contracting walls. However, they find that even the strongest moral values may crack beneath the weight of peer pressure, new ideas, and new experiences.

The stress continues to build until many teens feel like they're going to explode. With the resilience of youth, though, most teens adapt to the incessant pressure. Their discomfort soon seems to be a given in life. But just when they believe they have developed a tolerance, everything changes. New pressures appear. Old pressures intensify.

As the walls continue to close in on them, some teens collapse in despair. Others discover that deep inside themselves diamonds have formed from the pressures of their lives. They recognize jewels of hope, their dreams.

WENDY
OLSZEWSKI
LTHS

Chapter 9.

Teens and Materialism

"Friday at last," sighed Justin Adaise as he stumbled through his front door and crashed on the living room floor, exhausted by yet another week of doing as little as possible at school. He had a date that night so he dragged himself up from the floor to check out the pile of clothes in his room. "No problem," thought Justin, as he surveyed his wardrobe. His favorite faded Levis were clean, his favorite faded polo shirt was clean, and his Nike sneakers were ready to go. Clean underwear, though, was another story. Justin grabbed his dirty Sears underwear and started to head for the laundry room. Suddenly he stopped, threw the underwear back in his room, and went to the kitchen to grab a Coke.

"Hell," Justin thought. "I can always turn the underwear inside-out."

He collapsed on the living room floor again with his Coke and took a couple of gulps. The caffeine buzz got to him right away—he was usually a 7-Up drinker. But heck, it was Friday so why not be a little wild?

He reached out, pulled the remote control off the end table, and clicked on the tube. CNN, the Cable News Network, was on. They were running a special on Mother Theresa of Calcutta and her work for the poor. Justin really enjoyed the show, but not because of Mother Theresa.

"I really love those baggy cotton pants these Indian guys are wearing. They're so faded," Justin said.

Justin quickly became bored with Mother Theresa and switched to his old favorite, MTV. Justin bopped along to the catchy tune of a Madonna video, "Material Girl." He wondered whether Madonna would still look sexy if she dressed like Mother Theresa. Soon, though, he felt the caffeine buzz wearing off and his eyes closed. His snores grew louder as the Madonna video ended and the VJ introduced the next song.

Justin's subconscious, however, was busy taking Justin to a world far away from his faded Levis and dirty underwear. He was in a bright, shiny world where everything was very new, very fashionable, and very, very hip. Justin walked slowly through this foreign land, not knowing what to do. In the background, Justin could hear the song "Material Girl" by Madonna being played, except it had a bizarre, Indian sound. To Justin, it seemed like the synthesizer had been replaced by a sitar. He cleaned out his ear with his finger and kept on walking.

Suddenly, a bright white flash appeared in front of him, and then slowly, a person materialized. She looked like Madonna except that she wore a nun's habit and smock made entirely of see-through white lace. The woman smiled at Justin, licked her lips, and purred.

"Who are you?" Justin asked.

"I am Mother Madonna of Giorgio," she replied.

Justin gazed in wonder at the beautiful vision in lingerie and thought for a moment that he had died and gone to heaven.

"Am I dead?" Justin asked her.

"Only as far as your wardrobe is concerned," she replied.

"Then why are you here, oh Mother Madonna?" Justin asked.

"To help someone as immaterial as yourself," she answered.

Mother Madonna took Justin's hand, and Justin found himself surrounded by her white glow. They began to glide gently through the strange land. They moved so smoothly Justin thought they must be flying.

"Oh Mother Madonna, are we borne upon the winds?" he asked.

"No, my child," she chuckled. "The smooth sensation you feel is because you are now walking in your very own Bass Weejuns. They are so comfortable that you feel like you are walking on air."

Justin glanced down at his footwear. Indeed, his battered Nikes were replaced by new Bass Weejuns. The rest of his old clothes were also brand new.

"Yes, my formerly slovenly child, you shall now glance at your new garments, and you shall learn of fashion," Mother Madonna said, noticing Justin's amazement.

"Your trousers are Guess jeans. Your shirt is the finest pure cotton Oxford from L. L. Bean. And your watch is a 24-karat gold Rolex," Mother Madonna continued. "Gaze into this mirror, and see how I have changed you in one swift stroke from très gauche to très chic," she said, smiling proudly.

Justin stared at his reflection in the mirror, and he barely recognized himself. This was not the Justin Adaise he had known before. Indeed, he now fit perfectly with the other people in this strange land.

"Am I now a Material Guy?" he asked.

"Very nearly, but not quite," Mother Madonna answered.

She snapped her fingers. Nothing happened. Justin looked around anxiously, hoping to see another miracle occur, but he could not see anything new.

"Unzip your fly," Mother Madonna ordered.

Shyly, Justin turned away from her and undid his fly a tiny bit. Under his Guess jeans he saw a most amazing sight: bright blue, pinstriped Calvin Klein bikini underwear. Justin gasped and then stared at Mother Madonna in wonder.

"You are truly a worker of miracles, oh Mother Madonna," Justin exclaimed.

"Oh, borderline miracles, perhaps," she replied with a smile.

The tour of this amazing land continued. Justin began to feel a bit uneasy though he did not know why. He suddenly longed to see his old friends, to chow on some Cheeze-Its, to guzzle a 7-Up and belch aloud, and to drive his '77 Pinto while listening to the AM radio. But he quelled these desires for the moment and turned his attention back to Mother Madonna and her Strange Land.

"Is there anything else to learn, oh Great Mother?" Justin asked.

"Oh, yes, my child. Much more. You now have fashion, but you still need class, attitude, and finally, lifestyle," she stated firmly.

Justin now noticed that all the people in this place looked similar. They dressed the same, wore their hair the same, talked the same, even smelled the same. He began to get worried.

"Oh, Mother Madonna, what is that scent that abounds everywhere?" Justin asked.

"That most pleasant of odors is a mixture of the women's Giorgio perfume and the men's Cartier cologne," she replied.

They stopped next to a shiny, fire-engine red car. A man was leaning against the car, drinking something out of a clear green bottle.

"And now for your next lesson, my child, a lesson in class," Mother Madonna began. "You shall always drive a BMW 325i, and you shall always drink Perrier when available."

A lady walked by, wearing long, baggy shorts in the most obnoxious combination of bright, garish colors Justin had ever seen.

"And when the temperature is hot enough outdoors," Mother Madonna continued, pointing to the lady in shorts, "you shall wear those shorts that are called..."

Justin slipped away from her before she could finish her statement. He had heard some strange sounds emanating from a small, nondescript concrete building off to the side. As he neared the door, he heard a mixture of chanting and screaming. Timidly, Justin opened the door and stepped in.

Inside, Justin found he had entered some sort of classroom. MTV was playing on a wide-screen TV on each wall. The front room was filled with several rows of men and women, all fashionably dressed. Their faces, however, were expressionless, like zombies. The zombies were strapped into their seats. At the front of the room, a woman instructor pointed at some words written on a chalkboard and ordered the zombies to repeat the words.

"Yah, dude. Which way to the beach?" the zombies replied in a low, monotone voice.

"Again!" the instructor barked.

"Yah, dude. Which way to the beach?" the zombies repeated. Over and over, the entire chant continued.

Someone touched Justin's shoulder, and he turned quickly to see that Mother Madonna had found him.

"And why are you here, my child?" she asked.

"Well, I, uh, heard some strange noises, and..." he started to reply. The crack of a whip, followed by a long, painful shriek from the back room suddenly cut him short.

"What was that?" Justin asked nervously.

Teens and Technology   157

"Oh, nothing," Mother Madonna replied cheerfully. "This is our Materialism Re-education Center. These beautiful, re-educated, materialistic people you see in this room have successfully passed the program and will soon graduate.

"Mother Madonna, what is the name of this strange land where all are so fashionable?" Justin asked. He was trembling with fear.

"Why, my child, we are in the heart of the Material World," she replied with a chuckle.

Justin's worst fears were confirmed. Mother Madonna was about to put a pair of Vuarnet sunglasses on his face when Justin let out a terrified scream.

"Please, no, stop, nooooo!"

Justin awoke from his nightmare with a start and glanced at his Timex watch. He had to pick up his date in half an hour. He ran to his room and put on his faded polo shirt and began to put on his faded Levis. He could have just turned his Sears underwear inside-out and worn it again. For some reason, though, he decided to wear his only clean underwear, a pair of Calvin Klein jockey shorts he had received as a Christmas present. They had never even been removed from their box.

Justin smiled to himself as he pulled on the brand new red and pink striped underwear. "What the hell," he said to himself, "it *is* Friday."

Erik Landahl

Conflicts

Every year . . . the cost of popularity gets higher and higher. In elementary school, you need hand-held electronic games to be a hit. In junior high . . . the right shoes and hair. But in high school . . . people with cars, particularly new, expensive, and foreign, are at the top of the social ladder. Behind them are girls with expensive wardrobes and the kids with the speakers and stereo components. . . . If you don't have these things, you still can be popular, but they help.

For the poorer kids, it's harder to make friends. They don't have the flashy magnet that draws people to them. They just have to get by with what they have. . . . Every time I hear about some girl's Daddy buying her a car, I get upset. . . . It's just that they are getting another wedge in the trivial pursuit of popularity.

Jeff Field, 16
Kansas City, Missouri

A friend at school got a brand-new car. . . . The kid's best friend was so jealous that he absolutely had to have a car. He just could not live without it. . . . The boy knew his father couldn't pay for it, and he knew he couldn't afford it on his own. So he decided to steal one right off the dealer's lot. . . . He kept the car at a friend's house.

Everything was cool for about a month until he got caught. . . . He ended up in jail for five years. His father lost his job because his advertising firm did advertising for the victimized dealership. The last I heard the rest of the family was out on the street.

17-year-old male
Illinois

Materialism is one of the biggest traps of adolescence. Often . . . not only as a teenager but also as an adult, possessions become more important than anything else. I have friends that think nothing of spending their whole paychecks on records or tapes and yet, when it comes to giving money for a worthwhile cause at school or elsewhere, they are as stingy as can be.

I think that materialism . . . causes you to forget about the things in life that are really important like love, friendship, and peace. People should learn to set their priorities straight. After all, when you die, your possessions don't go with you.

Lisa Del Mar, 17
Auburn, Washington

Materialism is the most prevalant evil in our society. Emphasis on success and possessions fills our daily routines so much that, unwittingly, it has become as natural to think about them as about eating. . . .

Lynn Wilkins, 16
Little Silver, New Jersey

In grade school, people never judged you on what you wore or what you looked like. . . . Now that I've got to junior high, people laugh if you wear clothes they don't like. If they think you're ugly, they tease you. If you don't have as much money as they do, then you're gross or scum. They don't want you around them.

I've had it happen to me. When I'm at school, I get called names and teased because I'm not as pretty or as smart as someone else. It really hurts. . . .

I thought junior high wouldn't be any worse than grade school. . . . I was wrong. . . . I just pray that I don't get a bad attitude as time goes by.

Ageanna Boucher, 14
Independence, Missouri

When I was a freshman, I always had to have the newest fashions. . . . This did get me a lot of friends because they thought that I really had money, but my materialistic attitude was breaking my mother. This year I still try to look good in no matter what I wear.

Cars are very important to teenagers. Having your own car is like totally running your whole life. Having almost any kind of car will win you friends.

Christine Taylor, 15
Kansas City, Missouri

People in school react by judging others for what clothes they are wearing—they never get to really know a person. We should be able to ignore this, . . . but the label will always be on the clothes.

Gretchen Gardner, 16
Munster, Indiana

The values of kindness, generosity, and love seem to get lost in the shuffle of a materialistic society. . . . Maybe if love had a price, it would become more important.

Colleen Murphy, 17
Munster, Indiana

Materialism affects relationships with other people in a negative way. It forces the people with the expensive things to look down on the people with inexpensive things and to treat them badly.

Materialism is not just a way of dressing. It's a way of . . . being. Materialistic people tend to be close-minded. They stifle their true self and don't let their individualism come out. In my school, certain people are carbon copies of each other. . . . Money holds them together. In the long run, they can base their relationships on money—the clothes they wear, the

houses they live in, the purses they carry, and the places they shop.

Katherine Searl
La Grange, Illinois

Materialism is a very big here in my town. . . . The snobs are all very rich. Their big deal is to take daddy's American Express Gold Card, jump in their nice sports car, go to the nearest clothing store, and start signing all daddy's hard work away. . . .

I consider myself one of the middle class. The middle class are the ones who get dumped on. We get a bad reputation because the snobs don't like the way we dress. . . .

I hate it here because my father does have a lot of money, and he happens to be friends with all the snobs' parents. . . . In my family, we've always been taught not to flaunt what we own so I don't. The girls love to pick on me because they know I have the money. . . . Most of the girls here are vicious little brats and think they have it all. I hate it here.

16-year-old female
Indiana

Television . . . tends to glamorize the wealth and power which add up to materialism. . . . Weekly television shows make heroes out of those powerful, rich leaders. These shows draw big audiences due to . . . the average American's fantasy, which is to be rich, famous, and powerful.

David Sundstrom, 17
La Grange, Illinois

There is an unwritten, but known by everyone, contract of who sets the clothing trends and who doesn't. This contract can definitely affect the emotional growth of teenagers. A teenager can truly believe that he is less of a person because of material wealth. . . . This may also affect their grades which are directly proportional to how much they believe they can do. . . .

Even though this is what I believe,

I find myself being a hypocrite. I find myself judging people from the outside. I just wish we could all give each other a chance.

Carolyn Szczembara, 16
Hillsdale, Michigan

Many, if not most, of the people I know couldn't tell you the first thing about South Africa or Nicaragua. Many of them wouldn't know where France, England, or even Utah were if there weren't required classes that expected students to know such basic material. However, they could speak for hours about their new clothes.

Abbey Duke, 16
Grinnell, Iowa

Should I save my money for college survival, or should I spend the money on items my mother thinks are frivolous but I think are necessities?

Of course, I will need the money next year for food, shelter, clothing. . . . Yet, my heart still yearns for that newly released record album, and my fingers still twitch toward those super cool sunglasses. I can feel my will power collapsing under these kinds of pressures. Soon the thought begins to slowly edge into my mind: Perhaps I can buy these luxuries now and be frugal next year.

Chris Haine, 17
Stevens Point, Wisconsin

I'm scared to death of my future, whether I'm going to make my life successful . . . and how I'm going to do it. I think if society's view of success was not so high, if people could look at my life later on and not say, "Oh, she only makes $20,000 a year—she's not successful," I wouldn't be so afraid of my future.

Theresa Tenpas, 17
Whitmore Lake, Michigan

Materialism is impossible to avoid, and unfortunately idealism is merely a creation of a liberal society. Idealism is certainly a goal worth working

for, . . . but it is impossible to expect a teenager to be an idealist.

15-year-old male
California

Trying to "fit in" causes hardships on . . . families. Some parents can't afford the materials their child wants, and the child becomes rebellious towards his parents and feels the only way out is to leave. The child runs away and steals the material things that he wants.

Diane Nichols, 16
Bluefield, West Virginia

Materialism destroys. It distorts a person's mind and shapes even personal goals. What we have now is a nation of conformists setting standards of success on possessions—a prestigious neighborhood, a BMW, brand-name clothes, a particular restaurant, etc.

So what do we have underneath it all? A nation of wanting adults, those who never knew quite what their goals were and allowed society to dictate them. And now they are trapped into a lifestyle, convinced it's too late to change.

Katie McCarthy, 16
Little Silver, New Jersey

Discussion

Boston *guidance counselor:* We've gotten fat and lazy. Easy come, easy go. This generation has become more materialistic than any generation that I've known. There's no social consciousness in this generation. There's no reverence of God or people of lower classes or anybody who's different. The name of the game is that you have good stereos, good cars, a good condo, and a good job that pays well. Make sure that you have a lot of leisure time and that you wear yuppie clothes. That's America's youth.

Larry: I know a girl who is a junior and is surrounded by possessions. She has a brand new car. Dad owns a Rolls Royce. Brother has a Corvette and goes to USC. She has an American Express card with a $500 limit. That was at 16. At 17 it was increased to $1000. I wonder what she would do if her parents lost their money. She probably wouldn't know how to cope with life.

Steve: A lot of people whom I know won't say they're from Beverly Hills. They will say they're from West Los Angeles because otherwise you have to prove that you're not stuck up. All the little stereotypes set in just with the words Beverly Hills.

Larry: Whenever people ask me where I go to school, it's always "West LA High School." Where do I live—West LA.

Steve: We have a reputation. We'd be lying to say that there are not a lot of very wealthy people who go to this school. But I think our reputation outdoes the reality. People can't believe that there are students who go to Beverly Hills who aren't extremely wealthy. We are like any other school. It's interesting to see the people who drive their BMWs to school compared to the people who take the bus to school.

Sue: The people who are the most wealthy are the ones who are the least pretentious about it. There's the class of people that's very, very wealthy but you wouldn't know it. Below that, there's the class of people who are utterly obnoxious and showy. They're the ones who drive the BMWs to school. They're the ones who

make you feel like dirt.

Steve: I was the only one from our school at a yearbook camp. When I told someone that I was from Beverly Hills High School, I got reactions and people started looking me over. They immediately thought, "He's stuck up. He's from Beverly Hills." People who have never been to Beverly Hills think the sidewalks are lined with gold.

Hilary: It's been a struggle living in Beverly Hills because it's so expensive. I know how important it is to make money, but I don't consider myself materialistic. I just know that money is a real necessity. You can't even generalize about whether a person is totally materialistic.

Sue: When people talk about what they want to do after college, they say, "I want to be a lawyer because it pays well." Fundamentally, fewer people believe that they want to do something because they enjoy it. They're conditioned to that mentality—that they have to have a well-paying job.

Hilary: TV perpetrates materialism. It shows that you're not successful unless you have your BMW.

Steve: TV equates materialism with happiness. Our society does that to us. I don't think that's something that's inherent in Beverly Hills. It's something inherent in our society that everybody wants. It's the idea of the American dream. The whole object of anything is to better yourself. That's how it has been defined to us. To better yourself is to make more money and be successful.

I don't think you can set success as making so much money. You have to set success as looking at something, saying that's where I'd like to be, and getting there.

People who have money tend to

think it is the savior. They think their money can get them out of everything. They've never learned how to be a good friend or stick to anything because they never had to.

Morgan: I am encouraged to have money and other things like big cars. I want it. I want everything. You can't do anything without money.

Debbie: If someone has a Cadillac, I want a Lincoln. Everyone tries to beat everyone else.

Morgan: You can see it in some people by which sneakers they wear.

Debbie: People are influenced by others in what they wear.

Eva Marie: People like to imagine themselves in the position that they see on TV. They say, "That could be me." That is why they buy the product.

Jesse: What other people think doesn't influence me. Neither do the things that I see on TV.

Connie Fry *mother:* Actually, we're stewards of God, and everything belongs to Him. Anything we have when we die, we are going to lose. It's only the spiritual things we will have. God is important. That's priority number one. People are very important. That's priority number two. So when you talk about materialism, it should not be a priority. But we're a capitalistic society, and we should stay that way. You have to have incentives, or people won't work.

Lee Fry *father:* With materialism, you're never satisfied. You are always going after a larger goal. If you have a million dollars, you're going to strive for a second million. Your goal is the art of making money. Some people like to play golf. Some like to play tennis. And some people would like to see how much money they can make by the end of their lifetime.

Connie: It becomes a priority when it becomes the most important thing in a person's life. It's not just having money but having things. It's more pay-oriented instead of people-oriented.

Jason *teenager*: It gets in the way of your family. You might go to work instead of going to church.

Lee: Actually, you don't ask God for help because you have everything. Then you go on your own, and you get caught up in yourself. You won't get spiritual help, and then you will just go downhill because you need help the whole way through life.

Jason: I can't see any reason for wanting to become a multi-millionaire—as long as you make enough money to get by.

As a car salesperson, do you feel any conflict in selling materialistic goods to people?

Lee: I just go with the program.

Connie: Sometimes you feel badly when people go so far in debt for

a car. But if they don't buy it at your dealership, they will buy it somewhere else. They come in because they want to buy a car. We don't go out and pull them off the streets and say, "Come on, you really need this." It would be bad if someone came in for a $2000 car, but we sold them a $5000 car.

Lee: When teens come down to the garage for a job, they usually want money to buy a car. "I want to drive around and show off to my friends." The automobile is like a god to them, and they motivate themselves towards a car.

Connie: Then they quit the band and football and all the electives.

They can work the rest of their lives after high school. It seems such a waste for them to spend all of their time working for money for a car.

Jason: If you're confident about yourself, then you don't have to try and prove yourself with nice cars. If you have everything you've ever wanted and you've achieved all your goals, then what is there to strive for?

Connie: If we compare ourselves to people from Chicago or New York, we all have our interests, and we buy according to that. If we compare ourselves to people outside the country, Americans are materialistic.

Jason: The Amish and Mennonite people do without the things that could make their lives easier. They make us realize some of the things we take for granted. We see how hard they work and how hard their life is, but they still enjoy it.

Connie: There is a large number of kids out there who are starting to do what they can to help others. Then there's a lot of others who are interested only in themselves. Their goals and priorities are different. And if you asked them to give something away, they probably wouldn't. But that's not true just of young people. It's people of all ages. There are a lot of people who could care less about the people around them. Then there are people who give of themselves. You can't say all youth are materialistic. They spend money where their interests lie.

Chicago suburb
A private home

Father: Our 15-year-old son likes cars. He gets *Road and Track* magazine, and I take him to the auto show every year. He has a real good knowledge of cars.

One of the girls who lives in a really nice neighborhood found the keys to her parents' Audi 5000. She was only 15. She drove into town over country roads and picked up my son. Then she headed back towards her home because she was supposed to be watching her younger brother and sister.

They were on a dark country road that was winding and hilly. I guess she was out to impress my son. One of the neighbors who saw the accident claimed they were going at least 70 mph. They hit a telephone pole head on. The collision popped the engine and the transmission out of the car and across the road ten feet. Our son smashed and broke both ankles, both wrists, his right femur. He had a gash in his head, on his jaw, a black eye, and bruises all over his body.

An insurance agent told me that in the last year, all the high school age accidents are coming from two towns where all the money is. He said it's amazing the kind of cars being wrecked—Datsun 280zxs, Audis, or Corvettes, not old beaters or older cars that kids are fixing up. It's evident that materialism has definitely affected some of these people.

Mother: The attitude is that money can buy everything. We discovered the young lady had done this before. And the parents knew that she had been driving.

Father: Here you've got some materialistic things like the Audi. The parents have a Lincoln Town car and a nice home. They have not tried to teach the value of material things to their daughter.

Mother: Isn't failing to curtail her an act of encouraging her? If you know that your daughter has been taking the car, do you leave the car and the keys behind when you are going out?

Father: Our son was in the hospital for three months and continues to go for therapy. The father's attitude was, "Well, I couldn't give a damn. I've got a million dollar blanket insurance policy. I could care less." In other words, because he had taken out this million dollar policy, he could do anything—he could kill somebody on the street. Let the insurance take care of it. That's a good case of materialism. They have money, and they don't even care. They don't care that their daughter cracked someone up.

Mother: I view materialism as a pressure and a negative influence. It pressures people into living lives that they might not otherwise lead. The biggest effect is that so many women are in the working world. It's not simply for personal fulfillment. Women want money because they are pressured to provide a certain environment for their children. The pressure exists to own the latest model car because your neighbors have one.

Father: People can't just buy a car that is three or four years old and save some money. They have to have the newest car. If you try to keep up with the Joneses, you have to have money to do that. It's not worthwhile to try and keep up with them.

Mother: Materialism can be good because it gives people a goal to work for and they like to see, in some physical form, a reward. It can be bad because people can be so busy getting and spending that they don't have a lot of time to relate to one another. They are often uptight and nervous because they're so busy hurrying from one place to another. Life becomes a "rat race."

Are teenagers today more materialistic than they were during your teenage years?

Father: Young people are spending their paychecks on either having a good time or buying clothes. When we grew up, it was a big deal to go to the movie and spend 75 cents for a ticket and buy some popcorn. Now teens think nothing of spending $20 to go see some rock band.

Mother: Kids are materialistic, or is it the parents? I can't believe that all the kids who are spending the money on rock concerts are actually earning the money. Also, I can't believe how many kids have jobs during the school week. That's a sign of materialism.

Young people have great concerns about things that are superficial. They're very much involved with their appearance and fitting into their groups. Materialism is bound up with that.

Atlanta, Georgia
Marist High School

Wes: Most of the people in our school are from the upper class. The average income is from $40,000–$60,000. The tuition is pretty high—$3,500.

Sue: People want to go to a good college because they want to be like their parents. They want to be in at least the same income bracket as their parents are.

What are the status symbols for teenagers?

Carl: Cars—to Mercedes or a Jaguar.

Sue: There are a lot of popular girls who drive VW convertible rabbits. The green ones with a tan top.

Wes: It started in the last three weeks. First, one girl got one. Now you see about four in the parking lot.

Carl: Last year a kid bought his own Jaguar and left the price tag on it for three weeks.

Sue: Not everyone has a Mercedes. You see a lot of BMW and Jaguar stickers in the parking lot, but they really belong to the parents.

Bob: It's like wanting to go to school to be the best. They feel like they have to stomp on people to get to where they want to be. You have to get into the best school, and you have to provide the best for your family in the future.

Wes: It's the American ideal to get ahead in life. They're always talking about from rags to riches. Everyone wants to be President of the United States. We've all been taught that since we were little.

Jeff: When you grow older, you step on people below you because you want money. You can ruin someone's life just because you want money.

Wes: Teenagers won't be able to relate to people very well. If they put materialistic things first in life, there's not going to be good communication between people.

We have become too self-indulgent. Everything centers

around the individual. We should always have that interaction with other people because we can always learn things from other people.

There are very few people who are going to put somebody else before themselves. If I'm trapped in a burning building—it's negative and it's bad—but I know I'm going to save myself rather than somebody else.

Since the majority of the people are money centered and the most important thing in their lives is the materialistic thing, it would be very tough to get those people to change.

Jamie: If everyone was making about the same amount of money, the people who are lazy would just be handed this money. The hard workers wouldn't have any inspiration to work harder or go higher. Then there's the poor people who've done everything. The level of society they're born into and their location decide their economic situation. They get stuck at the bottom of the ladder.

Lombard, Illinois
Glenbard East High School

Brad: Kids don't worry about money. They just take it for granted. We worry about it when it's not there. The only way that I worry about money is from day to day—like where am I going to get my money to go out on the weekends. Money is not that important to me because I don't have to worry about it.

Sue: I don't think people are becoming more materialistic. I think people are noticing it more because of the media.

Meaghan: I think there is a lot of materialism.

Brad: It seems like now everyone is going into business to make money, but it doesn't seem like that was the case before. You had people who wanted to self-sacrifice, like teachers or religious figures.

Gerri Long *parent:* People are not going to college for the sake of learning. They are going to make money.

Meaghan: I have difficulty with materialism because I think people are becoming more external and like robots. In college, what I want to do is not going to be determined by how much money I will make.

Sue: But Meaghan, if you had a chance between two jobs that you enjoyed—one that paid you enough to just get by and the other paid so you could live luxuriously—which one would you choose? (long pause-no answer) See, no one wants to be poor.

Meaghan: My dad told me that when he was a kid, there were the poor kids, the middle-class kids, and the upper-class kids. They all played together. It's not like that anymore.

Brad: You want to be judged by the people you're with.

Pat Meyer *teacher:* Brad, is that really true? Do you really choose your friends that way?

Brad: Idealistically I'd say no.

Meyer: No, you Brad—not idealistically.

Brad: Yes and no.

Long: You choose your friends by what they can do for you. In essence, that's what you're saying.

Brad: I realize that in essence that's what I'm saying. I'd like to say no, but in some cases—yes. Everyone does. We'd like to think otherwise, but we all do that to some degree.

Meyer: You mean you don't choose people as friends just

because they seem interesting?

Brad: Yeah I do, but still you're inclined to be friendly to people if they're popular. People act like that. They'll be friendly to someone if they think they can get something.

Wheaton Illinois
Interview with a high school graduate

Lorrie: If we hadn't moved to Wheaton, I wouldn't have felt such pressure to buy clothes as I did. The biggest group at my school had a lot of different clothes, and they dressed pretty nicely. The popular group wore the things that were in style. Their choices greatly influenced what I had. Everyone had penny loafers so I went out and bought penny loafers. I didn't buy anything that I didn't like, though.

Some people didn't care what the popular group thought, and they would wear whatever they wanted. But I cared. I felt like I was under some pressure. I did feel self-conscious about other things too. They really cared about what kind of car you had. It bothered me when my parents would pick me up in an old green Maverick. That's how much pressure I felt.

Evanston, Illinois
Jeanne Vail Chapel

Robert Longo *Northwestern*

University student: In the United States the greatest measure of personal success seems to be money. Too often ambition seems to be dominated by the desire for wealth. People work all their lives simply to be able to drive a Porsche 928 or to vacation in Europe. Too many times personal relationships, whether they be with the Lord, with friends, or with family members, are subordinated to the monomaniacal desire for the almighty dollar. We are all socialized into the apparent reality that once we can afford a Mercedes 560SL, a house in Kenilworth, or to send our kids to Northwestern University, others will perceive us as succesful. After all, don't these things simply represent the complete realization of the American dream?

When we say that we want our kids to live a better life than we have lived, what does that mean? Is their success measured in dollars and cents? The Lord does not buy into this empty vision of the American dream. The Lord certainly does not condone the sacrifice of human relationships in order to achieve financial gain. We cannot afford to delay our caring for others until a more convenient time, such as after the important presentation or after several superfluous hours of overtime.

Compiled by Gina Nolan

Solutions

I don't care what I wear as long as I look presentable to people. . . . My family cannot afford to buy me pants, shirts, shoes, and cars just so I can be well-known.

> *Chris Martin, 16*
> *Hillsdale, Michigan*

Society encourages materialsim by putting people who have a lot of things on a pedestal. The media urge everyone to believe that the more you have, the better you are.

The family, school, and community should try to discourage materialism. They should be concerned if the children are always bragging about what they have. Everyone should be shown to share things with people who are less fortunate. Schools can show how some people are poorer and that they don't always need material things to be happy.

The family, school, and community should discourage materialism because if they don't, . . . people will be so concerned with themselves that they will ignore the poor and needy. They won't understand how to share and give.

> *Stacey Stonum, 14*
> *Portland, Oregon*

It usually hinders an individual if he or she has too much. A less well-off person develops a more ambitious attitude for his future life because he has probably seen others that were well off. Seeing how well they live, the individual will set more goals for himself. The well-off person will probably have fewer ambitions because he feels he is living a comfortable life already.

> *Ginny Chung, 15*
> *Scotch Plains, New Jersey*

We are, through advertisements, constantly hearing how possessing a certain object will make us more desirable. . . . The more a person has

is supposedly making him that much more important. And society scorns those who have nothing. Whatever happened to looking at a person individually as a person? . . .

We have to open our eyes and close our ears to what others say, what others think. Individuality has to be developed.

Carey Seatter, 17
Western Springs, Illinois

Materialism can be very helpful if used right. When teens want something bad enough, they'll go to great lengths to get it—even if it means giving up some of their free time to get a job. . . . But if parents are always willing to buy their teens what they want, teens will never learn . . . responsibility. Nor will they learn that you don't get anything for free today.

Tobi Basore, 15
Clearwater Beach, Florida

You don't need materials to help someone; you need love. I am from a regular middle-class family. . . . I could go out and spend money on new clothes and jewelry . . . to make me feel happy. My parents would do anything for me. . . . But we have something more than materials; we have Christ. That makes a big difference in whether . . . you have an okay family and social life or a great family and social life.

Kim Wilson, 14
Clearwater, Florida

The main source of motivation stems from my religious ideals. Success means not only achieving my goals but achieving them with right attitudes and actions. . . . Money is not the equivalent of success. I would rather be content with myself and happy as I work than making an executive salary and unhappy.

Cyndi Smith, 17
Stockton, California

Young people in modern society should cope with materialism by developing strong personal value systems. There are a myriad of sources for inspiration in literature like the Holy Bible, Thoreau's Walden, and Ayn Rand's The Fountainhead. Spirited leaders and committed artists can also help. Kids should recognize materialism in society and deal with it according to their own beliefs.

I for one choose to resist it. Living in affluent Orange County, California has conditioned me to value highly things of materialistic worth: cars, houses, clothes, etc. Therefore, I long to lead a simple life, isolated in the woods perhaps, where I will not feel the pressures of materialism.

Corba Tushla, 18
La Habra, California

This is where the question lies: Will you spend all that money and meet society's demand to feel a part of it all, or will you be happy with yourself for who you are inside—not who the world thinks you are? It's quite a challenge to dare to be different, but in the end true happiness is found in achievement, self-worth, living a full life—not in "acceptance" by a world that cares only about their possessions.

For me, my view against materialism comes from a strong Christian background in which I understand that I will leave this world with only those things I came into the world with—myself. Though I could pile up millions of dollars worth of possessions, I can take none of the things with me. What glory do these things bring? None.

Glory comes in serving others. Are great men remembered for their wealth, or are men noted for their deeds? . . . . There is no doubt in my mind that who we are is more important than the things we possess.

Heather Butler, 16
Little Silver, New Jersey

Materialism in our society is evident through the onset of the yuppie generation . . . who usually play racquetball, drink Perrier, and drive a BMW. . . . Some would say that this "shop-till-you-drop" attitude is wrong and undermines certain religious and moral values. But is possessing the items one desires all so bad if one can afford them?

There should be, however, concern that human values might be trampled on in pursuit of material wealth. The fact that money can't buy happiness or love should not be overlooked.

Tamara Carter, 15
Bluefield, West Virginia

People need to own to feel good about themselves. This isn't just America. This is the world. A girl in our school just moved here, and the school was buzzing about, "She's so rich!" As if I care. All the empty shells, carrying their Guccis, sporting Generra, are fake. I can't tell teenagers what to think, but I recommend judging a person on personality, not possessions.

Kim Barker, 16
Laramie, Wyoming

Asking teenagers today to resist materialism seems almost ridiculous. Teenagers spend more money on non-necessities than anyone else, and with advertisers pushing cars, watches, music. sweaters, everything at us—well, it's hard to ignore. We give in to it. . . .

The way I've learned not to place too much value on material things is through backpacking. Once you learn how little you can live with, it stays with you. You never actually need more than what you can carry on your back, warm clothes, and a good pair of boots. You need feet; you need friendship; you need music. But you don't have to turn to tapes for that—you can make it yourself.

It saddens me to see the people my age falling for the money-and-things routine. There's a saying in backpacking—"Whoever makes it to the end of the trail with the most toys wins!"—that we use to poke fun at people who invest in all sorts of silly, high-tech gadgets.

There's another one—"The load expands to exceed the space available"—which is what happens to a lot of us teenagers who are bored.

Michelle Moon, 17
Red Bank, New Jersey

Materialism is the prime cause of class divisions in young people. People with money and lots of material goods are matched against people with little or no money. There is a lot of dislike and animosity between these groups because of materialism. This conflict is stupid.

Materialism should be resisted by young people. It is a rampant problem which usually causes more problems. Materialism is something which is no good for man and should be gotten rid of completely.

Eric Parker, 15
Bluefield, West Virginia

Society often blames television and the media for its problems. . . . In fact, parents are the most immature role models. Only with heart-to-heart talks about what is truly important in life can these problems with materialism be resolved.

Christine Oyakawa, 18
Montebello, California

Parents are usually always trying to give their children the best that they can. If parents teach their children the difference between materialism and necessity, then there would be less confusion.

Harriet Hicks, 16
Bluefield, West Virginia

I am now living with my father and enjoying something approximating prosperity since he has remarried and I live in a two-paycheck family. Most of the money I have is in the bank. The money I have left goes into my two main hobbies: Doctor Who memorabilia and a small comic book collection.

I walk by the Walkmans, pass over the Porsches, and don't even watch lots of TV. I don't think I need it. Others disagree. I am an individual who wishes to remain that way. I'm not going to sermonize on how you should spend your money. I'll leave that to Oral Roberts. I am simply saying, "The choice is yours, choose wisely."

Bill Thomas, 17
Red Bank, New Jersey

Kristin Bolf LTHS

Chapter 10.

Teens and Morals

"Hi, honey, I'm home," yelled Mom Reamer, beaming as she walked through the front door.

"Shit. She's two hours early," thought Heather Reamer as she heard her mom's ringing voice. "Hi, Mom! Great to see you back" were the words that actually came out of her mouth. "How was Sun City?" Heather asked, pretending to be interested.

"It was terrific. I don't know where all these stories of so-called unrest in South Africa come from. Probably those damn liberal yellow journalists," Mom Reamer said. "We were there two whole weeks, and all we ever saw were these nice, attentive, clean-cut Negroes. They waited on your dad and me like we were royalty," she continued.

Heather winced at her mom's use of the word Negro, as if blacks were a separate species. Suddenly, she noticed a crumpled-up beer can under the table. As Mom Reamer continued lavishing praise on Sun City, Heather tried to slide the beer can out from under the table with her foot, without attracting her mother's attention.

"And the Negress who was specially assigned to your dad and me, well, she always had the biggest smile on her face, and she was as plump and jolly as can be. She didn't seem oppressed to me. I'm sure she was fed and bathed regularly...." Mom Reamer rambled on. Heather had the can out from under the table. She was trying to slip it into the garbage can which was only a couple of feet away.

"In fact, we liked our Negress so much that your dad wanted to bring her home with us. He was just joking. You aren't allowed to, of course. But your dad did leave her a whole carton of cigarettes as a sort of special tip, to show our appreciation," continued Mom Reamer.

"Six more inches, and it's in the can," thought Heather. She quietly opened the lid, moved the incriminating evidence over the open garbage pail, was about to drop it in....

"All in all, it was a great time. And I really got a great tan too. I tell you, dear, those South Africans really have their act together, because ... Heather D. Reamer! Is that a beer can you just dropped in the garbage?" asked Mom Reamer in an accusatory tone.

"Shit. Here it comes," Heather thought. "Yes, Mom, it's a beer can. I had a few friends over while you were gone," Heather said, hoping to make it sound like no big deal.

"You mean you had a beer-drinking party! Are you 21 year's old? Hmmm? Are you?"

"No, Mom, but...." Heather started.

"No, of course you're not. You are 17 years old, young lady. Therefore, not only is your beer-guzzling immoral, it is illegal. They have laws for a reason, you know, namely, to be obeyed," said Mom Reamer in her best high-and-mighty voice.

"I know, Mom, but..." Heather started again.

"No buts about it, young lady. We'll just have to talk to your dad about this," Mom Reamer said.

Heather sighed. "Oh well. The worst that can happen is that I'll lose the car for a couple of days. But it just isn't right," Heather thought. "My parents get furious over a can of beer but gladly spend a few thousand dollars in support of apartheid. Something is wrong here."

"Where is Dad, anyway?" Heather asked.

"Oh, he had to go straight over to the office from the airport. He has to handle some important litigation for his company," Mom Reamer said. "Some environmentalist group is suing. They want the company to stop dumping chemicals into the Clear River. They say it's killing the fish or something stupid like that."

"But isn't it killing the fish?" asked Heather.

"Fish, smish!" yelled Mom Reamer. "You want your dad to lose his job? You want his company to go broke? Who needs those fish? I get my fish from the store."

"I guess," Heather said. "By the way, I'm going out in a little bit. Bob is picking me up."

"Oh, Bob," said Mom Reamer in a sarcastic tone. "And what are you two lovebirds going to do tonight?"

"Nothing much," said Heather. "Just drive around, hang out, you know."

"You mean smooch and pet and have sex in the back seat of Bobby's car, don't you?" said Mom Reamer. "Don't think I don't know what goes on. I wasn't born yesterday."

"But Mom, you don't understand," Heather said.

"But nothing! You're only 17 years old, and what you're doing is not right," Mom Reamer said.

"You and Dad were married when you were 18," countered Heather.

"And what has that got to do with the price of tea in China?" Mom Reamer asked. "The simple fact is that having sex at your age is immoral. If I ever catch you and Bob at it, I'll have him arrested for statuatory rape!"

"Right, Mom. Sure," Heather said. She was disgusted once again by her mother's hypocrisy. Her mom was an expert at it. She was invincible. Nothing penetrated her thick skull and blatant ignorance. Time to slink away and wait for Bob out front. Heather needed some fresh air.

"Don't forget...," Mom Reamer yelled as Heather reached the front door. "You start Christian Youth Camp next weekend."

Heather stopped in her tracks. She hated Christian Youth Camp. "You signed me up for that again?" she asked incredulously.

"Of course, dear. It's good for you," Mom Reamer said.

"But I already know how to be a Christian," Heather countered.

"You do not. True Christians do not drink beer and have sex, young lady."

"Yeah. Right," muttered Heather as she slammed the front door behind her.

Smiling to herself, Mom Reamer called out from behind the closed door, "We'll bring you up right, in spite of yourself, young lady. You'll develop some moral fiber yet."

Erik Landahl

A Supplier's Dilemma

This summer is going to be different. I'm 18 now, just graduated from high school. Mom and Dad finally are ready to treat me like an adult.

They eliminated my curfew. No more sneaking in twenty minutes late and worrying about being grounded. Of course, I don't abuse it. I'm usually in by 1 a.m. Nothing happens around this dull town after then anyway.

Mom and Dad also realized that I drink. Yea! No more sneaking off to a party after telling them I've gone to a movie. They even buy beer for me at the ballpark. I don't have to hide anything anymore.

Well, that's not exactly true. I haven't told them about the fake ID I bought. While they let me drink, I don't think they would approve of a fake ID.

That ID makes life easy for me. I can buy for my friends when we go out. Sure, I'm breaking the law, but who will ever know?

My 16-year-old sister, that's who. She wants me to buy alcohol for her and her friends. The problem is, I don't think it's right.

I suppose I'm a hypocrite. I drink all the time. But I can control it. I've been drinking long enough to know my limit, and I never drive after drinking. I never get in a car with a drunk driver. I'm not stupid.

My sister isn't stupid either. But somehow I don't trust the combination of alcohol and brand-new drivers. They don't know how to drink, and they don't know how to drive. I worry about that.

I know what she's going through, though. I remember how the big adventure of sophomore year was finding alcohol and getting smashed. Because I didn't have many older friends, I didn't have easy access to alcohol when I was 16. My friends and I drank rarely because we had no connections.

When I found easy connections, I began to drink like a fish. I didn't even like the taste of beer. But I drank because my friends did. I wanted to be cool. So I did a lot of stupid things like throwing up on Lisa's Oriental rug. What a mess. I drank so much that night that I passed out on the way home. If I had been driving, I would have been dead. My sister doesn't need to repeat my mistakes.

Unfortunately, I think everyone goes through a phase when they drink too much. Mine was short, thank God. I wish we could grow up without having to face the pressure to drink. I felt so out of it when I couldn't share stories about my weekend drinking adventures. So I went through a phase of drinking anything I could get my hands on. But my sister, should she be going through that phase already?

She will always be "my little sister." I need to protect her from the dangers of the world. I don't want her to progress from alcohol to harder drugs. I need to keep her straight.

I feel like a pusher. I don't want to be known as the alcohol supplier for the entire sophomore class. It disgusts me. I try to warn her about alcohol. But how can I expect her to listen to me when I wouldn't listen to Mom or Dad?

The problem is, my sister is counting on me. I never should have bought her alcohol for that birthday party. Now she expects it.

She'll be mad at me. I love my sister, and I want her to love me. But I don't want to buy her love with alcohol. I don't want to ruin her social life. But even more so, I don't want to help her ruin her life.

I'm being hypocritical, I know. I break the law all the time. My conscience doesn't bother me when I buy for myself. Why does it bother me to buy alcohol for her?

Mike Hamilton

Conflicts

One guy made me change many of my moral values and standards that I had set for myself. I liked this guy very much. In fact, for a while I thought I was in love with him. . . . At a party . . . I sort of flirted with this guy. He was very reluctant to flirt back, but then he did. I thought, "Oh boy, he does like me". . . .

I thought that when he kissed me, it meant that he wanted to be with me, not just to fool around. I have fooled around before with a lot of guys in the past three years. But during my junior year, this was diminishing. I tried to concentrate on just liking guys and not to give in so easily to them. . . .

Well, another party came around, and this guy decided that we should try some more and some more. I was so sure that he liked me that I let him do some things to me that other guys have never done. Then he coldly left me and stopped talking to me that night.

I felt guilty; I felt like trash. I felt like hell.

> 17-year-old female
> Illinois

I never thought I'd be tempted by a cigarette or drugs until my friends got me involved. Now I smoke and take uppers almost every day to stay awake. Drinking was never a big deal until recently when my friends started.

> 16-year-old male
> South Carolina

One of my biggest inner conflicts has to do with peer pressure and conforming to high school norms. Sometimes I feel so lost. All I want to do is fit in.

More frequently and more recently, . . . I feel good about myself. I don't need to impress anyone. When you try to impress others, you often try to identify with their supposed moral values, which they most likely picked up from someone else. . . .

I have observed . . . cliques that seem to revolve around one person and his idea of moral values. In a group, upper middle class, intelligent . . . juniors or mostly seniors, one individual stands out. He is the basis for the group's activities.

On weekends when he wants to date girls other than his girlfriend, . . . all the guys in the group disregard their own girlfriends and tag along with him.

If he wants to get drunk, the whole group drinks. If he abstains, the whole group frowns on drinking.

It is a bit frightening.

> Jennifer Sheriff, 18
> West Chicago, Illinois

I met him about three months ago. We have become very close, but my moral values have changed . . . due to his influence. I was brought up to be strongly against drugs and alcohol. The first time we went out, I had a little beer, nothing big. But now it's a habitual thing. . . .

He wants me to experiment with drugs, and I know I will. They fascinate me. . . .

Inside I feel I'm trying to do right, but the will to do wrong is too strong. I just don't care anymore. I do what I feel like.

I know that the good and straight side will eventually come back out for good. But until then, it worries me what I might do now.

> 17-year-old female
> South Carolina

Conflicts arise when the teenager's values do not match the values of his parents and especially his friends. . . . The person may be strong enough to do what he feels is right, but he may decide that it is easier . . . to do what others want. . . . At least then he will be accepted by others, or his parents will stop nagging him for a while.

> Cheryl Petrarca, 16
> Cranston, Rhode Island

One reason I believed sex should only happen within the marriage vows came

from the example my parents "supposedly" set. When I found out a year ago that my parents were married in '69 instead of '68, making me a child conceived out of wedlock, I was shocked and confused.

My mother told me that they would have been married anyway, but how does that make it right? I decided then that even if my parents couldn't wait, I would.

Now I am faced with another dilemma. I am dating a guy whom I feel I love and whom I find attractive physically. He knows my views on sex and respects them, but he disagrees with me.

He feels that having sex before marriage . . . will only enhance the

beauty of it on the wedding night. To marry with no experience could be a mistake, in his opinion.

I am now faced with the decision of doing what I want or what I believe. No longer is there black and white; I'm surrounded with gray.

16-year-old female
South Carolina

When teens go out on dates, one of them . . . might want to have sex . . . and the other may not. But in most cases, just because of the pressure, the one will give in and do what the other one wants. . . . If you go out with someone, you shouldn't have to do anything you don't want to. . . .

Many parents of teens are always telling them that you shouldn't have sex before you are married. These kinds of pressures can also lead the teen into sexual experiments. . . .

15-year-old female
Illinois

Teenagers see other teenagers do something wrong and get away with it and figure if other people can do it and not get caught, then so can I. So they try it, don't get caught, and keep on doing it. . . .

Another reason for teenagers changing their moral values is because their parents just don't care. . . . Both parents nowadays are working. . . . They just don't seem to have enough time for their children. So the children decide . . . "Well, my parents don't care enough about me to spend time with me so I'm not going to be the perfect child they think I should be."

Anne Cassidy, 17
Columbia, South Carolina

I was completely for capital punishment. I thought it equaled justice. I heard my peers saying, "They deserve it," and I listened.

Then I watched a movie called Faces of Death. We got to see a real criminal fry in an electric chair. They had to give him two long jolts while he jerked and spit, and finally blood trickled out from underneath the pads

that covered his eyes. I truly felt sick. And, God, when we saw another guy walk down death row, I could feel his fright through the TV screen.

So the next day, my mind was changed about capital punishment. . . . I feel that teenagers' minds are fairly easily changed because with delicate issues, teenagers are especially compassionate—such as what happened to me.

Elizabeth Dehning, 14
Stockton, California

People in our society make much too big a deal out of premarital sex. . . . I believe it should be done out of love not lust. . . . I don't feel that just because you're married, you're having sex for the love of your partner. Many relationships dealing with unmarried couples are far more mature and respectful than relationships dealing with married couples.

For instance . . . John gets Suzy pregnant and neither . . . loves the other. John . . . marries Suzy. Now that John and Suzy are married, does that make it any less sinful to engage in sexual activities? Society seems to think so. . . .

No one commandment was ever said to be any worse in God's eyes than the others. So every time you . . . say, "God bless it," . . . you're sinning. But people understand; . . . you're forgiven. If you have sexual intercourse out of wedlock, you're a sinner in the eyes of God. If you're lucky, you'll make it to heaven. This is nonsense.

Max Anderson, 16
Wheeling, Illinois

The majority of the teenagers in the United States do not think premarital sexual relationships are wrong. . . . The main outcome of this issue is the girl ending up pregnant. . . . All it really takes is to say "no". . . .

As . . . American teenage girls, the responsibilities fall on our shoulders. All we simply have to say is "no". . . . We must gain respect from the guys. We must take control of our

relationships with guys.

They are ready and willing. If we are able to hold ourselves back, problems like abortion will decrease. Not only that, but the problems of unwanted children will never occur.

Yes, it is true that we . . . can take precautions before any sexual relationships. But there are also wide possibilities that the precautions will fail us.

Mary Maran, 15
Bakersfield, California

Most adults have lost their sense of mischief and adventure . . . so they usually don't approve of most things. You couldn't tell them . . . the whole truth. . . . I'm not saying it's good to lie because it's not, but you can leave out the details—the details that would get you grounded, that is.

Stacy Thelander, 17
Lincoln, Nebraska

Your friend dares you to do something ridiculously stupid, and you have no reply. You become speechless because you are afraid and shocked. . . . Afraid to go along with your friend's dangerous idea and shocked your friends even mentioned the idea. After all, friends are supposed to care.

Dawn Chimelewski, 15
Cranston, Rhode Island

Teens today fit the description of teens on TV. . . . The saying of today could be, "I want to be a clone." We're too busy trying to be so cool . . . that we don't take time to . . . decide what our morals are. . . .

Our parents are too busy trying to make and save money. They don't talk to us about morals, just about how much clothes and education cost. . . . Church used to be a good place to acquire morals, but today some churches are corrupt. Instead of a Bible study with the youth group, it's a keg party.

Holly Hislop, 17
Columbia, South Carolina

Mandik 88

Discussion

Chicago suburb

Female: I don't regret having my baby because I love her and we have fun together. I know I'm young to be a mother, but I wouldn't say too young.

During my pregnancy, people would glare at me, but I don't care what anyone else thinks. If I worried about what they all thought, I would be a nervous wreck.

People make it out to be so hard to keep a baby, but it's not hard. My teen years are not over yet. I've been able to do whatever I did before. My baby goes where I go. If I want to go out some weekend, my mother or my grandma will watch her. I wash, feed, and play with my baby. Just my TV time is taken away.

My mom didn't say it was okay to have my baby, but since it was already done, she said I didn't have to run off and get married. My grandma asked me when the wedding was. I said there was not going to be a wedding. I never thought about having an abortion, and it was out of the question to give my baby away.

I love her father, but I doubt we'll get married—maybe after college and I have a career.

Male: My brother was a burnout. My parents always said he'd never amount to anything. Now he's on the World Board of Trade and makes some outrageous amount of money.

The only thing I wasn't straight with my parents about was getting high. I would get high every day before math, but I did well in the class anyway.

I'm not immoral. I'm not going to go around getting a bunch of girls pregnant and not care about the kids. My parents once told me, "Party as much as you want as

long as you take care of your responsibilities."

Pornogaphy

Olympia, Washington
Evergreen State College Summer Journalism Workshop

Beth *Seattle*: Pornography is public sex.

Jenny *Seattle*: Pornography is displaying sexual acts in the media.

Susan *Seattle*: Some people see it as an art. I've heard that some sculpture is considered pornographic.

Lindsey *Mercer Island, Washington*: Pornography is trying to portray a sexual feeling. Tapes can be pornographic because of the sounds.

Diane *Auburn, Washington*: Some TV movies are pornographic. They go to the extremes. They go as far as they can go without showing everything.

Beth: There are porno movies. It is just like going in and seeing a peep show.

Becky *Seattle*: There are also places where you can call and can hear stimulating talk. Tapes are designed to play with people's minds and to arouse callers by what they are saying. That's supposed to be pleasurable. When people call, the businesses make money. They exploit sex for their own purposes.

Dee *Auburn, Washington:* Pornography makes everything that has to do with sex dirty and awful. Sex should be something you share with somebody.

Roberta *Auburn, Washington:* The American people have been brought up very Puritanical. Sex is a no-no. "Save yourself for marriage." Pornography is flirting with danger, and a lot of people like to do that.

Beth: An R-rated movie is not pornographic. It is not explicit sex. People don't go to that movie to get their jollies.

Melody *Redmond, Washington:* In an R-rated movie, sex has something to do with the plot. In X-rated movies, it is sex for the sake of having sex.

Roberta: Some of my friends have older brothers or sisters who rent pornographic videos. Teenagers have never seen a porno film so they want to find out what one is like.

Beth: We see all types of slimy movie theaters in Seattle. For a lot of people, pornography is their only sexual outlet.

Susan: I don't see why people would watch a pornographic movie, especially if it has no plot and no famous actors and actresses.

Roberta: Pornogrpahy only has a sexual value for people who need sexual arousal. I think a lot of it has to do with conditioning. For guys, it's okay. You're supposed to get experience. "Prove you're a man." For girls, it is more like, "You don't do that." That's why they exploit women. Boys are brought up to show that they are men. Women aren't supposed to think such thoughts.

Lindsey: On Mercer Island, the stores had to pull all the "pornographic magazines." The town was concerned that the children were being exposed to pornography.

Becky: *Playboy* is bad, but it is not so bad.

Susan: The whole thing is not all sex. They have a lot of articles on current issues.

Beth: And they aren't showing sex. They are just showing nude women. There's a big difference. They are not showing action photos.

Lindsey: A woman's body is beautiful. I'm not saying that *Playboy* is a work of art, but I don't get as offended seeing nude women as seeing a woman exploited.

Roberta: It is more tastefully done. They are exploiting the women, but not so grossly that we get offended by it. I see a naked woman there and big deal. It's better than a woman who is getting whipped and acts as though she is enjoying it.

Jenny: *Playboy* is not that bad compared to movies in which women are getting raped.

Roberta: I'm offended as a female, but *Playboy* does not show women doing degrading things to each other or having degrading things done to them. It is soft porn.

Becky: It also depends on how the woman is shown. In a lot of older art, the naked body is displayed as an art form. It depends on the pose. You can get some weird poses in some of the tacky magazines.

Susan: In Japanese art, for a long time, artists did pretty explicit drawings with men and women— orgy farms and stuff. People buy that, not as something for sexual arousement but as an art form.

Is pornography detrimental to society?

Jenny: We cannot censor pornography because that would limit freedom of choice. My sister had a chance to be in *Playboy*. She is a stripper, and she goes all the way in front of large audiences. Strippers mostly do dancing with moves that arouse men. She started when she was 18 because she had a lot of expenses and it was an easy way to make money. She enjoys it.

Melody: My sister is a topless dancer. She told me she makes about $4,000 a month. She's earning money for college.

Jenny: I disapprove of child porn because you are abusing children without their knowledge of what they are doing. But when adults go into pornograpy, it is their choice whether they do it or not.

Beth: We can't censor pornography because people have the right to say and do whatever they want to do.

Susan: If they start censoring pornography, they will go and go and go and not stop. Pretty soon, they'll say you can't have nude art. We'll have to put little black boxes over things on a $1,000 painting.

Roberta: Pornography falls under freedom of speech. They want to express themselves that way. It would be more damaging to start censoring. It would be like Big Brother.

Jenny: It is the family's responsibility. If the parents don't want their kids to see pornography, then they should watch their kids.

Nashville
Southern Baptist Christian Life Commission

Harry Hollis *associate executive director:* Pornography presents human beings as one dimensional sex-machines. "A person is the sum of his or her private parts." The problem with pornography is not that it tells too much about sex, but that it tells too little about sex. It doesn't really show people.

Many teenagers turn to pornography out of curiosity—to find out more about sex. People who look at pornography are often exploited. They're taught that this is the way human beings really act, but it's very doubtful that most human beings act the way that people act in pornography. However, that's not the impression that's given.

Seattle
University Congregational Church
  (UCC)

Paul Flucke *senior minister:* Pornography is an issue that I cannot get terribly excited about. I don't think that it is as pernicious and as pervasive as a number of other problems. As a number of people have pointed out, the presence of pornography in our society is a pretty clear indication of some pretty warped values that are shot through our whole society. Our love of violence—we fill our theaters with films like *Rambo.* It's not surprising that people carry that one step further and make video cassettes which relate that same violence to sex.

The attitude toward women in our society has been one of exploitation. Pornography makes a logical mating of violence and exploitation of women.

Gail Crouch *coordinator for outreach and adult education:* What bothers me most about pornography is that so much of it is violence against women. It is not only the beautiful body in *Playboy,* but it really is graphically showing that it is okay to be violent toward women.

Flucke: People can make elaborate arguments for the legitimacy of erotica, but people are demeaned and abused when pornography is coupled with violence. I don't think censorship is the issue. The

long term cure for that is instilling in people values that hold human life as sacred so that people are not turned on by sex and violence but revolted by that combination.

Olympia, Washington

What makes pornography a moral issue?

Douglas Gardner *governor's son/ missionary with World Vision:* Pornography is scary. Fathers are raping kids. Kids are running to their neighbor, who says, "Okay, you can come here," then rapes the child. My mom and dad get videotapes of all the programs that are being done about pornography. Sometimes they share those with me. It's become evident to me that there is a great problem and that it needs attention.

Teenage Sex

Chicago suburb

Sexually active male: I always carry a rubber with me—like right now I have one in my pocket even though I'm in school. That's just in case something comes up. It's better to be prepared and not have sex than to screw someone without being prepared.

I see a lot of my friends getting into trouble. They'll be driving home from school and start kissing. One of my friends did that and wound up having sex with her without a rubber. She lied and said she was on the pill. After he fucked her, she said it wasn't true. They went through several weeks of torture till they found out she wasn't pregnant. They had to go through all these tests—he wasn't himself for weeks.

Lots of girls have asked me to have sex with them. It's hard not to give in. On the one hand, there's the urge to go for it. On

the other, there's the moral concern, which is something I feel real strong about. I don't get drunk, and I don't do drugs. But sex—that's something I like as long as I'm not abusing a girl or myself.

One of the better times I've had sex was with a really close friend—a girl I talk to confidentially but not a girl I date. She's like, "I want sex, and you want sex. Why can't we have sex together?" So we had sex. It was special because it was planned, and sex was an expression of my relation with her. It was her first time, but we both were pretty pleased. I felt really good that she wanted me to be her first person. That was kind of a compliment.

Girls are making the moves and actually setting guys up. With me, that's pretty common. They think I'm weird if I discourage sex, but they respect me afterwards. Being able to say no is one thing that keeps me unique from other people.

My first experience was when I was a freshman in high school and I had gone out with a senior for about a week. She drove me to a movie. Afterward she asked me what I thought about going and parking and screwing around. I said "That'd be great." I knew if I had sex, I'd be one of the cool guys, part of the "in" crowd.

After we drove over to a local park, we talked for about five minutes and started making out—started feeling each other. She unzipped my pants and unbuttoned her shirt and put my hand in there. She guided me through it—and got on top of me. She pretty much did everything.

Being my first time, I was really scared. I must have looked hilarious. I was shaking and wide-eyed. I couldn't believe it was happening to me. I was thinking, "This is great, but it's not as good as I thought it would be." It

happened too fast. We kind of jumped right into it.

The second time was with another older girl—at a church camp in Wisconsin. During the day we had been playing and touching. By night I was feeling pretty horny so I was eager to respond to her invitation. After crossing the camp grounds to her tent, I crawled into her sleeping bag and fucked her. I was scared shitless because there were two other girls sleeping in the tent. But once I became sexually excited, I just thought, "I got to have sex, I got to have it." I didn't use a condom. I had never used one so that was the last thing on my mind.

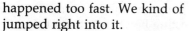

Teens and Morals

PAM LIVINGSTON
LTHS

I was feeling pretty low about myself—like I was really weak. I wasn't happy with my choice of having sex at such an early age. I felt I was doing it for the wrong reasons.

I kind of talked to myself. "Do you want to keep doing this? Do you want to get yourself into trouble? Do you want sex to lead to other things? What if you become a sex maniac, someone who has sex with every girl?" I felt like I could have gotten myself into trouble. That fear of starting too early still haunts me even though I'm a senior.

Now I've worked out a way to enjoy sex without screwing a girl. I encourage foreplay. I like to touch her and have her touch me. We'll be lying on the couch watching a movie. I'll put my arm around her and start kissing her.

Maybe I'll open her shirt, and she'll open my pants or something. It gets better as we keep touching and exploring. Obviously, this isn't a first date.

We make each other come—bring ourselves to mutual orgasms. I've found it's pretty much as sexually stimulating as screwing a girl. It helps me feel really good. Also, it's easier on myself, and I know she's comfortable. I don't have any problem morally because I don't have to worry about getting her pregnant.

That's really the main thing that keeps me from fucking a girl. Later, when I find a person that I want to spend my life with, I won't have to be afraid of getting her pregnant. Then having sex will be no problem at all. Sex is marriage in a sense—one of the

more interesting parts.

Most high school kids don't think about the consequences. They just have sex—during the week as well as on weekends. And summers can be pretty interesting because kids find that they can screw around at the beach, in parks, under trees, even in the backyard. They're more vulnerable because you don't have to say, "Come to my house and watch a movie." You can just say, "Let's go to the park." Guys don't worry about being seen or getting caught. Girls are more worried about a person walking by.

Of course, a lot of sex occurs at parties. It's often get in bed and out of bed. Or guys, "Oh God, it would be awesome to lay a virgin—so I could break her in." That's the kind of sex that bothers me.

Also, kids aren't concerned enough about safe sex. They're too concerned about what they're doing right now. The only fear of AIDS is if you're doing it with an older girl—in college or out of college—or with somebody from another town. This weekend a friend had sex with a girl in Ohio. When he got back, he told me, "I don't have any idea what she was like. I don't know if she was clean or not."

I don't think adults should even bother discouraging teenage sex. They should realize that teenagers are going to go out and have sex whether their parents like it or not. It would help, though, if the teens communicated with their parents. My parents know I've had sex. They know the kind of sex I'm having now—they'd rather have me doing that than screwing girls so they let me alone. They don't come intruding.

Sex is a thing teenagers will always have on their minds till the end of time.

Lombard, Illinois
Glenbard East High School

Is there pressure to engage in premarital sex?

Magnus Seng *parent:* I think there is a lot more pressure than when I was younger. There is more pressure because it is more accepted: "Everybody is doing it so how come you don't?"

Sue: I never went out with a guy who said, "Come on, sleep with me." I've heard people say that they've been pressured that way, and it made them feel uncomfortable. When a guy tries to go too far, the girl can say, "Stop." But then you never see him again. The boys have other guys saying, "Why don't you do it with her?" Or, "Did you get it?"

Kris: It bothers me. It should bother everyone. It just puts everyone down. Having sex with someone is what makes the girl a slut and the guy a stud.

Seng: It cheapens sex.

What are the moral issues concerning sex?

Sue: My parents never told me not to have sex before I was married. They told me not to have sex before I was sure I was in love. My mom said, "Every time before you have sex, think, 'This could be a baby.' Every time you have sex ask. 'Do I want this baby?' "

In a movie or on TV, sex seems like it's just for fun. You never see someone have a wonderful one-night stand and end up pregnant in the movies.

Gerri Long *parent:* Society is more accepting of premarital sex than it was when we were growing up. I think the TV and other media reflect that.

Seng: But there is a double standard. If a girl walks down the hall and says, "Boy, I got laid last night," we look down on her. If he's male, we say, "You're really doing a good job." There is a performance expectation from males. Why is there that double standard?

Kris: Because men are supposed to be the aggressors, and women are supposed to be timid.

Long: Society seems to put the responsibility not to get pregnant on girls.

What are your sexual morals?

Sue: I wouldn't make love to anyone unless I was positive that I loved him.

Brad: The Catholics believe that you are not supposed to do anything until you're married. That's where my parents get most of their beliefs. And from that, it goes on to me.

What is the connection between love, sex, and when you have sex?

Long: Sex is an expression of love.

Seng: One time this guy said, "I've had sex with a whole bunch of girls, but I've only made love twice." Sex is a biological act. You can have sex with a dog for that matter. But love is entirely different. There is a difference between the sex that you see on TV and sex as an expression of love.

Olympia, Washington

Jenni *Gig Harbor, Washington*: I think sex before marriage is okay. If the person you are with is special enough, you can share that together. But if a person isn't going to be responsible to take care of birth control, then they shouldn't kill the baby. They should consider adoption if they cannot afford a baby.

Tammi *Sumner, Washington*: I don't know if I would want to go through the whole thing, have the child, then give it up. What if you are raped?

Jenni: Then abortion is okay. I would never consider having that child because I would go through life looking at the child as the person who raped you.

Is sex accepted among friends?

Tammi: I have two separate sets of friends—my school friends and my church friends. Among my school friends, sex is very common. They are popping up pregnant. With my Christian friends, it doesn't happen.

Chris *Olympia, Washington*: I have a Catholic friend. In the Catholic church there is no sex before marriage and no contraception. My friend who is 15 and her boyfriend, who is also Catholic, had sex and used contraceptives.

Jenni: In my school, sex is no big deal. I'd say over 85 percent of my school is having sexual relations.

Tammi: To me, it is very important to stay a virgin until I am married. I am a Christian, and my parents have stressed it, too. Now, my decision to remain a virgin until marriage is not because my parents are stressing it but because I believe in the Bible and Christianity.

Stacey *Issaquah, Washington*: A lot of my friends who go to my church have sex. It is no big deal.

Jenni: I think the unpopular people are the ones having sex because they need the love.

Jennifer *Seattle*: All I ever hear is "Sex is bad." Why do teenagers go out and do it? All you ever hear is, "You are going to get pregnant." To me, I think that I have a whole future ahead of me. I think there are better things. I don't see why kids would go out and hurt themselves.

Jenni: My parents have always been very open about sex. They talked to me about it when I was very young. They always told me that if I ever needed help with birth control, they would always be there for me. They didn't expect me to stay a virgin until I get married. They know what is going on.

Chris: Men today feel that they have to have sex.

Jenni: It comes from their fathers. And from coaches—"You have to be a man."

Chris: They think of it more as a conquest. I've heard guys come back and say, "I got it ten times this weekend." It is to brag.

Jenni: There is a double standard. Guys who have sex are cool. Girls who do are sluts.

Jennifer: The male image is intimidating. "All they want from me is sex. They don't want to know what kind of person I am."

Are organizations like Planned Parenthood moral?

Jenni: Yes, they are moral. If kids have to go to their parents, they just say, "Forget it. I'm not going

to do it." My parents would just freak out.

Jennifer: When a 15-year-old finds out that she is pregnant, think about how scared she is. If she doesn't have her parents to turn to, at least she has somebody to go to who understands her problem. Even though it doesn't sound like the right thing, at least the organizations are there for the kids.

Tammi: Teenage sex is going to go on with or without places like that so they might as well do what good they can. But I don't think that birth control should be distributed in school. It is a learning facility. If teens can get contraceptives there, it teaches them that premarital sex is okay and condones it.

Chris: Think about the kids who don't have any money so they can't get to Planned Parenthood.

Washington, D.C.
Children's Defense Fund headquarters

Carol Holland *staff member of the education division*: Girls are getting pregnant because their girlfriends are pregnant. They think it's real exciting to have a little family. Kids get bored, drop out of school, and get pregnant.

Amy Taylor-Wilkens *staff member in the child and family support services division*: The problem is that young women don't have an agenda for themselves. When I was in high school, I knew that I wanted to go to college. I knew that I wanted to get a job. But others are provoked by the starlet moms. It's hard for a lot of adolescents to separate themselves from these women. Zillions of dollars separate Suzy down the street from Jerry Hall. But Suzy doesn't understand that she can't be Jerry Hall and have a baby. Then the media rams irresponsibile sex in our face.

There is an idea that "nice girls don't think about contraception." That means that you aren't supposed to plan ahead because sex just happens. If girls think about sex, then somehow they are dirty. Because of this weirdo message, a lot of girls don't take the steps to prevent pregnancy. We send teenagers incredibly mixed messages about what sex should be, what it is, and who's responsible. There is no consistent, clear voice.

Holland: It's a parental responsibility. It's the responsibilty of schools, churches, and community organizations. They need to have one clear message. I don't think everybody will be saying the same thing, but it should be a positive message: "Keep yourself on track, get your education, and make something of yourself."

That's something that really needs to be pressed into kids. Fun is fun, but business is business. Kids should be able to find a happy combination, but often they take the extreme.

Washington, D.C.
American Life League office

James Deger *government information officer*: Abortion is a symptom of deeper problems. When a teenager gets pregnant, the present trend is to have the teenager get an abortion. All the abortion does is wipe out the symptom, but it doesn't address how the teenager got pregnant or what could have been done to prevent it. That's why we take a more comprehensive viewpoint— pro-life.

In our society, it's accepted for a teenager to be sexually active. The federal government promotes it by extending the availability of free contraceptives. All the studies show that when you increase contraceptive use, you're going to increase, not decrease, the number of pregnancies.

There's only one 100 percent effective form of birth control, saying no. All other forms of contraceptives, like the pill and IUDs, have failure rates. Contraceptives create a false impression of security among the users. When a teen has an abortion, she experiences a lot of guilt. Some women who have an abortion break down and cry when they see a child or baby clothing. They have nightmares of children saying, "Mommy, mommy!" There are severe psychological side effects to abortion.

Abortion doesn't recognize that a pre-born child has the same civil rights as you and I have. The second problem is saying that abortion is a woman's right. The third problem is saying the government not only should sanction this denial of civil rights but also should be actively involved in promoting and financing abortions.

Portland, Oregon
Administration office
of Portland Public Schools

Dr. Matthew Prophet
superintendent: We have continuing education for girls who are pregnant. The health needs of kids are immense. As a result, clinics started in Dallas and Minnesota, but from a public perspective, people focus on the family planning component. But the clinics check everything, from your heart to your liver to your head.

We do not dispense contraceptives. We do recommend where the students may go. We can give them a prescription. I don't think it was a philosophical difference as much as a reality of how far we could go locally. Even then there were reactions. However, we had the students behind us. I met with the student president who said there were only three or four dissenters at Roosevelt High School. Some of them, by virtue of their moral convictions, said, "Sorry, I don't want it." A majority of students did. They weren't focusing merely on what the media said, the aspects of the contraceptives and family planning, but they were looking at the comprehensive care.

We chose that area because Roosevelt had a high percentage of pregnancies. Usually pregnancies run consistent with the socio-economic status. Also, the

185

carolyn wolcott

relationship between teenage pregnancies and dropouts is not one-to-one, but it is pretty high. We estimate that more than 600 young women in Portland schools became pregnant last year.

Someone said that the parents of the males who father children should be responsible for providing a percentage of the care for the kids. Also, in certain low socio-economic areas, particularly where many of those young men are incarcerated, many think it is best to stay in prison because their wives get more when the husbands are in prison.

Lombard, Illinois

Where should teenagers learn about sex?

Kris: Schools.

Sue: Family.

Seng: There is a debate about a Chicago school that has a birth control clinic.

Long: You don't receive contraceptives if you do not have your parents' permission to receive birth control.

Sue: I don't think they should need parental consent. A lot of people don't tell their mom and dad when they have sex. If they're getting birth control behind their parents' back, at least they're using the birth control. That's better than having a baby.

Brad: The first thing I learned about sex was from my friends.

Long: But are friends accurate?

Brad: They are not accurate, but you get an idea.

Sue: I learned everything from my friends and older brothers and sisters. It's hard to pinpoint when you found out. You just acquired it. My mom has always said, "When you think you are ready to have sex, come to me and we'll talk about it." But she didn't say, "Yes, I think you are at a point in your relationship where you can go ahead and have sex."

Kris: When we had our sex education unit in health class, the teacher said he didn't like to teach sex education because he thought it should be taught in the home. You get your basics from the home, but your parents can't sit down and whip out a graph and everything. I can remember my mom telling me about the birds and the bees when she was doing dishes. She sat me down at the kitchen table, but I think I knew everything from going to school and hearing the other kids. She used terms which I thought were funny, but I think it should be taught in school, too.

Irving, Texas
Irving High School

Whose responsibility is it to inform teens about sex?

David C.: It should be the parents', but a lot of the parents don't care. They have live-in boyfriends or girlfriends. They have sex on the couch when Bobby Joe comes home from school. They can't teach about sex or the responsibility that goes along with it.

Gene: I don't see what the issue is about sex. I guess it's supposed to be fun. Why are people making such a big deal about it? Teenage pregnancy is bad, but it's going to happen.

David L.: But it doesn't have to happen.

Jason: I think the stigma against teen pregnancy is caused by an image. People have a reputation— they want to be perfect. A pregnancy would ruin their reputation. Abortion wasn't practiced that much during the '60s, but now everyone's worried

about their weight, their figure, and their hair. That's why there's such a big deal about abortion.

Cindy: I personally am against abortion unless the mother is hurt or mentally torn apart. If you do become pregnant, the girl should have the morals to have the child and give it up for adoption.

Gene: The only two ways abortion is acceptable are if you're going to die or if you've been raped.

David L.: When someone gets raped, that's real sad, but is it the baby's fault that his father is a weirdo? Why should you kill someone for it? It is someone, not something. It's someone right after conception.

Jason: It's about two cells, and it can't feel anything. Would you like to grow up knowing your dad was a maniac running around raping people? I know I'd be upset if I found out my dad was some idiot running around raping people.

Cindy: It's kind of sad that so many teenagers have abortions when there are so many families who wait for years to adopt a baby.

World Issues

Seattle

Crouch: The nuclear issue has to be at the top of the moral issues. Many jobs in this area of the country are related to the military. Making choices about whether to take a job that pays well but may further the instability of the world is difficult.

Flucke: Another moral issue is U.S. foreign policy in Central America. At 7 o'clock this morning, I was standing on the plaza of the federal building with 100 other people in protest. It was rather moving to me to see two young men, who were not more than 20 years old, standing in the door of the federal building

blocking the entrance and holding their signs of protest until they were arrested.

I think political issues are fundamentally moral issues. Issues that have to do with how a society orders itself, uses its resources, and takes or enhances lives are what religious faith and ethics are all about. At base, every significant political issue is a moral issue.

Crouch: A lot of teenagers are aware of moral issues, but they are bewildered. They haven't the vaguest ideas where to start understanding them or protesting them. So they tend to walk away from them. But when the problem starts affecting them personally, they are ready to learn.

Flucke: One difficulty is that many of our adults suffer from the bewilderment that young people do. Problems have become so massive and interlocked that they are not black and white. Consequently, it is hard for adults to get their own thinking straightened out so that they can share their values with their children.

I think the parents' generation has been intimidated by our own failures. We were the generation that did not deal very well with civil rights and Vietnam. It makes us reluctant to say, "This is right, and this is wrong." We think, "Who are we to talk? We screwed up the world pretty badly. Maybe they can find a way through this jungle that we couldn't find." But that view abdicates our responsibilities as parents, as teachers, and as church.

Crouch: My son came home one day and said some kid had a locker full of Vuarnet sunglasses that had been ripped off. The boy was selling them to the kids for $5. My son's question was, "Should I buy these glasses?" I was stopped by that. He was disturbed enough to check it out with me, but it didn't occur to him to say, "No." He said kids were buying right and left because they knew the glasses were a good deal. He said, "I know what store they were taken from. What should I do with that?" He struggled with it. He finally went up to the store and told them. He gave a description of the student and left the store to deal with it.

Those kinds of situations happen all the time. Kids struggle with questions like, "To cheat or not to cheat? How do you deal with buying something stolen?" The smaller moral issues build for making the major moral issues.

How can teens be coached to deal with moral issues?

Flucke: In part, it is parents setting an example by their own behavior. I think we need to ask,

"What are our children learning by watching us?" We can all sound terribly moral while we are BSing, but what do our kids see by the way we live?

What is the major moral issue surrounding apartheid?

Crouch: Apartheid legalizes discrimination. Legalizing discrimination makes it especially wrong. In America, the fact that we have supported the administration of South Africa, and thereby the system, is the moral issue. It's not as simple as divestment.

Portland, Oregon
A private home

Why is apartheid a moral issue?

Betsy: Everyone believes apartheid as a system is wrong. Inhumanity is involved. The black people in

South Africa are being treated as subhumans. That's absolutely wrong.

Marshall: The tenet of freedom versus slavery—that's a moral belief. Should man subjugate another man? We all recognize that it is wrong, but we also believe that South Africa has a right to self-determination. Where do we step in?

Betsy: I think that the kids at our school have a pretty good understanding of apartheid. If not the full picture, they have a concept of what it is.

Laura: A lot of kids take their parents' views. They say, "My parents think this and that," but the kids don't really think about it. We did a special on apartheid in our newspaper to help teenagers know more about it. They are going to be adults, and it is important that they know what is happening in the world around them.

Betsy: There aren't that many ways to get involved in the apartheid issue. You can protest and have a firm belief, but there is not much we can do.

Marshall: To get teenagers involved, people have to prove that the issue is going to affect them. People don't want to step out for an issue that doesn't affect them. "It's okay if it happens to somebody else as long as it doesn't happen to me." If the issue is important enough to teenagers, they will seek out information on their own. All they have to do is turn on the TV set.

Perspectives

Irving, Texas

Melissa: Blacks have different morals than white people. Have you heard about the epidemic they have with being pregnant? I was so embarrassed. People think they should keep their babies while

Mandik 87

white people think they should abort. That's a moral difference.

David L.: Morals don't seem to be as important when you get older. When I was little, I didn't lie or cuss. But then I got older and got the attitude, "I really don't care."

Gene: But you have to be able to defend your morals. Morals let you know what's right and wrong. But people do what they want to do anyway. Teenagers look for the easy way out. If it's easier to cheat on a test, they're going to cheat. That's just the way they do it.

What is an immoral person?

Cindy: I think people are immoral when they intrude on someone else's morals and hurt them.

David C.: Times are changing. Parents and teachers are trying to judge us by their time. But morals have become more modern.

Dallas
First Baptist Church

Doug Wood *Director of youth ministries*: The morals of our country are changing. I have the feeling that this is what it must have felt like to be a Roman citizen—seeing your country going to pot and not knowing what to do about it.

Kids, whether they're Christian or not, are searching for answers. They think they can find the answers in a bottle of beer on Friday night, in the back seat of a car on Saturday night, or by snorting coke. That seems to be the way they're trying to get their thrills and fill their lives. My perspective is that a kid who is committed to God can fill his or her life without that stuff.

Jesus is real. I think it's about the only answer some kids can get to the problems they face. I'm not sure psychology and psychiatry can answer all the questions.

The best witness to this is kids who have made the change. One boy who graduated from high school two years ago told me he was the biggest hellraiser in high school. He said, "I was as big a drinker and wild a guy as you've ever seen. I was bananas. I'd do anything in the world."

And he said, "There was a point where I finally realized that everything I was looking for was empty. I woke up in the morning as empty as I was the night before. I realized that I needed to have God in my life."

He also told me he just helped perform a funeral of one of his drinking buddies from high school. His friend was selling coke and was going to the University of Texas to make a deal. He had a car wreck and was killed. The boy added, "I saw my entire senior class sitting out there. All I could say was, 'Brian was wrong.' Now he's dead, and there's no hope for him. He constantly searched for fulfillment in money, sex, or alcohol, but he never found it. God rescued me, or I would have been in the car with him."

What can the church do to change morals?

Wood: The church can give kids an alternative. The alternative is that they can see that it's enjoyable to go off and not drink and get wasted but come back excited and happy. There's a natural, clean way to laugh without getting bombed to do it.

Teens and Morals

The church has to meet kids' needs where they are—love and care about them—not try to cram something down their throats. We need to show them that there is a wonderful and exciting life that God created for them.

For example, I went to an Amy Grant concert at the Reunion Amphitheater. I just looked around and thought, "They're 15,000 kids in this room, and they're eating it up." The effects, staging, and lighting were every bit as good as I've seen at any concert. But Amy Grant was singing about God, and she didn't mind telling you she was.

One teenager said, "This is the first rock concert I've been to where the air wasn't heavy with pot." That role model is very important.

Nashville

Hollis: I find that my value system is shaped by the experience I gain in life. Also, I think television has a monumental impact on the shaping of values. All television is educational, but it's educating people in a positive or negative way. Television demonstrates different behavior systems. It tends to lead people to do experimentation because they've witnessed the experiences secondhand.

The media do not have a responsibility to program so that every program would fit into Baptist values. I oppose that vigorously. But they have a responsibility to program so that they don't violate the values that are essential for any society to function. Human beings should not be exploited.

How can churches help teens cope with conflicts?

David Lockard *director of organization:* In an age where social

pressure is so strong, there are other factors to guide a young Christian person concerning what is right, what is wise, and the part of God's will that he or she sees in Scripture and prayer. There is significant ethical and moral guidance in Scripture.

Hollis: One of the real problems in dealing with values and ethical issues in our society is that these issues are abandoned before they are properly dealt with. I call it bumper sticker morality. We see a car with a bumper sticker proclaiming, "Fight Pollution," but the car is spewing out fumes.

Primarily, the energizing power of the gospel within the church gives Christian teenagers the opportunity to keep dealing with issues and struggles. To the extent that Christian young people are able to emulate and follow the example of Jesus, they're able to practice a high standard of morality.

The church's responsibility is not to tell teenagers what to do but to help teenagers develop a value system whereby they may make decisions. I feel strongly that churches have a responsibility to help teens develop the method for making decisions and their own ways to go. Teenagers need to learn how to make moral decisions themselves because there will arise a situation where the church is not around.

Lockard: I think the church teaches teens who they are and whose they are—the motivation that comes that way. The church has to counter peer pressure. The young people in the church see the kind of fellowship that they enjoy. And it saves that youngster from the cop-out of "Everybody's doing it." The motivation and support come from fellowship with others who value Christian principles.

Lancaster County, Pennsylvania
Roots Market

Mrs. Daniel Fox: To solve society's problems, it is our business to see that we behave. The only hope is to take the Lord as your Savior. There are some people who are morally good. They don't steal; they don't kill; they're kind—and this is all wonderful. But when they die, their goodness dies with them. The good deeds they did while they lived here won't give them a ticket to heaven.

The Mennonite ways are easy for me to follow because the Bible gives guidelines. It's no hardship for me to live like this because I have a peace I wouldn't give up for anything. The Bible spoke that in the time of Moses people would rather enjoy the pleasures of sin for a season than be counted among the people of God. People still would rather do like everybody else does. They want to look prettier so they wear cosmetics. They want to be in style so the girls wear pants. I'm not throwing stones, but 20 years ago teens' grandmothers wouldn't have walked around in pants. There's a verse in the Bible that says it's an abomination when a woman wears what pertains to a man, or the other way around.

Do young people want some standards to be upheld, or do they want to go their own way? I think they respect standards and they need parents and teachers who have enough grit to enforce these standards.

Tucson, Arizona
A local high school

Steve: When I was younger, my parents and I had different views on just about everything. They thought black, and I thought white. It was rebellion. As I got older, we agreed on a lot. I respect their opinions. I have accepted a

LINDA RETZLAFF
LTHS

lot of their morals and views.

We need to be able to defend our morals because it's all we have sometimes. Friends mean a lot in high school. You want their respect, and you want to do what their friends do. But if the crowd is going to do something you don't want to do, they'll call you a wimp and you have to be able to say, "Hey, that's not my thing. I don't do that." It's important to let people know where you stand, or else they'll walk all over you.

Maggie: A boyfriend or girlfriend could try to change your morals. They try and make you just like them. They are doing it so you'll think they are perfect and you'll have a lesser view of yourself.

Lisa: Usually you're so eager to please them that you'll do it.

Steve: It's also possible to find out through experience that your viewpoint is wrong. Maybe you are giving in to someone at the bottom of the barrel. I didn't care because I've been there. I treated other people pretty crappy. I didn't care for myself or anybody. I saw myself biting my mom's head off when she came in to get my dirty clothes. I'd tell my dad what an asshole he was for doing something—just blowing up for no reason. I saw that it was really myself that I hated. It took a lot of time to bring myself back up.

Compiled by Michelle Jao and Chris Anderson

Solutions

I changed my moral values drastically during my junior year. . . . I was the outgoing 4.0 that was everyone's friend. I began going to parties when my best friend got a car. I drank a little just because it was there. I started smoking cloves and cigarettes a little, too.

Pretty soon I became the "party girl." All I cared about was going out on weekends. I started neglecting my school work and cutting classes for every reason under the sun. My parents didn't know I was cutting or that my excellent school work was dwindling into nothing. My whole attitude about life and people and myself changed into something I could not recognize.

Things went on this way until December—report cards. My straight A's had fallen to C's and one D. . . . Around February, my parents discovered my excessive cutting . . . and restricted me until June from absolutely everything.

I acted like a horrible monster. But it also gave me a lot of time to evaluate what I had turned into . . . every parent's view of a teenager. . . . I was a phoney person, and I hated myself.

I decided to do some changes. I finished the . . . year by the skin of my teeth. I got a job, stopped drinking and smoking . . . and began standing off to the sides silently watching the people around me. I saw different people going down the same paths and ending up with the same major problems. I began looking to see if I was beginning to make the same

mistakes and would stop the problem before it started. . . .

Now I'm getting better grades, and I feel much better than I ever did about myself.

> *17-year-old female*
> *California*

I . . . do not believe in premarital sex. I even get upset if I hear some friends have done it. Virginity is something that should be saved. Girls who have not done it should be glad; they'll find a husband who'll be very happy to find he's marrying a virgin. I think the couple would have more respect for each other if they both are virgins.

> *Amy Anderson, 15*
> *Mount Prospect, Illinois*

I decide what is right and what is wrong by my religious background. I was brought up in the church and have a firm faith in my religious beliefs.

> *Thelma Ross, 16*
> *Eagle, Nebraska*

I agree totally with my parents' judgment. For example, truthfulness to parents—there is no such thing as lying to parents or anyone. You just don't do it.

> *Michele Berman, 16*
> *Wheeling, Illinois*

In order to know what is right or wrong . . . consult the Bible. Unfortunately, in an increasingly immoral society, people succumb to their natural urges rather than overcome them. . . .

The only thing we as human beings can hope for is that society will try to regain some innocence. . . . I, myself, will not participate in sex before marriage, nor will I support the homosexual's cause. I know, however, that the position I take is becoming increasingly unpopular with each passing year. This scares me.

> *Megan E. McKinney, 17*
> *Abilene, Texas*

If I choose to use drugs because I enjoy the way they make me feel, is that really different from someone participating in a dangerous sport? . . . In both cases, people are taking risks for something that they enjoy. I don't think that other people should try to tell us that something is wrong just because they don't believe in it.

> *15-year-old female*
> *Illinois*

Some of the decisions that I make . . . may be seen as wrong . . . in the eyes of others. But if I were to base all my decisions on what other people think, then I would never be happy. . . .

The majority of people go along with this unwritten constitution even if they don't really believe it . . . simply because they're afraid of what others will think of them.

> *Chris Gedgaudas, 16*
> *Wheeling, Illinois*

The best way to decide what is right or wrong is to do what you yourself know . . . is right. A person will go about this by taking into consideration their moral standards, how they were raised, and although it's not always a good idea, what their friends would think. . . .

In sexual issues . . . it's not fair for partners to pressure individuals into anything. They themselves will know when the time is right.

I feel . . . every person has a right to do what they want as long as it is not harmful to them or anyone else.

> *Kim Pond, 16*
> *Waverly, Nebraska*

If you have to make a decision on something like confidentiality for a friendship, you really should think about how this might affect your friendship. If your friend has seriously been talking about killing himself or herself, before doing anything else you should try to talk to him or her. If, after that, they are still talking about it, maybe you should try to talk to a counselor. Your friend will probably be mad at you for a while. But once they realize that you did it because you care and don't want them hurt, you will probably be better friends than before.

Barbara Gilliam, 15
Wheeling, Illinois

When I was . . . in junior high . . . I made all these decisions about what I could and couldn't do. Abortion was murder; premarital sex was a sin; smoking and drinking and drugs were out of the question. But I made most of these decisions before having any experience with them.

My sophomore and junior years, I had a steady boyfriend. The more I loved him, the easier it was for me to believe that premarital sex is all right, as long as there is love. Since I had the idea that premarital sex is wrong, I didn't have to worry about myself having an abortion. But once I was sexually active, my views started changing.

The . . . inner conflict I felt concerned my parents. . . . I began to wonder what my parents would think. . . . I resolved my conflict by realizing that this is my life and the only one I will ever have. Even though I may do some things my parents may not be proud of, I still do many things that do make them proud.

17-year-old female
Illinois

Insecurity is probably the biggest factor connected with a change in moral values. Teens want to be recognized for doing the socially accepted activities such as narcotics or sexual involvement. They don't want to be isolated from their peers.

If there is a lack of communication between a parent and child, . . . a child may tend to develop morals which deliberately contradict his upbringing, in order to express the bitterness he withholds. . . .

To overcome . . . inner conflicts, a teenager must first become acquainted with himself. He has to develop his

own individual morals and stand by them. Friends and fads change and disappear; . . . personal ethics will remain yours forever.

Tara Thaler, 16
Cranston, Rhode Island

Anything that you do not feel right about or have been told . . . is questionable is usually wrong. This is my guide. Anything I do that just doesn't click right inside, I know that this is wrong or generally not in my best interest.

Some things which may be wrong are sometimes necessary . . . to keep a certain social status. . . . For some, doing those things that are wrong inside tends to build up and may result in suicide or insanity. . . . Those who do those things that feel right usually enjoy themselves . . . and are free from guilt feelings. . . .

Regardless of choice, individuals must be free to make the decision of

doing right or wrong, as long as it doesn't hurt society.

Paul Flack, 17
Waverly, Nebraska

Once I transferred to a public school, . . . I had a lot more decisions to make. I thank God that I'm a happy person and not too concerned that the "in" group accepts me because I probably would have . . . taken the drugs, booze, and cigarettes . . . shoved in my face. Many others my age try something once and then to become accepted, they try it again. . . .

If just one person who was influential would turn and say no, I think the others would follow. I also believe more parent, teacher, and teenager communication would help. Problems I've had have been solved . . . with the advice of adults who have been through it.

Julie Barra, 17
Cranston, Rhode Island

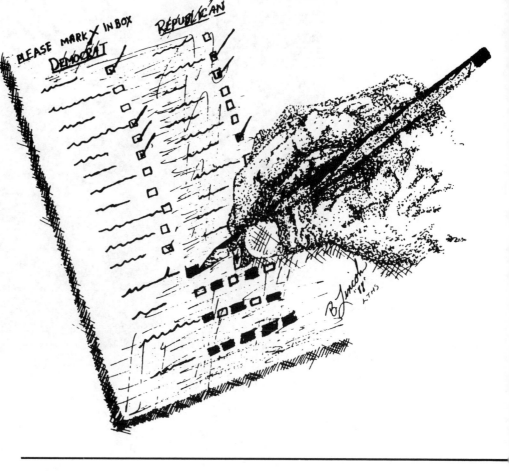

DAN O'BRIEN LTHS

Chapter 11.

Teens and Stress

Hum-zap, Hum-zap, you watch your temple pulse in the bathroom mirror. Your throat is tight and dry, your eyes narrowed to slits. The pounding is a crashing surf in your head.

The door bangs open and you jump as if a high power line landed on your foot. Jerk your hand through your hair, wish for a cigarette, feel your mouth twist into a jagged line. Two deep breaths, drawn too quickly, not exhaled.

The corridor stretches wide and fluorescent, empty as a church at 2 o'clock in the morning. Your stomach rolls 360 degrees, and you can see it, a red balloon in a laundromat washer.

Pencils!

A burning sensation scorches your insides and makes your eyes tear. Your tightly wound stride falters. Nail breaks as hand dives into pocket and traces the reassuring bump of the eraser, spongy, resilient. The lungs kick back in. With sharp gasps, you lie back against a locker.

The drinking fountain hums to match and mock the buzz of the blood in your hands. The water, bouncing futilely off your lips, won't flow through clenched teeth.

Time! Your arm arcs up. Your eyes blink and strain blindly to comprehend: hours, minutes, seconds. Five minutes, there is still time—the watch is ticking, the hands are moving, five minutes.

And you are almost there, three more classrooms. The first is filled, stacked with pale victims of some horrible deprivation, watching a fat man slash geometry on a green chalkboard and raise enormous clouds of dust.

The second is crammed with accident cases, spouting blood, some on fire. Others, shining with embedded glass fragments, mix orange and green fluids in test tubes, hold screens over Bunsen burners, roll their eyes behind safety goggles. All turn to watch as you pass the open door.

And arrive at the room. You see yourself sitting alone in the middle of the room chewing on a pencil. You melt, sink into your body, and everything falls into place with a dead calm.

You sit amid your peers, and they feel as you do: the calm, centered looks on their faces say so. The tall, bald man enters slowly. Everyone is encased in syrup, smooth and steady, as the dot sheets are passed out and the man carefully notates the time on the chalkboard. His hand comes down, and the stopwatch clicks as loudly as a gunshot.

You haven't slept for three days, but everything is under control. You watch yourself laugh, laugh until you break into a cold sweat. The droplets mix with the pencil lead as you blacken each dot darkly, A through E, then on to the next question.

Eric Kammerer

Success Paradox

The kid had everything. She was smart, involved, athletic—a leader. She liked being active. She had hopes of scholarships and honors, and she had praise from both peers and adults to keep her smiling.

First came the hard classes she knew she could handle. And they wouldn't have been a problem if it weren't for band, volleyball, student council, and a weekend job behind the check-out counter.

Then came the people who began to depend on her. The competence she showed was wonderful, they all said. Dependability became a priority. Pleasing others pleased her.

Then came competition. In the classroom to earn the best grades, in the band to be first chair, and on the court to be the best player. She never had to worry about being the best and certainly not the worst.

As homework stacked up, she noticed her grades began to slip. There were other losses. She didn't make first chair, and she wasn't the team's strongest player.

But then a lot of her friends got B's and C's, and many were worse at music and sports.

So, she just laughed about "blowing it off."

The solo contest came along. She practiced hard and played well. She started in the final game of the season. Pretty soon she had time to study a little more. So much time, in fact, that she had to find another after-school activity. She tried out for the play, and to nobody's surprise, not even her own, she made it.

The pressure built up once again. Lines to memorize, band tryouts to practice for, dance decorations to plan, and a research paper to write.

She began to live for Fridays. The drinking crowd was sure a lot of fun. Besides, she was no longer a stuck-up, brainy introvert. Now she was becoming accepted by doing what was "cool" on the weekends.

The grades were slipping again, but only a little. After all, most of her friends received B's and C's. She really didn't like the band so why should she want to be at the top of her section? And drama was interesting, sure, but she never wanted to be a successful actress.

But there was a high point to everything. The new guy she was seeing was cute and popular. He could make her happy, and she wanted to make him happy. She had always been pretty liberal about sex so she let him take advantage of that attitude. And when he was around, the two of them had a great time.

Finding out what he once thought of her was kind of interesting. She knew people were wondering what happened to the quiet, smart girl. Actually, she liked breaking down her image. She liked being the exception to the straight-honors-student-with-low-esteem-but-high-hopes-for-the-future rule.

Pretty soon she partied every weekend. Smart enough to know when to stop and not become dependent, she knew the social drinking and the occasional pot she smoked would do her no damage. Her close friends were probably a little worried, but she ignored them. It was better that way because, frankly, she didn't care.

In fact, she didn't care about much. "Who cares?" and "blow it off" became common vocabulary. She was plain sick of everything, and it wouldn't go away.

She would never turn to drugs. That was stupid. For a while, she had fun getting drunk, but she also found the high was completely temporary. And the fun she had on the weekends made her realize how depressing the weekdays were.

She went home after school and enjoyed the natural high of sleep. But sleep was only temporary, too. The next day she would always find herself lost in the anxiety of lack of preparation.

The paper was due the next week. She had all week so why worry now? The play would run in two weeks, but her lines were pretty much learned. The student council president said she wasn't working hard enough. She stayed late after play practice doing his work. Her boss at the store complained that she was taking too much time off so she went in early to help stock the shelves.

She didn't like to be at home anymore. Her obnoxious sister and brother never shut up or left her alone. All she wanted was a little privacy. But her family interpreted her complaints as hostile acts and hassled her even more.

The paper was due the following day. She had math to finish. She had cues to learn. Her family was yelling again. She was exhausted, but she wanted to talk to her friends on the phone.

She checked again. Her period still had not come. She hoped it was the stress, but she had been hoping for two weeks. She called his house for the fourth time that evening, but he still wasn't home. She couldn't concentrate, but the paper was still due. She was upset, but there was no way to make the problems go away.

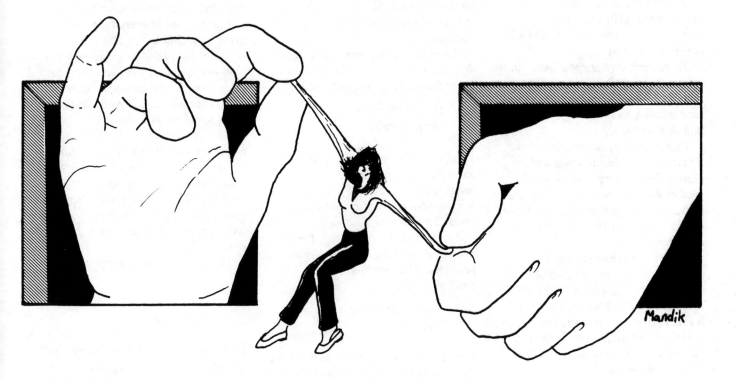

She hated writing. She hated school. She hated the friends who were no longer there when she needed them. She hated her family for never shutting up. And she hated him for not being home. He probably wouldn't believe she was pregnant anyway. And she probably wasn't. But right now she wanted to believe it, and she did.

It wasn't self-pity. When she thought about it, she knew she had put the pressures on herself. But no matter how good her grades were, no matter what she did after school, no matter whom she dated, she decided that she could never be happy.

She had never wanted to think of herself as weak. She was proud of her accomplishments and of her ability to work under pressure. But all her drive had run out. She wanted happiness and had hoped to find it in so many ways. But happiness, like life, can be only temporary.

Although knowing how everyone would react made her sad, she was smart enough to know that no one was going to feel sorry for her. But she didn't care. She wasn't happy. She owed it to herself.

The suicide was a surprise to everyone but her. The mourners grieved, but out of anger instead of out of pity or guilt. "She wasted a beautiful life."

Sara Corrough

Conflicts

Pressure is one of the major reasons why half the kids I know are crazy. . . . You can tell they all have something missing.

To me, pressure is not a word but a disease. It breaks kids down and plays with their brains. They feel like they have nowhere to turn unless they give into their pressures.

One of the biggest pressures that teenagers today face is drugs and alcohol. I know they make you feel good and bring you up when you are down. . . . I'm not putting drugs and alcohol down, but there is a limit to everything.

Some other pressures that we teenagers face are parents, homework, and teachers. These three things all sit on your back and play with your brain. Parents and teachers don't seem to realize that we are people too and that they would go crazy if they had all these pressures.

Laura Shaughnessy, 14
Brookfield, Connecticut

I attend an all-male prep school in New England. Living away for home and . . . isolated from the opposite sex . . . sexual identity is very important.

During the week one must almost perform to uphold a very macho

appearance. The pressure to perform on the athletic field is very high, and our school produces very fine athletes. . . .

There is a strong pressure to have sex, and if one doesn't also perform in the bedroom, he is frowned upon. . . .

16-year-old male
Massachusetts

I find myself always wanting to get away from everyone and everything. . . . Even if it was only five minutes of peace and an empty mind, I would take it. . . .

I just break down and cry. I'm 17, and I still can't deal with the smallest problems. Who out there has the answer?

17-year-old female
Pennsylvania

I feel the most pressure for teens in my school is grades. How many times have you come home with a 70, and your parents gave you the third degree over it?

The lowest grade I have ever gotten is a 79, and it was a devastating blow to my parents. . . . My parents just scare me to death about grades.

15-year-old male
Texas

Competition complicates teenagers' lives because it makes some teens want to be very good at everything and never be second best. . . .

When I get a worse grade on a test than my friends, I feel like I want to bitch them out for getting a better grade than me. . . . It really bugs me when somebody is better. . . .

I am competitive; I don't like it, especially when I was raised to think it's not very good. I try to ignore test grades when they come back. . . . I start to feel rotten if I get a better grade, but if I get a worse grade, I feel bad because I let them get a better grade. . . .

"Can you see how confusing this is?"

Judy DeGroot, 14
Maurice, Iowa

With some people, if there is any kind of competition, they'll cop out. . . . I know a girl who is great at basketball, but when she found out there was going to be cuts on the team, she decided not to even try out.

I thought it was a waste because she's really good, and I know she would have made the team. . . .

Sandy Van Hill, 15
Alton, Iowa

these demands placed on them. Why should my life be all screwed up because someone somewhere decided that we must excel, and to excel, we must place the demand for excellence on the new generation?

It's not my fault that the world is as it is so why should I pay the price to make it better?

16-year-old female
South Carolina

The following appeared in the **Trapeze,** *the student newspaper of Oak Park-River Forest High School (Illinois).*

Josh was only 17. On Wednesday, Feb. 2, he ended his life.

I hope that people learn something from this. Yes, I think he chose to end his short life partly because many students at this high school made fun of him, just so they could look cool by picking on someone.

I'm not saying that's the only reason. He had a case of epilepsy which often caused him to have seizures. It wasn't hard to notice that he was different.

Josh wanted to be noticed and appreciated. How many of you had fifth period lunch last semester and saw the robot that won the Halloween costume contest? Remember the light for its nose that blinked on and off, controlled by the robot's turning hand? The robot did that during all its classes and even when it was walking down the hall by itself. The person inside did it for attention; that person was Josh.

Just like anybody else, Josh wanted friends who cared. What did he get for that? He got people in his gym class who liked to throw balls in his face. When he played soccer, some kids thought it was fun to trip and kick him, especially since they didn't get in trouble. They thought it was great when they could get the whole class to laugh at him. . . .

Even though many people were unkind to Josh, he wasn't mean to anyone. The day before he died, we

honor a group of students that made honor society. the principal got up and told us how we should strive to be like them. This puts a lot of pressure on the people who try but really can't be as smart. . . .

I feel the biggest problem is with alcohol. . . . Most of the students in our school drink.

I hang around in a group that doesn't go to parties. . . . There are people who don't talk to us and consider us snots because of the fact that we don't drink. . . .

Charlotte Kraviec, 16
Wahoo, Nebraska

Sometimes I don't think people realize I am human. . . . I'm only 16 years old. "Don't make me grow up before I'm ready" is what I want to scream sometimes.

I know my parents didn't have

One of the bigger pressures that I feel is to excel at sports. . . . If you want to be really popular and be accepted, you have to be really good in sports. . . .

Another big pressure in my school is to get good grades. Just the other day, we had a school assembly to

Sometimes I wonder how the American population ever made it into adulthood without going crazy. . . .

Parents cause one of the largest pressures for a teenager. They expect so much of their child, and then nag them to death when things don't go exactly the way they wanted.

Parents don't praise kids enough for their successes, but be sure that when kids get into trouble parents are ready and waiting to "kick their butts."

17-year-old female
Connecticut

My parents always tell me to study, study, study! I hate that. It gets me so mad that I feel like failing all my subjects.

If I get a B, my parents . . . say, "How come you couldn't do better?". . . . I can't be perfect!. . . . When I sit at home and try to study, my parents start fighting. It annoys me so much. Then I get scared because they might get me involved in their fight, and I will get hit.

The next day . . . I can't pay attention in class. I start worrying about what's going to happen when I get home or what they are doing right now. . . . Are they talking about putting me in an all-girls school?

16-year-old female
New Jersey

In the beginning of the year a guy whom I knew shot himself in the head with a shotgun. I couldn't believe it because he was really smart and had everything to live for. There were some rumors afterwards that being in high school with bigger guys put pressure on him and made him nervous.

Randy Brown, 15
Dallas, Texas

In high school, everyone is so paranoid to be around someone who isn't popular. As one of my friends puts it, "When I'm around her, she makes me look bad."

Each day I feel I'm forced into a clique—"the smart kids' group." I

were playing water polo in gym. I had the ball, and he went for it and accidentally dunked me. He then stopped and said he was very sorry. Before this, Josh must have been dunked ten or fifteen times by other classmates.

Now Josh is dead; people are going to find someone else to pick on. While he was alive, nobody really noticed him, but now that he's gone people

will know who he is. There are a lot of other people out there who try very hard to make friends and be liked, but no one realizes this until after they've given up hope.

Think before you throw that ball in someone's face and laugh at them. It's really not that cool.

Brian Fischer, 16
Oak Park-River Forest High School

really hate it a lot, but all the "smart kids" are in my classes. I have no choice but to follow them.

14-year-old female
Connecticut

The problem that causes the most pressure for this teen is too much responsibility. Ever since I was young, around eight-years-old, I've had to take care of my household by doing chores, contributing finances to balance the budget, and always worrying if I have food to eat.

To this day it hasn't changed. . . . I work at a hospital so a good three-fourths of my take-home pay goes for upkeep of the house.

17-year-old female
Michigan

My oldest brother broke the state track record in long jump, was an all-state baseball player, and was an outstanding basketball player. He had good grades and is now in medical school.

My other brother was a four-year varsity starter in baseball, a two-year varsity basketball player, and is an outstanding student.

I feel a great amount of pressure trying to follow in their footsteps. Teachers and coaches expect me to be as good as they were.

Todd Miedema, 15
Hospers, Iowa

Discussion

Academic Stress

San Francisco
Lowell High School

What causes academic pressure?

Marc: Parents hope that you can be as successful or more successful than they are. They're pushing you, but they don't come to school with you so they don't know what you have to face.

Alexandria: They think school is easy. They don't realize that sometimes you're stuck in there a whole day not understanding something. Then your dad comes home and complains about how he's working hard at the office while you just have to go to school. They don't understand that it's not all fun at school.

If I don't do well in school, my parents get a very upset look as though I hurt them in some way. If I get a B in something, they'll say, "Very good dear, but we know you can do better."

Stephen: Parents bitch a lot. They're always comparing you to other kids. If you do well, they always say, "Well, you can always do better."

Alexandria: Parents don't understand that if you've got lots of stress from studying, you need to take out some of the pressure. They think that if you're really worried about the tests coming up, you should stay home and study instead of going out.

You can envy those people that seem oh so cool and collected. But then you realize they put on this total facade at school. And at home they start ranting and raving.

How is stress apparent?

Alexandria: When I get really stressed out, I get really stupid and do stupid things. For example, I may go through the halls with a toy gun or a water pistol and shoot people.

Gigi: You're supposed to be so smart and cram all this information into your head. To do something that stupid feels good.

Can pressure lead to suicide?

Gigi: At this school everyone thinks suicide is just stupid. It's not a big thing because it's going to mess up your future.

Alexandria: Suicide is found at high schools where kids don't think they have a future.

Eric: I don't think kids commit suicide because of school. It's outside troubles. Maybe their parents are divorced, or maybe the kid is abused. I don't think you're going to commit suicide because you get a D in math class.

Marc: You might consider killing your teacher but not yourself.

Gigi: Or the guy in the front row who screwed up the class curve.

Lombard, Illinois
Glenbard East High School

Pat Meyer *Teacher:* I wish school put more stress on students than it does. I don't find that very many people are under that much stress.

Brad: Back in freshman and sophomore years, grades were everything. Some of my friends would get so upset that they wouldn't be able to sleep at night because of their grades. You pressure yourself. My parents will say, "Just do the best you can." Yet if I come home with a C, then they're all upset because they're used to A's and B's.

Kris: After a weekend, if I didn't do my homework, I cannot get to sleep. I just lie in bed, like last night, thinking, "I can't believe I didn't study." It affects me physically. I wake up in the morning and say, "Mom, I'm sick. There's something wrong with me." She says, "You didn't do your homework."

Brad: Last night I stayed up all night thinking about how bad I was going to do on the next calculus test. My calculus book

Mandik 2·23·87

was next to me, but I didn't even think of studying.

Is pressure necessary for motivation?

Brad: Sometimes. I've had some weekends where I'll do four or five papers. The thing is, though, I always do a good job when I'm under pressure.

Magnus Seng *Parent*: I couldn't relax and enjoy myself if I had all this stuff hanging over me. I was one of those nuts who went into a class, and if there was a paper assigned, I'd get it out of the way.

Meaghan: When I was a freshman and sophomore, I was always studying, especially for finals. The weekend before, I'd be locked up in my room. I would get so nervous. I can actually say I have not studied at all yet this year.

Xuong: Freshman year, during finals, I watched TV the whole week. There are a lot of funny shows on TV.

Kris: I got real nervous just last week. I was taking a trig test, and I knew I was going to do well. But I was nervous when I walked out after I finished. What is wrong with me?

Xuong: It could be the teacher. You feel like you have to live up to what the teacher expects of you.

Kris: Well, no, because I do average work in trig. I was thinking, "God, I can get an A on this test because I know everything." The test was pressure.

Is there pressure from others' expectations?

Seng: If you're not living up to someone's expectations, then that person has the problem with the expectation, not you. The problem is when you make other people's problems your problems.

Brad: How can you lower your expectations?

Xuong: I know if I can't get an A

on something, it wouldn't be so bad if I got a B. That's my attitude towards everything. For example, you don't have to be the richest person in the world.

Kris: You can accept one failure. It will not kill you.

Brad: I'm not talking about A's or B's. I'm talking about the things that you want to do in life. I don't know how I could accept less than what I want to be.

Xuong: What expectations do you have that you can't lower?

Brad: The expectations of myself as a person. My expectations as far as success and what I want to do for God. Those are what makes me me.

Manhattan Beach, California
Pacific Shores High School

Robert Babb *program director of Program Touch:* A lot of the kids in this school are in troubled homes or troubled situations. I see kids who have sometimes stayed up all night long because the family is fighting. Drugs are as evident in the parents as they are in the kids. We have people who were using drugs heavily in the '60s and '70s now parenting. The parents have continued in the drug scene. The disorganization of the family is an incredible factor.

In one of my recent surveys, I had two intact families out of 30

kids I was working with. Twenty-eight families were single or stepfamilies. The kids have been incurring major losses. It could be death. It could be they never had a parent to begin with—they were raised by a single mother or father their whole lives. It could be happening right at the moment.

Under those kinds of stress, the kid isn't functioning on too high a level. They haven't got much supervision. You don't know if they have been eating properly or getting the right kind of rest.

They are certainly distracted by all the goings-on in the family. It is a very volatile situation. You get a lot of abuse and neglect.

What I see is a cycle for failure. The kids will get behind in a class setting, and they give up. They don't have the support system to say, "Wait a second, hang in there. Do some extra credit. Catch up."

Their self-esteem just spirals downward, and pretty soon one failure builds on another one. They choose peer groups that are identified with being losers or failures. And the other kids push them into that category, too. Now it becomes trendy to be a failure.

Social Stress

Lombard, Illinois
Meaghan: I've always moved away

from being pressured by my friends or by people around me. I don't go to parties and drink. I don't smoke. I've never had sex even though I know the pressure is there. I don't let myself do it because I know it's wrong.

I look at drinking, and I see what it's done to people. Everybody believes my uncle was an alcoholic, and he committed suicide. My friend was drunk and fell over. She got hurt and was acting like a little baby. I could not deal with it. She was literally like an infant, and she had to be treated that way and carried around. It makes me so sad.

Kris: Drinking is a group thing. A social thing. I don't think I'd just sit by myself and stare at a can of beer.

Brad: Mostly people sit around, socialize, and drink beer. Pot's kind of the same way. If you succumb to drugs, you can't blame it on your friends because it was your decision. I don't think peer pressure can provide an excuse for your own actions, but it may be a reason.

Seng: I never knew a bunch of guys sitting around saying, "You've got to get stoned, Seng." Because they didn't have to force me. I would join the party anyway. One of the reasons I wouldn't do some stuff is not because it's morally wrong. It's because I'm scared.

Meaghan: Maybe the most courageous thing you can do is to go against your peers and say, "I don't believe in this."

Seng: That's not the point. I had friends who wanted to go rip off some place. What I'm trying to say is I did not go along with that because I was scared of being caught.

Brad: The virtuous idea seems to die out pretty quickly, depending on how hard the peer pressure gets and on how things go in your

own life. Your mind starts getting kind of accustomed to something until it doesn't seem so bad anymore. I drink some, but I try to keep it under control. For a long time I was really hypocritical because I criticized other people for it.

Kris: Peer pressure is standing around at a party when someone says, "Do you want a beer?" and you say, "Yeah." I was caught smoking my freshman year. I said, "Mom, I don't like it. I just wanted to try it." She said, "Oh, well, if somebody wanted you to try cocaine, would you try that?" And I replied, "No, why would I ever do that?" "Then why did you try smoking?" she said. I said, "Well, I don't know. It's not as bad." I had a limit in my mind.

Brad: Your limit changes, too. I throught drinking would always be beyond my limit. Suddenly that limit changed. I tried smoking cigarettes once or twice just because I wanted to be accepted. It didn't do anything for me. But a lot of people had seen me do it,

and it changed their image of me.

But peer pressure can be good, too. I have friends who smoke pot, and they have always encouraged me not to. Drugs have a tendency, especially like alcohol, to remove your normal standards.

Kris: I've heard girls say, "Well, I was kind of drunk, and I couldn't help having sex," but that makes me sick to hear it. If you get that drunk, you'd be praying to the porcelain god in the bathroom.

Brad: If you're drunk, you don't think about it. You just do it.

Seng: The type of pressure is different. It's a one-on-one type peer pressure. Everybody having a beer is a different type of social pressure than the pressure of a one-on-one sexual encounter because ultimately sex comes down to two people.

Peer pressure doesn't go away when you grow up. Maybe one of the reasons that peer pressure is much more important in adolescence is because you have yet to find yourself. Therefore, the way that you define yourself is partly defined by the group you're with.

Manhattan Beach, California

Grace: Relationships with the people you respect cause the most stress because you never want to let them down. You try to be your best with everything you do.

In front of your friends, you can say, "No, I don't want to drink that." If you are not with your friends, the people are going to look at you and say, "Oh wow, she can't party." You want to look like you are having fun, too.

Someone says, "Hey, do you want a beer?" If you say no, everyone looks at you like, "Why not?" If you don't drink it, they sit there and look at you, saying, "You can't handle it?"

People make you feel uneasy. You were having the best time until the alcohol started. People think, "Well, she was really cool when we first started talking to her. But she can't drink so maybe she's not that cool."

Even if everybody thinks, "Hey wow, you drank all that beer and you're really cool," you feel bad because you know it's hurting your brain and your body. And maybe when you were drunk, you hurt your best friend in front of all those people. You hate yourself then.

Babb: I work with ninth and tenth graders on a regular basis. They resist saying that their peers are the ones who are influencing them. They identify with a group that holds their identity for them, and kids don't really learn how to find their own identity. They are forced to conform to their own little group, which is supposedly "a rebellion against society."

When I was growing up in the '60s, we all grew our hair long because we were trying to be different. Then we looked around, and we were all the same. Suddenly, in your twenties, you start saying, "Wait a second. We're really not all that different. What makes me me?" The kids are not allowed to be themselves in their peer group, but they don't even know it.

There is such a need to be liked, received, and loved. Kids are seaching for that so much, and they really don't get it from their peers. The typical peer group isn't set up to offer love. It is set up to encourage conformity. Kids are huddling together for comfort, but it doesn't really satisfy them. They are really still searching, and they seem very sad.

How does stress cause teenagers to turn to drugs and alcohol?

Babb: When you have single parents carrying a family, you've got parents who are dealing with their own issues. Parents don't have time to teach the kids. So, the stress is that the kids aren't prepared. They are put into situations that they can't handle. Drugs are great for that because you don't have to handle anything.

Some kids find their needs met by being in the drug culture because it provides a structure and an activity for them to pursue. Just getting the drugs is a big deal. Even if they don't smoke, they go through their whole day making the contact, setting it up, stealing to get the money, and bargaining for the dope. All this gives them something to belong to.

How does having sex put pressure on teens?

Babb: I've seen so many pregnant

14- and 15-year-old girls. They have to make an adult decision, but they're not adults. They either have to have the baby and think about supporting it or get an abortion. Some of them are worried about what's going to happen to their bodies. They talk about carrying the baby and giving it up for adoption, but they're afraid that they would be too connected to it.

At that age kids don't seem to have the capacity for being in an emotional relationship that requires "giving." The males particularly lag behind the females. I hear the girls complain a lot about the guys not being there and not being emotional. I just shake my head because it's not time for them to be there yet.

The guys have developed mentally only to the stage of going after "the big conquest." It's a very physical thing for the males. The girls are a little bit more emotionally developed so they're frustrated.

Duncanville, Texas
Duncanville High School

Craig: There's stress over prom. To go to the prom, you have to do it a certain way. For the prom, my friend and I are renting a stretch limo and a $90 tux. We're going somewhere to eat, which costs $55 on top of the ticket. Prom includes eating, but we're not going to eat there.

Karyn: You've got to keep up the image with your friends. You've got to keep up the image with your family. You've got to keep doing well, or it falls apart.

It's expected here that shortly after you get your license, sometimes even before you get your license, your parents are shopping for a car for you. It has to be a brand new one that is straight off the line. It puts a lot of stress on the students because they know their parents can't afford it. So they get a part-time job working more than they can handle so they can afford the car their friends expect them to have.

What is the major cause of teenagers' stress?

Lori: It's a lot of family problems. You hear people talk about how they get into a fight with their parents. Their parents kick them out of the house, and the teenagers move and look for ways to make their lives better. They start going out drinking and getting on with drugs.

Walker: A lot of times, the parent hasn't even told them to leave, but the kids go off and say that because they're looking for

sympathy from their peers.

Karyn: It's not all the parent's fault. It has a lot to do with the kids and their behavior—if they're on drugs and if they're drinking. My mom kicked my brother out of the house. He was gone for two months. He finally straightened up.

Craig: Kids will say that drugs and beer can be relaxants. I guess beer can be a relaxant if used properly. But the kids whose parents don't want them to drink and get high may do it, anyway. It causes the kid more stress, having to come home and deal with it—without anybody knowing they got really smashed the night before.

What other conflicts exist between parents and teens?

Steve: In four months, I'm going to be on my own. My parents say, "You have to be in by this time, or we'll take away the car for a week." It seems kind of stupid that there's a curfew. I'm sure it would be a lot easier if I learn at home so I won't make the same mistake twice when I go to college.

Karen: It would be better if my parents said, "Okay, you know when you have to work and you know what you have to do for us. So if you want to stay out all night, you can." When we go to college, it's going to be so easy to say, "Okay, great, no parents, no curfew, let's party all night." We need to deal with that now.

Suicide

Red Oak, Texas
Red Oak High School

Grace: He was here about four weeks. I thought he fit in really well with everybody. He was bright, a really intelligent dude. He was gone last Monday and Tuesday. He killed himself. It was a big shock to everybody. He

definitely had problems, but I don't think he showed it that much.

David: He was a class clown.

Belinda: I wonder why he didn't say anything to anybody. Me, I have to get it out. I talk to my brother, or I talk with a real close friend whom I've known since first grade.

David: It must have been something at home. He was hiding it at school.

Belinda: He did a good job of it.

Andy: There's a lot of stress around the school. There has been talk about other students after he killed himself.

David: A couple of students went up to one of our teachers and said they wanted to do the same thing.

Tracy: Our first period teacher took it really badly.

David: She was the first one to find out. She told me right then that she needed soemone to talk to. She was torn up bad.

Belinda: I have flashbacks of everytime that we were talking in class. I think about whether there was something that Bill might have said, indirectly, about some problem.

Lombard, Illinois

Meaghan: My uncle committed suicide. I guess he'd always been the favorite child. Anybody who had a problem would always tell him, and he'd go and break it to the parents. They'd always let the kids off because my uncle had the knack for using his words and making things turn out funny. That carried on to his adult life. He never learned how to really face things straight on. He always thought he could get himself out of it just by making people laugh. He wanted to be wealthy, to have a nice house, and to have all the things for his kids. Because he

could not sit down and do the work, he was not earning the money he needed. We think that he started gambling or going to loan sharks. And he just got in deeper and deeper because he always thought, "You know, I'll just get out of this somehow. I can just use my wit to do this." But it never worked for him.

He took out a health policy so his family could have money and waited until it was safe. Then he killed himself.

Seng: Suicide is a statement saying there's no hope. They can see no answer to whatever the problem is. The hard part is that suicide is not the answer. The point is to try to prevent it.

Brad: It's a plea for help. But it depends on how the person tries to commit suicide, if they really want to die. A lot of people who try to commit suicide want someone to take care of their problems. They don't know how to do it themselves.

Meaghan: You have to give them some hope. They have to accept things. They see anything below their goal as a failure. Sometimes it takes a lot of failures to achieve. They don't look beyond this and say, "Gradually I'm going to get there." They just say, "I'm failing. What's the use?"

Brad: You can't help such people. No matter how much you try to help them, the change is inside themselves. You can say, "Life's worth living," but they're not going to listen to it. All you can do is be a friend to them and try to be there when they need you. A lot of people want attention. They don't really want to kill themselves.

The people I know who have attempted suicide didn't realize what they were doing. Neither one of them wanted to die. I don't think they realized they were doing it for attention.

Jocelyn Miller LTHS

Xuong: But you're getting the wrong type of attention. You get people trying to sympathize, and you didn't want that. You wanted some friends. You might get attention from people who just look after you so that you don't commit suicide.

Seng: I think we all like attention. But when you get to the extreme where you have to take that kind of measure to get it, then there's something in your supply of attention that's missing.

Plano, Texas
Administrative Office
 of Plano Independent School District

Larry Guinn *director of student services:* We had six youngsters at

Plano Senior High take their own lives within a five-month period. It caught everybody by surprise because we had never had anything like that before. It woke up the community.

We tried to identify friends of the youngsters who committed suicide. We didn't want to blow it out of proportion because it can be very damaging. We tried to do everything one on one. We wanted everyone to know there's a place to get help. We had our teachers looking for people who might be under the stresses and strains so we could help them.

We used the SWAT team (Students Working All Together) to help us through that situation. I got a group of students together to

look at Plano Senior High School and say, "Hey, do we need to do more to make this a warm and friendly place to get an education?" A lot of people like to think it's suicide prevention, and some people think it's peer counseling. But it's really not that. SWAT is a friendship group.

When new students come in, we try to match them up by interests with a SWAT team member. We get a National Honor Society student with a National Honor Society student. Then they have something in common, something to talk about. They also introduce them to the people who have the same common interest.

They have to eat lunch with that person because lunch is a

critical time for most adolescents. Most adolescents don't eat lunch by themselves unless there is something going on. Sometimes it's because they're lonely. They don't know anybody, or they don't have any friends.

Also, we found out, most people move in the summer. And that's the worst time to move a teenager. In the summer they come into a new place and they have no way to make new friends unless they get immediately involved in a church setting. So we have a counselor on duty during the summer.

Then we said, "Okay, we're doing great with the new students, but what about students who are here?" There are always people who haven't adjusted or who haven't been able to find a nichê. The parents call me, and I match up the kids with somebody.

Is there value in peer counseling?

Guinn: I don't believe in peer counseling. If people are not particularly trained and they're dealing with a suicidal or a depressed person, it can do harm. If I went in and got a couple of training sessions on how to operate on brains, would you want me to operate on you if you have a brain tumor? If a person has serious problems, you don't want an amateur. You can listen, you can talk, but when it gets to be something that you can't deal with, you need to go and get that person professional help.

Also, sometimes a peer counseling group can get so involved in training that it becomes a social clique unto itself. They start electing officers and start having parties. And when you do that, you lose the purpose of reaching out to try to help somebody.

Why do teenagers commit suicide?

Guinn: To this day I can't explain

all of the reasons involved in the individual suicides because they were varied. People who try to generalize and say, "Well, these are the reasons these people are committing suicide," really haven't dealt with the problem.

The only one constant I can find is a feeling of hopelessness. Now that blows my mind because we have more hope in this country than anybody else. We're supposed to be the "Judeo-Christian reform" and the basis of all that is hope. But here we're seeing a whole generation of young people who feel like everything is hopeless. We've got to get back the doctrine of hope into our schools and churches. And we need to get off all this negativism.

As parents, we teach our values to our children. We've got to be careful of the role model we represent. If negativism is what we convey all the time, our children are going to be negative. If hopelessness is what we express all the time, our children are going to have that hopeless feeling.

Perspectives

Manhattan Beach, California

How can teenagers relieve stress?

Grace: Usually I call up someone who doesn't know the problem that I have had. I can talk to them because they are looking from the outside. You just go have fun with them, and they make you forget about whatever problems you were worried about. They are too busy showing you what they have done when you haven't been there. Get away from it all—go to the mountains. Different scenery gives you a different perspective on life. You will look at an idea differently.

Danny: When kids are young, parents should let them know that they are somebody. Parents should let their kids tell them whatever their kids want to tell them.

San Francisco

Alexandria: It helps to get out of the house. Do anything as long as it has nothing do with school.

Gigi: If you go home, you're surrounded by your parents, your books, and your desk. Your dictionary stares you in the face, and you think about all the homework you have to do and the finals coming up.

Marc: You can watch television in the den, but in your house you still get that feeling that you should be in your room studying.

Gigi: Try any other outlet. Sometimes it helps to read a book that you know is not a literary work, like a Harlequin romance.

Alexandria: Go home and relax with a cold brew.

Gigi: Or a joint.

Alexandria: Personally, we don't do that, but I'm sure there are people who do that, especially on the weekends.

Marc: There's still a whole group of people who go home at lunchtime and get stoned for their afternoon classes. Most of them are seniors, and they figure it doesn't matter. Whatever they haven't done, they aren't going to do.

I don't think it's the stress factor. I think they use that as an excuse. I think drugs promote more stress, worrying about whether you're going to get caught.

Marc: Drugs are a cop out. The kids are trying to use stress as an excuse to do the drugs because they know drugs are wrong. It's a form of rebellion rather than a form of relieving stress.

Do parents recognize teenagers' stress?

Marc: My parents are pretty cool about it. My mom will say, "Don't worry about your room. Don't worry about any chores. Studying is more important, and you don't need any other pressures."

Eric: My mother always brings me ice cream every hour and a half. It's something that she's always done that makes me feel better.

Gigi: Just to let you know they care. You do have a friend in the world besides your biology notes.

Alexandria: Sometimes it's annoying because my dad will say, "Is there anything I can do?" I'll say, "No, Dad. All this pressure is on me." "Are you sure there's nothing I can do?" "No, God dammit, stop asking. You can't." I feel like nobody else can help me.

Manhattan Beach, California

Babb: I would try to reach kids early and try to teach the processes that they are not learning at home. They are not seeing role models solve relationship problems. They are seeing parents fail on each other and walk out rather than work it out. They don't know how to be successful because they've never seen it.

I'd like to see a culture or society that allowed their young people time to develop rather than one that forces them into decisions. Adults need to teach kids how to develop their own views and integrate them into some kind of value system. We have to put faith in them to develop in a positive way and to make choices for surviving and taking care of each other.

Tricia Maxwell LTHS

The ideal society would have enough love for everybody. There would be such a scarcity of love. When people feel that there is a scarcity of love, they hog it for themselves rather than give it away.

How can people build self-esteem?

Babb: Parents should set up a challenge for the kid, one he is equipped to take on. They should be available to help the kid negotiate the situation. We've taken kids out on wilderness challenges. If it's challenging and scary enough, yet "do-able," then you've got potential for building self-esteem.

One kid last week came back from a 17-day outward bound where he was doing rock climbing and camping. He had to go out solo with a limited amount of food and manage for three days. He came back saying he had learned that you can't start your life over, but you can continually pick it up from where you are and move on. You never can go back and change what's happened, but you can change what's happening tomorrow. That kind of idea from a 16-year-old is profound. Self-esteem is the key.

Duncanville, Texas

Lori: People pick their own way of relieving their stress. I say with exercise, but it depends on what kind of stress it is.

Steve: Taking drugs or drinking will just postpone relieving the stress until a later date.

Karyn: They add to the problems because you're fighting your parents. You're fighting your teachers. You're fighting whoever knows about it.

Steve: So it really doesn't take care of the problem. It just makes you feel good for the time being.

Craig: One way to relieve stress is to be open with your parents—to reach a compromise. A lot of parents don't want to compromise. They're set in their own ways, and the kids set themselves in another way. But if you can meet halfway with your parents, a lot of stress can be knocked out. A lot of people should learn to talk to their parents. They think of them as the very last person to go to.

Karen: With peers, listening is the best way to help unless it's

Teens and Stress   211

Jana Fry CTHS

something like drugs or they're considering suicide. It's simply listening to them, giving them the chance to say it to someone. A lot of times you go to your counselors, to your teachers, or to your preacher, but you can't really talk to people who are looking down on you.

Craig: They talk like they've been through it.

Karen: They have, but you want to talk to someone who's going through the same things. Times have changed a whole lot since my mom was my age.

Lombard, Illinois

Xuong: Whatever happens to me, I just think, "Well, there's got to be someone out there worse than me." Because of the war in Vietnam, I know I never wanted to die. I've seen dying too much. When you went to sleep, you'd hear guns shooting. People were dying—getting shot or starving. I knew that my life was precious. Why should I kill myself?

I was lucky because my dad was a ship captain. He had to bring all these people out of Vietnam. The ship was just packed. They didn't have any food, and we didn't have enough to go around for the 2000-odd people. But there were people worse off than I was. People were getting killed. We just got as many people as we could on the ship and took off. People who were on the beach didn't make it.

Plano, Texas

How well do teenagers cope with stress?

Guinn: There are some people who are born with this innate ability to cope with things. Others have a good, strong family unit, and they've got people who communicate with them—people who are sensitive to them and vice-versa. But there are also youngsters, whose dad, for example, spends less than twenty seconds a day with them.

You have to open up some lines of communication. You have to be able to express yourself. You have to know that there is someone whom you can talk to about a problem, who's going to understand, and who will handle it the right way. When a crisis comes, I'm hearing from students that they don't want a buddy-buddy teacher or parent. They want someone who's going to listen to them and can give them some direction. In families and communities that have these communication situations, generally you will find youngsters who are able to cope and handle things.

But it is just as dangerous if parents totally monopolize their teenager's life. The kids are playing football because dad is reliving his life through his son. The parents don't cut him any slack and don't give him any independence.

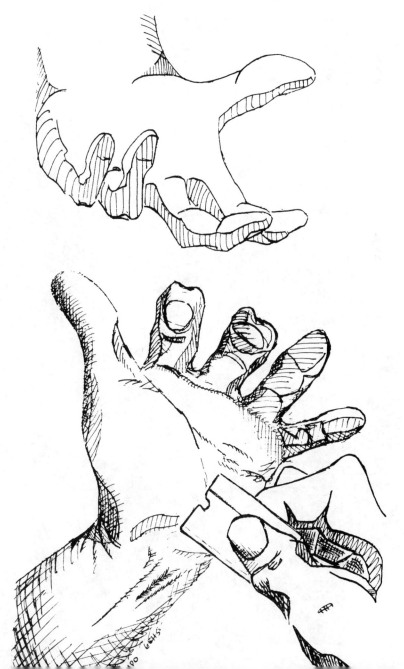

Teens and Stress

Youngsters who are under extreme pressure will send up warning signals. A sudden drop in grades or a sudden attendance problem could be a sign. A teacher should notice, "Hey, I need to look a little closer at this youngster to find out what's going on here." Most teachers, if they know someone is going through a hard time, are going to do everything they can to help them.

You can't put learning and curriculum in this "bag," adolescent stress in this "bag," and drugs and alcohol over in another "bag." They're all together. You get them off drugs. Then you'll see learning happen.

We have to sensitize the adult population—teachers, parents, ministers, police departments, everybody—to the world teenagers are growing up in today. Everybody needs to be sensitive to the pressure.

Compiled by Paulette Polinski

Solutions

People will use many different things to escape from reality. One of these is drugs. . . . I have a friend who takes drugs for this reason. I know that his group would exclude him if he didn't because I have been left out by them ever since I turned down a joint. If he would realize that he's ruining his life, he could find plenty of the right friends.

Mark Brown, 17
Grinnell, Iowa

The problems that cause the most pressures for me in school are drugs and alcohol—how to say no. . . . Other students ask you to try something that you know is wrong, but you do it anyway. You usually end up feeling guilty when it's over. I know I do. . . .

The easiest way to avoid many of these problems is to make friends . . . who don't do things that you don't wish to.

16-year-old male
Connecticut

The best way to handle pressure is to get involved in activities that you enjoy, not what your friends enjoy. Then when things get rough, you will feel motivated to work hard and make it through the bad time.

Michele Bloodworth, 18
Salem, Virginia

Teen views and adult views don't really differ . . . when it comes to handling pressure . . . because we handle it about the same way. Our parents drink, and so do we.

Sean Mix, 16
Seattle, Washington

The best way to handle pressure in high school is to acknowledge the pressure. I think after you acknowledge the pressure that it is easier to deal with. . . . You can do things with your friends and family to vent that pressure.

I also don't believe that I could handle the pressure if I weren't a Christian. My belief in God has helped me through a lot of situations.

James M. Thomas, 17
Lake Toxaway,
North Carolina

A good way to handle this pressure is cannabis. Not only smoking of this waky tabaky, but also growing and nurturing young plants to full productive adults. . . . If taken in limited amounts, it really can be effective.

18-year-old male
California

I find that dancing really helps me. I can let the music "set me free," and I turn my stressful feelings into energy. . . .

Put everything into perspective, and remember that what you can't change now will probably go away by itself—or become unimportant to you.

Laura Smith, 16
Little Silver, New Jersey

The best way to relieve myself of pressures after a rough week is to lock myself in my room and play my guitar. It relaxes me to play. When I compose something really worthwhile, it makes me feel really good about myself.

Lynwood Hall
Salem, Virginia

If you have faith, there is hope. I handle the pressures by way of the Lord. Although it looks big and hopeless to me, I ask him to help me learn from it. . . . So far it has done wonders.

Kay Frazen, 17
Seattle, Washington

Ignorance is the way to handle pressure. If you don't know the consequences of your actions, you can't be held responsible.

> Brian Herzog, 17
> Monmouth, Oregon

In high school sometimes, the best and only way to handle most pressures is to have a few drinks or maybe a reefer. It may not be a positive way, but since there is not much help offered from counselors and teachers are not concerned, it makes life pretty hard to endure. You can truly bury your troubles in drugs.

> 16-year-old male
> Idaho

The pressures that high school students must cope with seem unbearable at times. Parents, teachers, and peers are usually the sources of this pressure. Although there are many ways to cope with pressure, the best way is to get organized.

If a student has to study for three tests, write an essay, and go to track practice all in one day, he may feel so pressured that he can only stare at his work and say, "I'll never finish."

Organization would relieve the pressures on this student. A carefully planned schedule . . . would show the student that his work can be accomplished. . . .

Getting organized also means figuring out one's priorities. A student who feels that social acceptance is more important than good grades must give in to peer pressure and ignore pressures from teachers or parents concerning school, thus relieving some pressure.

> Heather Weiss, 16
> Little Silver, New Jersey

The best way to handle drug and alcohol pressure is to look at a good example and think of the possible outcomes.

When friends, if you want to call them that, pressure me into drugs or alcohol, I think about an adult, or even another person my age, who I admire that doesn't drink or use drugs. I try to model myself after that person.

I also think of what will happen later if I break down now, under pressure. I think of who my acts will affect and of all the possible dangers.

> Amy Cichanowski, 16
> Winona, Minnesota

I think we should be able to use drugs at our own will. It is our life, and we should live it like we want to. Parents think it makes us crazy.

They are wrong. If you have ever smoked pot, you would understand. It does not make me or any of my friends crazy. Parents believe anything they hear.

> 17-year-old male
> Illinois

When you feel all fed up about the world, it is nice to go out and have a laugh or two or three. Sometimes it feels like a whole world has been lifted from your shoulders.

> Kris Kohler, 15
> North Plainfield, New Jersey

When I am under pressure . . . I try to think positively. . . . For example, when I am in a fight with my parents, I think about my friends and how much they mean to me. . . .

I also have faith in God. I know he is with me and will make everything turn out all right.

> Holly Havnaer, 17
> Seattle, Washington

The best way to handle pressures in high school is to remember that every obstacle in a road does not mean a dead end.

> Vera Vaughan, 16
> Little Silver, New Jersey

216

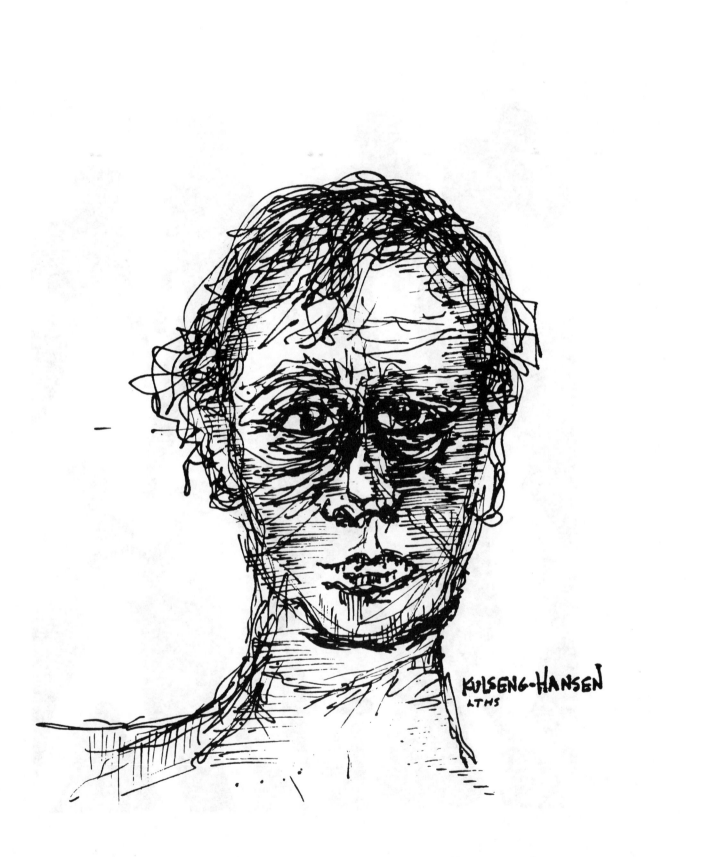

KULSENG-HANSEN
LTHS

Chapter 12.

Teens and Change

The sun rode high, a fiery orb that seared through the body until nothing remained but a bare soul, scorched bone-dry and running for shelter. Days like these often drove people a bit loco, made them listen to their trigger finger instead of their common sense. The Teens of Dodge City were no exception.

"I hate Change," Hoss Teen growled as he tossed a fifty-cent piece into the air, drew his Colt .45, and blasted the coin to smithereens. Hoss and his brothers—Bart, Jake, and Tex—marched through the dusty street at the center of town, their broad shoulders lined up side by side. Their pace was slow and deliberate; their eyes, dark and menacing; their wills, indomitable and all-powerful. Clouds of dust rose from beneath their feet with each mighty stride, enshrouding them like four demi-gods forged from the very earth.

The Teens were waiting to do battle with Change. In contrast to the Teens, Change was calm and cool. He had endured many tough battles throughout the course of history. The Golden Age of Greece. The rise and fall of the Roman Empire. The Renaissance. Copernicus. Newton. The American Revolution. The Industrial Revolution. The Civil War. Edison. Marx. World War I. Hitler. World War II. The Atomic Age. The Space Age. The Civil Rights movement. The Vietnam War. Countless other wars, revolutions, political upheavals, social changes, scientific advancements. Yet Change had always emerged victorious. Thus, as mighty as the Teens were, or imagined themselves to be, they had no chance for victory. They could not resist omnipresent and omnipotent Change. Nothing could.

Change did not want to fight. He never did. He was destined to win anyway so fighting was a waste of time. It was merely a tiresome way to delay the inevitable. Change would rather rest quietly until something really big came along, such as another revolution, or a major medical breakthrough, or at least a presidential election. But when challenged, Change was obliged to fight. The Teens had issued just such a challenge: Gunfight at Reality Corral.

Change took up his position in the corral. He seemed bored as he hefted his rifle, but he waited patiently for the Teens to arrive. The blistering heat rising off the ground caused the air to shimmer. Suddenly, a cloud of dust appeared in the distance. Change nodded his head in recognition of the approaching cloud. The Teens had arrived.

This wasn't going to be too tough of a fight as far as Change was concerned. Just another day's work. From the Teens' point of view, however, this was everything. The big showdown. The Teens knew in their hearts that they would resist Change, defeat it even, no matter what everyone else said about Change being invincible. They didn't want any Change. They felt safe, happy, protected. They loved the status quo. But could they stop a force as irresistible as Change?

The Teens reached the entrance to the corral at last. Hoss Teen kicked open the gate. The Teens marched to the center of the corral and stopped. Hoss spit a giant cud of chaw into the dust, then thundered, "We don't want no Change."

Jake Teen stepped forward. "Now look here," he began. "We is tired of all this here Change. Dodge City jes' ain't a-big enough for the both of us. So before we gits to shootin', we's givin' y'all one more chance. Git outta town, Change, if ya knows what's good fer ya."

There was no answer. Only silence greeted Jake's feeble threat. The Teens looked around anxiously, hoping to see some movement, straining to hear a reply. It was not to be, however. Change was well hidden, waiting for the right moment to strike. He hoped that the Teens would deviate from their foolish decision. Silence was his weapon.

The silence grew and then swelled to the unbearable din of a cacophonous symphony, with the burning sun as its demonic conductor. Bart Teen could take it no longer. He screamed, a long, terrified scream, and began to shoot wildly at every stable, wagon, and fence he could see. The other Teens panicked and began shooting at every movement they thought they saw. All the while, Change crouched behind a low stone wall, not moving. He had achieved another victory without even firing a shot.

Soon the last wasted bullet ricocheted into the afternoon sky. The Teens had run out of ammunition. They had fired enough rounds to fell the Apache nation, but the only evidence of damage was the wagons, fences, and stables they had blown to pieces. As the symphony of silence began an encore, Change himself rose from behind his barricade. He was tall, mighty, an awesome vision of immortality. His body was a murky gray mass through which his eyes glowed. As the Teens stared into these eyes, transfixed by the gaze of Change, they saw the unclear depths of the past and the uncertain paths of the future.

Change began to stride forward, to accept the Teens' surrender as they lie cowering in the dust. Tex Teen, however, was not quite ready to give up. As he grovelled on the ground, he had found an unused bullet. Quietly, he slipped it into his revolver. Summoning incredible courage, Tex whipped out his gun and, with a yell like a wounded bear, fired it directly between the eyes of Change.

Change collapsed, knocked backward by the force of this unexpected blow. He lay in the dust, momentarily stunned. The Teens all rose, inspired by Tex's courage and Change's apparent downfall. They began to whoop and cheer as they stared at the body of their enemy. The Teens had defeated Change!

Patting each other on the back, they congratulated Tex on his bull's-eye aim. After working up a big wad of chaw, Hoss walked over to spit in on Change's face. Suddenly, however, Change began to rise. Hoss stopped in his tracks and swallowed the chaw. Change whipped out his Winchester and with four shots knocked the gun out of each Teen's hand.

Suddenly, Change raised his arms, and a cold wind began to blow. The sky became cloudy. Dust was swirling everywhere. The Teens dropped to the ground, terrified, convinced that Change was ending their world. Change dropped his arms, and each Teen was enveloped in a kaleidoscope-like cocoon of dust. Frighteningly bright colors jumped out from the gray whirlwind.

The Teens began to see the many visions of Change. They saw personal changes, social changes, political changes, technological changes. They saw themselves bearing much more responsibility than they had ever borne before. They saw college, jobs, hard work, marriage, children, laughter, tears, joy, pain, life, death. In essence, they saw reality at last.

When the Teens were subdued, Change raised his arms again, and the visions ceased as unexpectedly as they began. The Teens were on the ground, shaking, moaning, too scared to open their eyes. Change ordered them to stand up. In a commanding voice, he said, "I am Change. Gaze upon me. I am invincible. Do you now accept me?"

Change regretted that he had to force himself upon the Teens. He liked it much more when people accepted him, worked with him, benefited from him. But so few people did. Why did so many people fight Change, hate Change? Their lives would be so much easier if they would not resist him so stubbornly. "Perhaps it is an innate part of the human soul to hate me," Change thought to himself, for the trillionth time, as he watched the Teens pitifully beg for mercy.

Each of the Teens whimpered that, yes, they would accept Change. Change made them swear an oath of loyalty to him. He had done his job. He had forced the Teens to accept him. "Now go back to your homes," Change commanded. "And do not forget the promise you have sworn to me, for I shall return."

With that command, the Teens scampered out of the corral like coyotes with their tails between their legs. Change walked over to a pile of hay and lay down, tired from his busy afternoon. "I'd better get some rest," he sighed as he looked at his schedule for the next day. "Tomorrow it's the Moral Majority."

Erik Landahl

Teens and Change

Conflicts

People resent change in others and in society because they are afraid of failure. People are basically insecure about the future because they have no control over it. . . .

People are secure as long as they know that they do not stand out in the crowd or when they are not vulnerable to criticism. The initiation of change always brings criticism, which most people tend to avoid.

Michelle Dall, 16
Dubuque, Iowa

The purpose of a new generation is new ideas and attitudes. No matter what the situation is, the new generation will have a different viewpoint. For example, our parents cannot accept the fact that high school kids drink because our parents didn't when they were young. But society has changed since then, and kids' drinking, unfortunately, has become accepted by people.

And when we have kids, what if drinking is acceptable social life for sixth graders? Of course, we couldn't accept it. The times are constantly changing, and we have no control of them. Because society changes so much within every generation, there will always be a generation gap.

Katy Turner, 16
Grosse Pointe, Michigan

Everyone always seems to oppose negative things, yet they seem defensive whenever someone tries to change things. Probably it's because people are content with what is going on the present system and are uncomfortable about changing anything, regardless of its worth or value.

Martin Luther King Jr., Gandhi, and Anwar Sadat found that out the hard way. . . .

Particularly whenever youth try to change things, adults become defensive. When I tried to get people to respect our youth group at church by sponsoring service projects, the

congregation frowned on us doing so and told us to go back where we belonged. They just distrust teens and want to keep us in our place.

Jeff Field, 16
Kansas City, Missouri

I had a close friend who got hooked on drugs. When you talked to her, she began to never hear what you had to say anymore, and changing her was probably the most difficult thing I ever attempted. I say attempted because I never was able to help her, no matter how hard I tried.

16-year-old female
Virginia

I have found it very difficult to implement change because of the obstructions set up by the adults in charge. In one . . . instance I tried to coordinate a demonstration concerning the proliferation of nuclear arms. . . .

A group of my friends and I wanted our school, which is a small, private institution, to be . . . involved. . . . The group who coordinated and conceived this event was called in to the office and verbally accosted, the threats beginning with demerits and ending with expulsion.

I can understand the administration's fear of involvement and complacency, but with the issues that we have today—nuclear genocide, apartheid, homelessness, poverty, hunger, suicide, cocaine . . . it is absolutely . . . life-threatening if we . . . let the adults . . . say, "That's the way it goes. Some things will never change." It is up to us, this new generation, to make the difference and to act like our parents did in the '60s.

Esther Cain, 16
Eiberon, New Jersey

Not many changes occur in the everyday life of a teenager. . . . When things are changed, a sense of security is lost. Changes are considered unsafe.

Pam Pauley, 16
Bluefield, West Virginia

I think the reason people resent changes in others is that they themselves wanted to change in that way but either didn't have the will to do it or failed while trying. . . .

People resent change in society . . . they don't want their lives to become more complicated or even simpler. . . .

People resent changes suggested by

other people like, "Boy you could lose some weight," . . . because they . . . don't want to have to evaluate their lives because they might find something that they aren't satisfied with and that would mean a change.

Terri Chapman, 15
Dubuque, Iowa

People resent changes in others because it usually forces people who do not want to change to change. . . . My step-mother has changed the relationship we have.

She used to take me places and go to my concerts and functions at school. Often she would be the only one—my father couldn't show up because he worked; my mother couldn't because sometimes she couldn't find the time. But my step-mother would try to make it even when she worked.

My stepmother got fed up and decided to withdraw or change her attitude towards me. This forced me to change, and that's why I resent her.

15-year-old male
Illinois

Studying . . . habits are the most seemingly impossible things to change about myself.

For instance, I usually start my school year off by promising myself that this will be the year I'll study every night and get my homework done before I do anything else. Oh sure, it lasts for about two weeks and then—bam—I've got the homework blahs. . . .

One of these days, I'm sure I'll change. After all, I've got all the time in the world. Besides, I don't feel too bad this way.

Janet McGinness, 14
Independence, Missouri

Teenagers are apt to reject and resent change because of the fear of the unknown. . . .

I moved when I was 16 years old. Like almost every teenager, initially I resented the change. . . . If the present environment is changing, . . . security is threatened. . . .

Kristin Swisten LTHS

224

When change is suggested by a friend or a parent, resentment is common. Suggestions of change are interpreted as an insult of the present procedure. If my mother suggests that I curl my hair different or that I wear something else, I assume that she disapproves of the way I look. Nobody enjoys rejection. . . .

Michelle Youtz, 18
Casper, Wyoming

I think the days have passed in which I and other students can bring about change in our school. I have heard stories in which students succeeded in changing unfair school policies or practices by organized protest. But something in our society has been lost, and I don't think my peers are capable of the things that students five or ten years ago were.

Laura Sayre, 15
Iowa City, Iowa

When a person changes, he places a weight on the people around him. The others must accept his violation of the norm. This change in people makes others nervous.

Punk rock is a change in society. Many people are finding they cannot accept this way of life. They are afraid of the change suggested by other non-conformists only because they are afraid to take a chance. Change is necessary, or life becomes monotonous. . . .

Lisa Leffer, 18
Mt. Prospect, Illinois

People resent change in others because sometimes they feel left out . . . because . . . they cannot keep up with it. People resent changes suggested by other people . . . to protect their pride.

Jeff Timmerman, 15
Dubuque, Iowa

When I was in eighth grade, I met a girl, and we became best friends for two years until she moved to Texas. I

miss her, but I can tell she is changing. Or maybe I am changing. I guess we both are. The secrets we shared will never be again. I have grown away from her and from how it used to be. I know it will never be that way again.

That seems to be why people resent change in others. They sense the possibility of change in themselves.

Kristin Zuerlein, 16
Casper, Wyoming

I'm one of those people who resent change in others. I don't really fully understand why I do. . . .

I, for example, had many friends that I was really close to and that I would talk to. . . . I can't recall when I started to lose contact with them, but it seemed like all of a sudden, they all went their separate ways. . . .

Sometimes, I'd lay awake at night staring at the ceiling reminiscing about the awesome times my friends and I shared. There would be a lump in my throat and tears forming in my eyes when I asked myself what I'm doing home on a Saturday night and why the phone has not rung in the last five hours.

When I do get together with most of them in some party, I don't know what the topic of conversation is. I often feel lost and like an outsider.

Life gets so complicated when someone changes because . . . you have to change with them.

17-year-old female
Illinois

When we started out we thought it would be easy, but we soon found out that changing our school team name, Brownies, would be quite difficult. We formed different committees which drew up petitions to circulate throughout the school and town.

After we accumulated a substantial amount of names, another committee was formed . . . to meet with the school. When the school heard our proposal, they said they would get back to us. It has now been two

months since the last meeting, and we haven't heard anything as of yet.

Keith Juzba, 16
Feeding Hills, Massachusetts

Discussion

Adolescence

Plano, Texas
Plano High School

Johnny: We have matured a lot more. We've started to realize our interests and what we want to do in life.

Jim: From junior high to my sophomore year, I saw a bit of change. I was a little more mature. I was a little more concerned about my world around me. When I moved here before my junior year, it was a bigger change because I saw a totally different part of the country and a totally different viewpoint. I took the two, and I made my own decison about what I think is right and what I want to do.

Cherrie: The best part of going from junior high to high school is responsibility. The more you act like you're responsible, the more people treat you like you're responsible. You learn what to do and what not to do and what they want from you. It helps a lot to be given more freedom.

Jim: Maturity is kind of indescribable, but it's a lot of pressure. The only way to deal with it is to keep going.

Johnny: You can't put your head down and feel sorry for yourself. Sure you get bogged down, get a lot of stress, but you've got to keep going. You've got people whom you can talk to and who are going to listen to you. You've got friends there to encourage you.

Holly: You kind of cushion

yourself from change by staying around friends. You need to reach out. When you come from junior high, everybody has a little group of friends. When you come here, it's a lot bigger and you have to spread yourself out.

Cherrie: People also cushion themselves by not getting involved. They say, "I like what I'm doing. I won't try anything else."

Johnny: You always have to experience change. You have to be flexible.

Jim: If you're not, you've stagnated.

Johnny: I always have to change even if it's only rearranging my room.

flow with change. It's easy to facilitate change. If people want it, they can make it.

Jim: Negative changes make people feel isolated. There's a big thing with suicide. Some people don't like the fact that they feel left out. We had a suicide recently, and it affected the whole school. Everyone was depressed and upset.

Johnny: Some people get involved in things, and they change. I've had friends who get involved with a new group. Then they find out they have a different interest so they start to go to another group. When we got to high school, my best friend in junior high wanted to be more punk so he started to hang around a punk group and

think about it all the time. You've just got to cope with it.

Generations

Atlanta
City Hall
What were the '60s like?

John Lewis *U.S. Congressman, former City Councilman, former leader of the Student Non-violent Coordinating Committee:* The late '50s and '60s were a period of a great deal of action. Millions of Americans were mobilized over the question of civil rights. During my leadership of the Student Non-violent Coordinating Committee, there were student groups around the world that would send contributions. They would send telegrams to the federal government that would say, "We support these young people."

The moral forces were on the side of the movement—the national political leadership, a large segment of the academic community, and the religious community. It took the non-violent movement and the raw, daring courage of young people, primarily students, to educate the larger community. We mobilized the American community and created a consensus.

By 1965 a majority of the people were saying, "Segregation is wrong. All people should have the right to eat in a restaurant. All people should have the right to vote." It took the courage of the people in the movement to bring out the dirt and filth from under the American rug and to deal with it.

Great movements come in cycles. We went through a very trying, turbulent period in the 1960s. Toward the end of the movement, we witnessed the assassination of the moral leaders of the country. Some of that hope died with

Environment

Johnny: I've lived here for eight years, and Plano has grown by about 60,000 people. Now there are many grocery stores, shopping centers, and malls. When I moved here, there was one small movie theater.

Cherrie: The attitude here is new and moving. You're encouraged to

ignored me. That hurt me. We're still friends, but. . . .

Jim: People are going to break off. You're not going to have only one group of friends forever. We'll deal with upcoming changes, like college, the same way we dealt with the other changes. Take it bit by bit, piece by piece.

Johnny: It's going to be weird. I

A GURU HELPS CLEAR UP A SOUL-SEARCHER'S SENSE OF DIRECTIONLESSNESS.

Martin Luther King, with Bobby Kennedy, and on the streets of Chicago.

It's a question of whether we want to have hope again. Of whether we want to go through a period of great change. We've been holding back. We've become a society that is very selfish. We've lost that sense of caring, that sense of sharing, and that sense of compassion. We've become a very inward people.

We went through a very difficult time. Everybody went on to do their own thing. We became "the Me generation." Young people wanted to get away from it all. But now you see some of that focus being restored around the question of South Africa and the question of nuclear freeze.

We are on the verge of another great struggle. It will deal not just with civil rights, but with the whole question of human rights,

peace, and the survival of humankind. We will not be concerned only about what happens to blacks or other minorities in America but also about all of the people who have been left out and left behind.

How are high school students getting involved?

Lewis: Some individuals have been involved in the demonstrations against South Africa. In the South. we have NAACP high school chapters. Young people can influence their parents, their teachers, their administrators, and the larger community the same way young students did in the '60s. Young people can appeal to the conscience of the older community.

The activism of youth is an untapped reservoir. Someone needs to transfer that energy, that

concern; and that organization into some of the big issues.

Young people will become involved. Humankind has been threatened. Young people sense that. Teenagers today are much more informed than a few years ago. The need is to find a way to vent their sense of discontent. We are going through a transitional period. The sons and daughters of my generation will be out in the forefront. I don't think there is going to be a particular issue. But there comes a time when a force is able to say, "Now is the time." You can't plan that. We are on the verge of something.

Cleveland
West Tech High School

Dora: I think environment has a lot to do with changes. When my dad was growing up, he had to drop out of junior high to support his family. Now you can't get a job that would support a family without a high school education.

Gloria: Back then, you would never see someone coming to school high or drunk. It was there, but it wasn't as common as it is today.

Dora: If they went to school and did something wrong, they knew they would get a whipping. They knew when they got home that

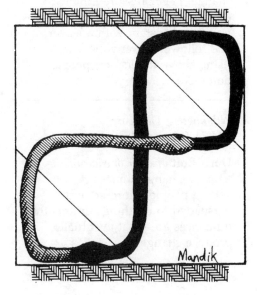

they'd get a whipping from their parents.

Lee: It was a lot stricter then. Today if you cut class or get caught smoking in the bathroom, they just tell you to put it out or give you a warning.

Kelvin: The teenagers now are maturing a lot faster then they used to. There used to be 16 or 17-year-olds who were just learning about the world. Nowadays, most 16 or 17-year-olds know more about the world than before.

Glen Ellyn, Illinois
Glenbard South High School

Richard Peck *author of young adult books:* Teenagers seem to want every day to be same—all the parties, all the music, all the clothes. They don't want anything new. They go to the library and say, "I like this book. Give me another one just like it." They want one more Harlequin romance just like the last.

Repeating yourself is easier than innovating and is less scary. I wish that there were more times in teenagers' lives when change was forced upon them. Today teenagers grow up only when they decide to. In my novels, it is always about people who decide to change, or have to decide to change. Peer pressure inhibits change because it is a tribal traditional system with a leader and followers. If anyone starts rising above the leader, people don't like it.

Wilmington, Delaware
YMCA Resource Center

Doris Bolt *director of educational services:* Change comes about by getting people informed and persuaded to do things differently. Influences are what eventually produce change in society's

attitude toward the use of alcohol. The hope is that all of these efforts put together will make it unacceptable for young people in our society to drink.

It's inevitable that people who get involved into thinking about national and state issues during their high school years are better equipped as adults to make social changes.

Pam Wright *senior prevention specialist:* Teens have the heartbeat of change. Change will take place when adults learn from kids.

Duncanville, Texas
Duncanville High School

Steve: Sometimes it seems like we can't influence change, but through our newspaper, we learned that we can. We helped the state pass a bond issue for a new stadium. We've done several things through the community, and we've had results. Students think, "We're not important." They underestimate their own power. The people will listen. The city government will listen. They may not do anything, but they do listen. They respect your opinions more than students feel they do.

Orlando Santiago *program director:* A way to create positive change is to allow people real responsiblity for their lives—really respecting or loving someone. We should focus on the positive things that someone does. It is unfortunate that we don't work like that as a society.

Most of the attention we get is the result of the negative. We don't get as much recognition for a lot of the positive things. No one walks up to you and says, "It's nice that you polished your shoes today." Or, "It's nice that you have a clean shirt on." We need to reinforce positive messages to inspire people to change instead of jumping on negative aspects.

Tucson, Arizona
Office of Tucson Tomorrow

Betsy Bolding *executive director:* It's human nature for people to be against change. Change is difficult. If someone tells you to cross your arms a way that you haven't been crossing your arms, you'll say, "I can't do that. It's uncomfortable." In the old days changes occurred so slowly that people had a chance to adapt, but now changes happen so fast that it's difficult to keep up. People are scared because they think that they are not a part of what is happening.

Change is inevitable. Growth is inevitable. Whether it's an evil or a good change depends on how you approach it and the way you sell it. You have to convince people that it will be in their best interest.

People don't change their minds because someone has told them to. They do so because they've figured out change is in their best interest. It took me lots of time of going to meetings with other parents of teenage alcoholics before I realized that I could not tell my daughter, "This is a bad thing. You're hurting yourself." Her decision to turn her life around would come only when she figured out that she was hurting herself.

Lombard, Illinois
Glenbard East High School

Dave: The older you get, the more you resist change. You get set in your ways.

Pat Meyer *teacher:* I'm not sure you resist change. You see that the world is a lot more complicated than you did when you were younger. I used to think there were very easy yes-no, right-wrong solutions to problems. The older I get, the more difficulty I see. It's not easy to change things overnight. Once you realize that, you grow out of the impatience of youth.

Dave: The knowledge that something needs changing comes from the ability to criticize what's there. I don't know when that develops.

Meaghan: Some changes are easier. At younger ages people are more likely to accept the peer pressure to try drugs and alcohol, but now you have your own set of beliefs. Fighting the administration was out of my reach when I was in junior high. Now I know what's

Eric Cederholm LTHS

going on so I can say to them, "This is what I want."

Personal change is usually gradual. I don't think one can sit down and consciously say, "Monday I'm going to change."

Dave: It comes down to self-image. From the time you start as a freshman to the time you leave as a senior, your self-image is different. Change occurs, but I don't think you sit down and consciously say, "When I'm a senior, I'm going to be this." If you don't change from the time you're a freshman to the time you graduate, you're in serious trouble.

Are there parts of yourself that you can't change?

Dave: You have to learn to like yourself, and part of liking yourself is accepting yourself with your limitations. The only person who doesn't change is the person who is totally satisfied, and there isn't such a person.

Doug: I don't think there is such a thing as negative change. There's negative change from the point of view of someone who judges that change, but I can't see somebody changing and embracing a point of view that is not positive. For somebody who would pick up smoking, smoking might be

positive even though we would look at that and say how dumb it is.

Gerri Long *parent:* I resist change. I don't like the idea of doing things differently. I don't like the idea of my child going to a different neighborhood school. I wouldn't like my husband to come home and say, "Come on. We're moving to the East Coast," because I'd have to find a new store. I'd have to find a new doctor.

Dave: There are different types of changes. With slow, subtle change, you don't even know it is occurring until you look back and say, "My God, the elephant has grown. It's gotten big." We're seniors, and we're in control. Next September, we'll be a freshman again. But we'll be different than when we came to high school, and we'll be different people four years later when we get out of college. We don't sit consciously and say, "I can see the difference. I can see this maturity."

Compiled by Gina Nolan

Solutions

I believe that for . . . teenagers especially, it is very hard for anyone to make a positive change. Most teenagers believe that partying, smoking, drinking, and sex are the only things to do to belong in the crowd. . . . Most teenagers are afraid to be different and be themselves because they fear being disliked.

Teenagers are too worried about being like everyone else. . . . That is why it is so hard for someone to make a positive change. If they were to stop smoking, they fear that their friends would no longer like them. . . .

Don't be afraid to stick up for what you believe in.

Jean Purdy, 17
Hillsdale, Michigan

In the last nine years, I have gone to seven different schools and lived in seventeen different houses. Many times when we moved, I got so negative about leaving that . . . things got worse.

Over the last few years, though, I've been trying to be more positive in my thinking. I found that when I was thinking positively, the changes I made were easier and better.

Fred Budd, 13
Independence, Missouri

Since the death of my father, a little over a month ago, changing seems to be a way of life. When something is taken away from you that has been such a constant in your life, everything is altered.

You go through a period where you feel that even the slightest change would take your loved one even farther away from you. You think that staying the same is a way to ensure that that person will never disappear, or be forgotten. Then you realize that you're only pretending. Staying the same will never bring them back, but, through changes, you will learn to cherish your memories to the utmost.

One of my friends lost a close friend over two years ago. Since then, she seems to seek out his personality in people, his traits, his fears. Though she thinks this is keeping him alive in her, it's only hurting both her and the person she is making out to be something they are not. . . .

A 17-year-old boy in my school lost his father five years ago. For two years he wouldn't even let his family talk about his father. He not only needed to change, but he also needed to grow. He is trying to do both now. Instead of cooping up his feelings, he is reliving memories and feelings that would have been lost without his changing.

Chrissy Levinson, 14
Los Angeles, California

Before I joined the church I now belong to, most of the people around me were mean, rude, and, in short, rather rowdy people. My church taught a message about missionary work. In the lesson, the teacher said that your good example is better or just as good as your active missionary work.

After the class, I started watching my classmates and friends. They changed. They started being nice, at least to me.

16-year-old male
Kansas

Being a sophomore this year and seeing my best friend, a senior, play his last baseball game and graduate, I have encouraged several changes in myself. By seeing him play throughout the year and his emotion after the game, I realize that I should give 100 percent all the time . . . so that after my last game I can walk away without any regrets because I will know that I gave my all.

David Wilson, 15
Bluefield, West Virginia

If you want something changed, you must lead an organized campaign or you will never reach your goal. Recently at my high school I was involved in organizing and starting a "peer counseling" program. . . .

We wrote letters to our superintendent, the chairperson of our school board, and thirteen other administrators, counselors, and teachers. A brief description was written; research was done on other schools in our area that have a similar program; and a very detailed survey was conducted that involved most of the student body. . . . An overwhelming 96% of the students surveyed said they would use such a program if it existed.

Three members of our committee were chosen to give a presentation to the superintendent of our school district. . . . After giving the presentation, the superintendent told us that he approved . . . and wants to help us. . . . So next school year . . . we will have a peer counseling program at our high school!

Joanna Zimmerman, 17
Gig Harbor, Washington

I have encouraged change by not succumbing to peer pressure. If I want to do something, say to go to a class or program that no one else wants to go to, I will attend it with or without them. I'm growing up, and I must start making my own decisions. I must move forward and not let my friends hold me back.

Stacey McFarlane, 15
Parkdale, Oregon

People resent changes in others. . . . My friend Jim is a handsome, athletic, but very shy person. When I knew him freshman year, he was always very quiet, not a party-goer, and wouldn't even try to talk to a girl.

But now . . . he has changed drastically. He has more friends, does a good share of party going, and is not girl-shy whatsoever. People resented

Jim's change because he wasn't the stable, good-old Jim we all knew.

I really didn't get angry. I was happy because he was happier.

16-year-old male
Illinois

When I passed from junior high school to senior high school, I noticed a new attitude and a new self-image of myself. The change took place over the summer after one of my closest friends was killed in an automobile accident.

Before then, I pictured myself as just another guy who acted cool, went to all the parties, and never really participated in things unless my friends did. But towards the end of the summer I picked up a new hobby . . . basketball. . . .

I now feel the need to be athletic and competitive. This change was encouraged by both my friends and myself.

Buddy A. Taxley, 16
Bluefield, West Virginia

I once had a friend who had a drinking problem. There were five people beside me telling him to stop drinking. He never really paid attention to us. Meanwhile, he kept on drinking beer.

One day he realized he was wrong. He came to us and told us he needed help. Then he enrolled in a group called Alcoholics Anonymous.

Lon Bachelle, 17
Union Beach, New Jersey

I try to encourage change in school by talking to students who are put down by the other students. I hate how people are prejudiced for no reason. I want to see real equal rights for minorities. If we keep trying, we can dilute prejudice.

I try to encourage younger kids to accept change and to make it happen. If you don't like something, why leave it the same and say, "Oh, well?" I get really mad at my friends for not accepting someone for the way they

dress or whatever. I know how much your feelings get hurt.

Kerry Murphy, 17
Sandpoint, Idaho

By choosing to abstain from alcohol and drugs, my friends are trying to adopt my idea . . . to have fun without being stoned. My example may keep my friends alive. . . . After all, as the song says, "It's hip to be square."

Tiffany Bost, 15
Bluefield, West Virginia

I have seen a great change in myself from frosh year to sophomore year. My attitude has changed towards my school work because now I see how important it is to me to get a good education so I leave high school and go on with a good life. Before I would just say, "Oh well, I just won't do it." But now I do my school work before anything else.

Carl Ashton, 16
Red Bank, New Jersey

I work on a school newspaper voicing the students' opinions. We discuss controversial ideas and what should be done about them. We also encourage various ideas about changes in our school. The newspaper points out things we feel are wrong. We bring these things to the attention of the students, who then sometimes participate in making a change.

Trianda Keramidas, 16
Los Angeles, California

I believe the most important change is in yourself. . . . If you feel good about yourself, you don't have to worry about what others think of you or try to prove you're better than anyone.

James Butler, 16
Union Beach, New Jersey

I have tried to encourage change in myself and others. First, I have developed a sense of myself and was brutally honest about my flaws. After I was convinced I was on my way to changing for the better, I joined an organization called Mental Health Players. . . .

We . . . perform for people of all ages, role playing improvisations about controversial topics. Most of the time the actors play horrible people with exaggerated flaws. People in the audience, when allowed to talk to these characters, yell and scream about how wrong we are.

In a broader sense, even if they don't realize it, they are criticizing themselves and things they do. I noticed . . . one day a girl who had all the right answers and arguments . . . about not discriminating. After it was over, I saw the same girl totally ignore a small boy trying to be friendly to her. She had snubbed him in the same way she had told us not to do.

I can't change people, but what I do is to try to start them looking at themselves and changing themselves for the better.

Lynn Wilkens, 16
Little Silver, New Jersey

ANTON DAVIS LTHS

11·3·86   G.E.H.S.   Mariann O'Malley

Chapter 13.

Teens and Dreams

Camelot. A place where What Should Be joined with What Could Be to become What Would Be. A place where dream became reality, where the freedom to dream the dream, to live the dream, to defend the dream, and to become the dream flourished. A place where dreaming was synonymous with living.

With a dream, King Arthur and Merlin carved a kingdom of light from a land of dark. Knights, nobles, and peasants feasted on dreams of the impossible: Righted Wrongs. Peace on Earth, the unity of all humankind. They expected it to occur, and it almost did. They reached for their Holy Grail and, through this pursuit, achieved greatness.

Now, however, we delude ourselves and say, "Camelot is gone. The Grail is lost. We must be pragmatic." We worship the mechanical god of Practicality.

In schools, our high priests, Science and Math, offer the arts as a sacrifice on the altar of expediency. Together with them, we pray to the god of Practicality to provide a four-year plan that will assure economic success. We discover that the sacrifice of the humanities reveals the miracle of an educational system that prepares us for a job without wasting time on the heresy of art.

We are believers in a modern religion that offers us a new heaven on earth. In service to our god, we choose our occupations for their monetary rewards. Before each career move, we invoke the name of Practicality to guide us.

Job satisfaction is an unexpected bonus rather than a goal. "How does it pay?" serves as the measure of work. "How enjoyable is your job?" dies on the bloody altar. The saint of quality is replaced by the icon of quantity. Short-term profits serve as the incense that pleases our god. Long-term benefits are excommunicated from our fellowship. Our offices resound with the hymn of immediate job advancement.

We join the ranks of the evangelists and proclaim the gospel of pragmatism on every street corner, at every store, and in every home. We indoctrinate our children with the epistles of practicality. "You have to be practical when you plan your life. You are a talented musician, but how much does it pay?" Our curses begin with, "You're a dreamer."

Practicality raises a Grand Inquisitor, The Fear of Failure, to conduct an inquisition. Its goal: to annihilate the last vestiges of Camelot on Earth. Camelot's citizens are burned on the stakes of public ridicule. Dreamers experience the torture on the rack of fickle public support.

The rest of society recants and worships in the Temple of Practicality. As the plate is passed along the pews, we offer the aspirations of a previous generation. Civil rights, social work, and humanitarian aid are left at the temple. We receive the blessings of materialism.

Our Kyrie eleison soars, "Lord of pragmatism, have mercy on our lives. Let not false hopes cloud our eyes. Prevent fickle aspirations from deceiving our minds. Have mercy, oh Practicality." Through our Te Deum, praise ascends to society's god. "We praise thee, oh practicality. Our hearts fill with thankfulness for the complacency to enjoy our world." Our doxology: "Praise our god who will bless me soon. I don't have time to right the wrongs of the world. But when I become successful, I will donate money to the needy."

The 1960s offered Camelot an opportunity to raise its banners. Like a flaming match, Camelot lit the world. Dreams became acceptable. The cult of the practical stumbled. But like a match, the ephemeral light of Camelot burned out.

To rekindle the flame, we must now embark on a quest for a holy relic that will exorcise the god of Practicality from the universe. A Holy Grail of Dreams. We must build a new Round Table and charter a league of brave knights who will pledge themselves to the pursuit of dreams.

We need to mount our steeds and charge into the world so we may wield our hopes. Dare to be champions for world peace. Joust against the villains of racial and sexual inequality. Confront ignorance and intolerance. Swear fealty to political and social progress. Summon heralds to announce our intention of creating a better world.

However, we have to learn to dream the personal dream. If we cannot dream for ourselves, we can never dream for others. Therefore, we must dare to dream that our families can openly and honestly communicate. Believe that we can attend a certain college or land a particular job. Attempt to pierce the veil of appearance and to discover the realities. Have faith that we will succeed as long as we are true to our vision of ourselves.

But where will we find the knights to join the quest? Will there be a Galahad to lead us? Will some die during the search? Despite the cost, we can restore the Realm of Camelot if we accept dreaming's risk: Failure. We may never see world peace, constructive communication in the family, or lasting happiness. But we must dream these seemingly impossible dreams because no other dreams are worth dreaming. And we must strive to turn these dreams into reality because idle dreams are useless. But even if we fail, our attempts are no less noble or great.

One could consider the Camelot of legend a failure. The kingdom did fall. People were killed. But take heart, Camelot did not fall because it dreamed. Camelot fell because its people lost the dream.

The original Camelot may have been in England, but the love of that place lingers today. Camelot is an attitude that dreams can come true. That dreaming is not the province of the mad. That dreaming is the value of the living.

Greg Jao

life just isn't a bowl of cherries.

there's no limit to your ability. To create, to build, to dream.

If you can dream it, you can do it.

Let your talents unfold to their fullest.

BE ALL YOU CAN BE.

G.E.H.S.

National

I want a society where any man, regardless of class, can fulfill his dreams. Where a person from the ghetto and a person from Beverly Hills have the same chance to become a doctor, lawyer, writer, or anything he is inspired enough to work for.

I would like a society where blacks and whites are thought of as equals, which they are. Where Americans and Soviets can be the best of friends. . . . I want no discrimination of any kind.

Matt Rider, 14
Irving, Texas

I would like to see America at peace with all countries. I would also like to see America with more power over Russia. When there are terrorist attacks, America should do something about it instead of letting them get away with it.

Jim Krause, 15
Portage, Indiana

There is no perfect society, but we

Americans have the best society that man can have.

Doug Alberhasky, 16
Iowa City, Iowa

I hope that ten or twenty years from now America will learn to open its mind to new kinds of people, ideas, and values. When they do, I think that Americans will see what they have been missing.

Bonnie Payne, 15
Tucson, Arizona

I think fear is our society's worst problem. Everyone lives in fear, all the time. . . . A utopian society for me would not be one where no one works or where everyone is happy all of the time, but one where no one fears.

Theresa Tenpas, 17
Whitmore Lake, Michigan

America . . . has to be more socially aware. A Cambodian teenager came to school and talked about this country's responsibilities after a war. . . . The people around me cringed, and some

even cried as he told about his father and mother who died from the war. The next week, they couldn't remember his name. . . . People just don't know how to apply these stories to their own lives.

Barbara Molini, 17
Catawissa, Missouri

My dream of a perfect society would be one without murder and kidnappings. . . .

If criminals could sit through the funerals of the people that they heartlessly killed and see all of the sadness, maybe it would make them stop and think. . . . Or if they could see what the parents go through or feel the pain that the parents are feeling— wondering if their child is dead or alive.

Rhonda Griffin, 18
LeClaire, Iowa

Ten and twenty years from now I would like to see the people of our country open their eyes to the rest of the world and realize how suicidal our good ol' American pride and spirit can really be.

Michelle Smock, 15
Lexington, Kentucky

My dream for a perfect society would be for all people to love one another. . . . All people would enjoy being together and not need laws to keep them in line. . . .

Teenagers could be treated equally as adults. . . . People should be able to do what they feel they want when they feel it's right.

Shelly Mills, 17
Irving, Texas

I would like to see America back in the number one position in education. . . .

I would like to see other countries depend on us, and I would like to see our country self-sufficient. . . . America is a gold mine, and we have to use it.

Misha Hammond, 18
Joplin, Missouri

Teens and Dreams

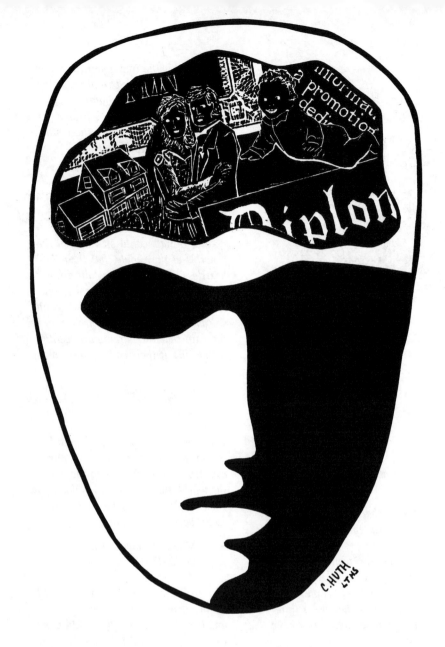

living room and find a mother and father with their children, sitting around communicating.

I'd like to see churches built where the X-rated movie houses are— and . . . families to spill onto the sidewalks in honor of our Creator.

I'd like to turn on the TV and see profound ideas and messages enacted through sensitive actors and actresses, not half-clad bodies rolling around in a bed.

I'd like to see America instilled with self-love and self-respect. I'd like to see America with a reason to be called the Land of the Free and Home of the Brave. I'd like to see us living the ultimate American dream.

Tondeleya Dumas, 16
Cleveland, Ohio

America, in ten years, should be stronger. Fewer homeless and jobless, more government aid to the elderly, to school systems, and to people on welfare. . . .

By then, maybe someone will realize that the way to help our country stay strong starts with caring for our people.

Sharon Malis, 15
Portage, Indiana

My dream for a perfect society begins when everyone has a job.

Amy Thornhill, 13
Red Oak, Texas

If the world would blow up, it would be better off than it is today.

Tommy Baldree, 17
Irving, Texas

A perfect society is one in which there are people who keep up with current issues and get off their lazy butts and vote because people get the kind of government they deserve.

17-year-old male
Iowa

A perfect society should be totally free of crime. . . .

Justice will be in the hands of common people, not authorities. It will be a crime to divorce once a couple has produced children.

Children will be taught all the essentials in life: learning how to cope with other children, saying "no" to drugs and alcohol. Calculus, physics, foreign languages will also be taught, making the school day a lengthy one for youths.

Chris Vecchio, 18
Scotch Plains, New Jersey

In twenty years, I'd like to be able to walk down American streets at midnight with the same ease I'd walk down the street at noon.

I'd like to walk into any American

Discussion

Los Angeles
University High School

What is your idea of the perfect self?

Josh: It's when there are no problems. My mind is at peace.

Abby: It's when your world and the real world coincide in a way that is harmonious.

Pat: It's when the consequences of

what you do aren't so important. It's when you are getting your needs met and everyone else's needs met. People only become perfect if they want to be perfect. You could become perfect, but you don't really want to.

Where would you like to see yourselves in ten years?

Josh: I'd like to be married with kids. I'd like to be an actor, well known, but not harassed. Not having to worry about where my next job is coming from. Enough money to say, "I can live through the day or week, and if something comes, it'll come." It's the peace, not having to worry. I want to be respected.

Chris: I'd like to be at least wealthy and powerful in politics. Unmarried. Without children. I'd like to have money. But I'd also like to be constantly on the edge. Never feeling always sure that I'm in the right place.

Pat: There's nothing I want to do more than say, "Fuck school. Fuck everything, except for what I'm dreaming of."

Josh: My dad has been a lawyer for the past 20 years, and he doesn't want to be. He never thought about being something else, and now he's unhappy. Now he's telling me he doesn't want me to be in show business because it is an unhappy business. And I will not listen to him until he quits law and tries something as a profession that he really wants to do. Adults are more scared to change because they have less time.

Abby: Also, they have you. Say your dad was into being a gardener. Maybe he would be happy, but as soon as you came into the world, he might have trouble feeding you and providing for you. And that would make him more unhappy.

Pat: I don't think your dream should be realistic. It should be above anything you can attain. I'd like to have a dream so high I could never achieve it. I'd like to have something above me that I want.

Abby: Half the fun of attaining a dream is the path along the way. It's the climb along the way. Rocky Horror said, "Be it, don't dream it."

What is your dream for the perfect society?

Pat: My dream of a perfect society is everybody in total conflict. If you stick a leg down, somebody's going to grab it to pull it down to pull themselves up.

Abby: It would be really hot if everyone was in a constant high. Everyone just spaced out all the time. Productive things would

happen, like good songs and poetry. Everyone is all stoked and flying around. Like a constant good trip.

Duncanville, Texas
Duncanville High School

Does everyone need a dream?

Naida: If you want to live.

Steve: There should always be some challenge. Most people want to achieve more, more, and more. More and more money. Have more and more friends. Bigger houses. Better car.

Too many people are willing to give up their dreams. They don't realize that dreams are going to take time. They're not willing to wait. The person who doesn't dream certainly would be boring.

Todd: America has become more competitive. It is harder to reach goals so a lot of people have dropped dreams. But if you don't have dreams, they can't ever come true.

What are your personal dreams?

Todd: College in Santa Barbara.

Naida: I want to be successful in whatever field. I don't necessarily want money, but I want people to know I am something.

Cheryl: I want to be successful. I want to know a lot of people and to see how they live.

Kim: I want to make my mom happy because she expects a lot. I just hope I can meet her needs.

Steve: Your family certainly influences what your dreams are. You want to do better than your parents. Do better than your older brother. You want to make your parents proud of you. The dream is always there.

What do you want ten years from now?

Steve: I will have a novel published. I will have someone to share my life with. I will have a job in some kind of journalism. I will have a Mercedes. I'm going to be happy.

Naida: I want some type of business in a high rise in Chicago and a subsidiary in Dallas. I want a warehouse apartment. I don't want anything in it.

Cheryl: I want to be independent and happy.

Todd: I will be sitting on a beach and will be very comfortable. A margarita in one hand and a pen in the other and be able to write. I will have the ocean in front of me and no one to bother me except a cute girl in the house. A speedboat parked and a plane. Maybe a Bell helicopter. Maybe an ultralight too.

Claire: Ten years from now, I will find someone and marry him. He is going to love me forever, and we're never going to get bored of each other. I want to have kids. I want to raise them. I don't even mind labor. I've got this little child, and I'm going to form its life. I want them to be little individuals.

Lombard, Illinois
Glenbard East High School

What would you like to be in ten years?

Dave: A professional fisherman with my own TV show.

Kris: I'd like to be happy with my life. Maybe with a couple of kids, maybe with a husband, maybe with my job. Not being frustrated, not getting a divorce, and not having a problem child.

Magnus Seng *parent:* I can't remember sitting down at 18 and saying, "What the hell do I want to do ten years from now?" My goal was to get to the next stage. I can't remember something that I always wanted. I've been undirected all these years. I just go from one thing to another. Ten years from now I want to open up a classical record store.

Xuong: At 28, I would hate to work the rest of my life. I want a lot of money so I wouldn't have to work. It could be lazy, but I dream that I wouldn't have to do something else.

Kris: Dreams are a form of escapism. I can sit there for 15 minutes and zone out and then zone back in.

Dave: I've sat in class, looked at a book, and zoned into my mind doing some kind of fishing show. I'm sitting there picturing every place I'd want to go. I'd like to have this boat and this kind of motor. It's not like a total fantasy that may never happen. It's just something you'd love to have happen. You can think about it, and after you're done, you're all relaxed and happy.

Julio: Goals come from dreams. You think about something, and that's your dream. Suddenly, you go out to do it. You're out to get what you were thinking about. For example, you dream about success in college so you start working towards that achievement.

Where would you like to see the world?

Seng: We all believe in Utopia, a world that is conflict-free, where everybody is happy. You can have a picture of something that does not seem within the realm of the achievable.

Kris: Clean. No prejudice.

Julio: I don't think there'd be any money. Whatever you want, it's yours. Keep on living. There's always something new to do. Something exciting. Nothing dangerous.

Dave: I'd get rid of the slums. I'd get people educated because without education people miss out a lot on life. Without people knowing what's wrong and

Teens and Dreams 241

realizing problems, they're not going to change.

People like to believe in a noble vision, but most people care about number one. Caring about people in Louisiana who are poor and the poor farmer is great, but I don't think too many people in America are going to go out and give their last paycheck to help a starving

the world, there is all this hatred between races. The world is great and lousy at the same time. You're never going to have total peace. You have to live within the problems. You're surrounded by the world, and you cannot really get out of it. Try to make it good for yourself and the people around you.

A dream is the furthermost point of a goal—the very most a goal could be.

What are your personal dreams?

Lee *Issaquah, Washington:* My dream sounds archaic and womanesque, but I want to have a successful career, a happy marriage, a house, and a dog.

Kelly *Port Orchard, Washington:* For me, it would be winning an Academy Award. My top dream is to be an actress. But acting is so hard to do. My second dream is to be an investigative broadcast journalist like Diane Sawyer. I see these women and how brave they are and how fascinating their lives look. You see that and that's what you look for. Sometimes you're sitting back and you see what other people are doing and you think, "Oh God, I would love to be there."

Matt: For me a dream would be winning the Masters Tournament in golf. I have a lot of fun playing golf, but I know someday I'll have to work to make a living and to have a family. But if I could make a living off golf, that would be perfect. It wouldn't be like work; it would be like fun.

Julie *Seattle:* I want to travel and see cultures and people who live and think differently than I do. I want to try and understand them. I got a taste of travel overseas, and it inspired me. Seeing how other people think and live can enlighten you about other things. Goals come from your strong points. You are good at some things so you have a desire in that direction.

Nathan: My dream is to find a career that would involve three of my major talents: photography, astronomy, and business, and along the way make several million. A lot of my dreams came from individual friendships. Somebody got me involved in something, and I said, "Wow, I

J.H. CHOU

farm family. If it means eating chuck roast instead of filet mignon, they'll definitely go for the filet mignon. It'd be great to help other people in the country, but you're not going to be achieving much if you don't help yourself first.

I don't think people think about the abstract. I don't think about world peace. Look at the United States. Freedom and all, but we persecute our own people. In the so-called greatest free country in

Olympia, Washington
The Evergreen State College
Summer Journalism Workshop

What is the difference between goals and dreams?

Nathan *Aberdeen, Washington:* A goal is something that you expect. If you work hard enough, you know you will get it. Your goal is a stepping stone to your dream. Each goal that you achieve gets you closer to that dream.

Matt *Battle Ground, Washington:*

really like that." Like astronomy. A friend took me out with his telescope, and we were looking at the stars. I thought, "This is really neat." I developed a talent for just knowing where the constellations are. Business, that was something innate. I knew how to start a business and work my way up. Dreams come from people you know and experiences you have.

Is it important to have a dream?

Julie: It is. Life would be boring; I couldn't function without my dream because dreams give you hope, an idealistic thing to strive for.

Lee: Without dreams, life would be meaningless. Also, if it is a realistic dream, and you can see it, and you are getting closer, you will work a lot harder. It's like a yearbook. In the beginning of the year, you're like, "Oh God. What am I going to do?" Then at the end of the year, you get so excited and know all the work was worth it.

A very idealistic dream gives you something to work towards. You always keep working towards it even though you are going forward three steps and getting hauled back two. You're still working for it. You are always making short little gains toward your dream.

Julie: The higher the dream, the higher you'll be able to reach. If you only set a goal so high, then you only get so high. If you set it even higher, you'll reach that much higher.

Matt: You have a dream. You try so much harder. It's not "I can" or "I might be able to," but "I will be able to do this."

What are the dangers of dreams?

Kelly: If you bank everything on your dream—"If I don't get this, my life will come to a crashing halt"—there is a chance, that it will not happen.

Julie: I had a dream that I would get a straight four point all through high school. It was unrealistic. When I got a B, I went, "This isn't supposed to happen. It's not in my dream." If you put too much on your dream, it can be too much stress.

Kelly: I know a girl like that. She got a B and was almost suicidal. She was crawling up the walls and talking to her counselors.

Lee: Sometimes people get obsessed with their dreams. They've got tunnel vision, and they're just looking at that one thing.

What happens if a person doesn't have a dream?

Nathan: They are dead. They would be too boring to live.

Matt: I would assume everyone has at least one dream. If they

don't, they aren't really alive.

Kelly: They have absolutely no ambition or drive. You can't relate to them. You're talking about the school you want to go to and about the things you want to do with your life. They say, "Well, I don't care."

What is your dream for the U.S.?

Kelly: I would love to be optimistic, to say, "Yeah, we could feed the world and have nuclear disarmament," but I don't think it's going to happen. It makes me feel helpless. What am I going to do? I'm one small voice.

We need more mature leaders. They're like little children. "You won't take away your missiles so we're not going to take away ours. And we're going to add ten more, so what are you going to do about that?" What are you people doing?

Teens and Dreams

You aren't talking about missiles. You're talking about people.

Julie: I'd like America to be a friendly nation because we're not friendly. When you hear some things in history that our country has done, it's sad. Even if you go up to someone in the streets in another nation, the response is, "Oh America. You did this. And you did that."

What's your responsibility to fulfill your dreams?

Lee: Speak out. Journalism is the best place to speak out. You can just about say whatever you want. That's what I love about writing. You can just lay it all out and speak your piece. Don't sit back and say, "Oh well, somebody will do it." Nobody ends up doing it when everybody thinks somebody else is going to do it.

Kelly: You should never be afraid. Even if you realize all of the western world is against you. You should always speak out because you never know if there are three or four people whose minds you will change. That'll make it worth it.

Matt: Never give up on a dream. You never know—the next day you might win the lottery. When your dreams die, you might as well die, too.

Washington, D.C.
Children's Defense Fund
headquarters

Where would you like to see the government in ten years?

Carol Holland *Staff member of the Education Division:* The government should take care of home. Taking care of home means improving social programs, education, child care, and child welfare. Getting the family structure back to a level like "Father Knows Best" but not as stiff.

Amy Tyler-Wilkins *Staff member in the Child Care and Family Support Services Division:* The government needs to stop protecting rich people and rich businesses. We need to begin to care about everybody. If you are rich, you got it. If you are poor, you don't. It should be each according to his ability and each according to his need, rather than based on status.

Holland: We will be getting back on an even keel if we get somebody in who is not like Reagan. If you have somebody in the vein of Reagan, then there will be no social programs, and we will probably be in a military state. Reagan doesn't think there are social problems out there. "Yeah, a few people can't afford to pay their rent, and the kids are being born out of wedlock. That doesn't matter." If we have somebody who's totally opposite of Reagan, then there will be more social programs.

Tyler-Wilkins: Americans don't want to look at their social realities. There were years of prosperity. Then we got our asses kicked around the block in Vietnam. Americans are scared of not being the baddest kids on the block. Part of the American image is being a world power. Americans can swallow this military waste because they don't like not being number 1.

What would the perfect educational system be?

Holland: Everything should be geared towards the student making it. Teachers should be there for the student. The curriculum should be designed individually so that the student can learn. Students should understand what they are doing and why they are doing it. There's got to be a lot of communication from the administration on down to the students so that the kids

participate in what goes on in their school.

You want to make sure they get the things they need. You also want to make sure it is cyclical— that they can give back to their state, district, or school in some way.

What would the perfect family be?

Tyler-Wilkins: I don't think that's for any of us to say. There are a number of family forms: the extended family, the nuclear family, and the single-parent family. We need to develop a national policy which is conducive to all of the family forms thriving. I don't think there is an ideal family.

How achievable are these hopes?

Tyler-Wilkins: I wouldn't come to work if I didn't believe in these hopes. I would slit my wrists. People's lives can be substantially better. I used to think that everybody could be happy. I certainly think that in our life there will be more people with more options. But it's never going to be great for everybody. You get closer.

People have a real responsibility to be involved in the process. Everybody has some part in making decisions about our society. It can be joining an organization, running for Congress, or making a donation to an organization that you think is good. Or voting. I get angry at people who don't do anything.

The role of government is to even things off. To redistribute income. The system of government is fine. Congress tries to act as though they are just a bunch of regular people, but most of them are wealthy. People have to have access, but too often they are shut out. Congress has to be made accountable to the public. That's our responsibility as

citizens—to hold them responsible.

What would you do to make society better?

Tyler-Wilkins: Give people more chances, which means giving them more money. Your options are limited by your economic means. Everybody would have the widest choice concerning how they are going to live their lives. We should have a government and an economy that affords every individual the most options. If you are poor, you have a very limited number of choices. If you are rich, you have a lot more choices.

Boston
English High School

Huston Crayton *social studies teacher:* There is a breakdown in society. That's why I'm going into the ministry. I'm leaving teaching. I can be more effective from the pulpit. I want to reach a larger audience. I want to stir up the thinking of people.

I like to get some dialogue going. When people stop talking, I have a problem. If I can at least talk to people about their attitude, and they can respond, then we are heading into some kind of direction that's out there. But when we become apathetic, then we are going down. Somebody has to stand up and say, "Look, this is a problem. We want you to be aware of it."

How can society encourage dialogue?

Crayton: Make an atmosphere that's conducive to talking. At school I make hot dogs. While we're eating, people like to talk. I make situations where we can get a little conversation going. I try to make it a relaxed environment.

There's a state of future shock. People say that we're going to wind up with everything being one big computer. No emotion, no nothing. Or people say that we're going to go back to very strong humanitarian interest. Everybody's going to be a part of the Moral Majority. Everybody's going to be concerned about social issues. Everybody's going to make sure everyone has his share, almost a utopian society. Or people say we're going to destroy ourselves in a nuclear confrontation.

I think the robot issue is out. It's either everybody becoming part of the Moral Majority and becoming concerned about feeding people, or we're going to blow ourselves up. I can see that in 30 years.

Wilmington, Delaware
State Chamber of Commerce office

Ruth Mankin *vice president:* I'm a great believer in self-fulfilling prophecy. You can make your dream come true. You set that goal, and you channel all your effort toward realization of that goal. You maximize every opportunity to make that dream come true. It's not only a dream of a profession but also of a home, a family, a community, a contribution to society.

We all fail. We all stumble. But if we don't learn from errors, we don't move ahead. Too many people say, "I goofed. I messed up again. I'll never be any good." That's a negative attitude. But if they say, "How can I learn not to make that mistake again?" they move on. You have to be a fighter. Will, strength, and courage can carry you a long way. You have to trust in yourself and other people.

The most direct way to make your voice heard is to be active and act on your belief on a political level. Work in your church. Work in your neighborhood organization. Everyone shares the responsibility

to make the community a better place to live.

Spring Hill, Tennessee
The Jenkins' home

What is your dream of a perfect society?

Peter Jenkins author of *A Walk Across America, The Walk West, The Road Unseen* and *Across China:* I've never really had a dream of a perfect society because I don't think one will ever exist. Our system is as close to perfect as humans can make. You have a democracy, and people have a say in their lives. You have the maximum kind of freedoms. We have so many freedoms that it's outrageous. I'm pretty sold on the United States of America.

I don't have this utopian dream of everybody sharing everything in common. I know it can't happen. It's not in human nature. I've lived in a commune in Tennessee. Everybody shared everything. Everybody supposedly did the same amount of work. Everybody shared the food. They shared the kids. I don't think they shared each other's wives though they would if they could. That type of society has been tried over and over again, and it's never worked because some human beings like to work and some don't. Some human beings want a lot; some don't. Some human beings are gifted with tremendous talent; some aren't. I don't believe that everybody's the same.

One of the things that is so important when you are young is to have a dream. I see nothing wrong with having the most idealistic possible dream. In life, you take your dream, drop back, and punt based on reality. But if you don't start out with a dream, then I don't think you can go as far. The people who have been the most successful are the people who have been dreamers, who have been able to take dreams and blend them with reality.

There are a lot of dreamers who can't face reality. They stay in a dream world all their lives. They escape through drugs and alcohol. If you can be a dreamer and be realistic, then that is the best of both worlds. It's easy to be a dreamer in the United States because most of us don't have to confront the reality of starving, freezing, going hungry, or having

Teens and Dreams

our children starving, freezing, and going hungry. Most of us never have to deal with the basics in life.

The idealism of youth is essential. It makes a lot of adults jealous and nervous because they forget what they used to be like. Maybe they didn't have the opportunity to dream as much as their children. There are a lot of parents who can't handle that. There are a lot of teachers who can't handle that. People should attempt to be idealistic. When you lose your ability to dream, you lose a lot. You become hard and cold, and all you think about is yourself. That becomes kind of a limited life.

Atlanta
Martin Luther King Jr. Center

How can dreams affect the present?

Reverend Leslie Carter *Co-ordinator of summer non-violent workshop:* We are carrying what we think is the logical extension of Dr. Martin Luther King Jr's works through social and institutional changes. The center has an induction program that looks at the implications of what Dr. King had to say and what he did to social issues today. We have a review for correctional officers about alternatives to using force. We have a variety of programs to teach young people basic literary skills, English, grammar, and math. We see all these things as connected and consistent to what Dr. King called his vision of a better world. Once communities relate and evolve to that point, we

LINDA RETZLAFF LTHS

will be able to attain justice, harmony, and positive peace.

The '60s showed what happens when people lose their vision—when there is a sense of despair. That is why the Center is doing what it can to say there is hope. It doesn't have to come about by revolutionary changes or by turning the government upside down. Success is going to come when people start getting involved in the issues rather than waiting for the government to solve them.

Why is there a lack of dreaming for the future?

Carter: When I was faced with the proposition of going to Vietnam to fight a war I thought was immoral, it wasn't hard to find a lot of other people to agree with me. We shared a lot of the outrage. Our constitutional government, a democracy, was going out to a Third World country and exploiting and killing these people.

We decided not to go. We decided not to hide. There had to be a connection between our thinking and our action. There was a lot of protesting in the '60s on college campuses, but it was ultimately translated to increased political participation. We read the Constitution, and we saw that our country is to pursue life, liberty, and happiness. We couldn't see it happening around us. We saw that there was something wrong with the way this older generation was interpreting our future, and we had to correct that. And we threw ourselves on the line. That kind of intensity concerning an issue is lacking in this generation. I don't see it being apathy as much as lack of focus on an issue.

But I see the free South African movement. Students are now saying, "We now have found something that strikes at our very moral character. We want to live in an America that does not support regimes that enslave people. That's not what this country is about."

Students are protesting in different ways. We had the rallies and walked the streets. They're going to the board of trustees. They're going to the corporate board rooms. They're sitting down saying, "I'm a stockholder, and I have a right to speak." They're talking about taking their investments out of South Africa.

These are students. This is the kind of movement potential that arises out of a fundamental question.

As long as a person was not directly supporting apartheid, it was an obscure issue. But when students began to realize that the money they paid for tuition was in South Africa, they saw a direct relationship between their participation and that issue.

Why should people be optimistic about the future?

Carter: I'm optimistic because I'm hearing young people articulate the issues. I'm seeing them become more aware. I'm seeing them not just rely on clichés and old adages about what life can be. I'm hearing them ask very important questions. I'm hearing them say, "What is the future?" I don't see the naiveté that my generation had when we walked blindly into adulthood.

I see much more communication going on. Adults don't like it. They have a problem because they never learned to communicate with young people. They'd rather not hear what young people have to say. They'd rather not see young people. When adults see them, they want them to act a certain way, talk a certain way. It's not conversation.

Young people have always been on the cutting edge of change. Young people have less to lose. They can be more idealistic. When Dr. King started, people said, "Upstart. Youngster. This young guy is trying to tell us what to do." Young people have a way of crystalizing what we are all about because of the ideals we teach them, ideals that we have forgotten and no longer believe in.

Compiled by Greg Jao

248

Teens and Dreams

Personal

I don't want to be caught up in all the hypocrisy and banality of many adults. I don't want to be a slave to money—someone whose only care is whether the stock market is looking good, or whether they're going out to lunch with a certain person.

Ron Eltanal, 17
Paradise Valley, Arizona

My dream of a perfect job would be a job that would keep my body in shape. Paying well would also be one of the main factors. I would also like to have some time to hunt, fish, camp, and just plain relax each year.

Chad Hope, 14
Red Oak, Texas

The perfect family would be one that is always there for you even if you're wrong, . . . one that understands the feelings of a teenager and realizes we will make plenty of mistakes.

Kimberly Aretta, 17
Uniontown, Pennsylvania

Ten years from now I would like to see myself with a Ph.D. in psychology. I want to be a counselor because I think there are a lot of social problems that people need help dealing with. I think the reasons for these problems is the high-stress, capitalistic society we've created.

Craig Rooney, 17
Jefferson City, Missouri

Ten years from now, I would like to see myself not wishing for the past and regretting childhood mistakes.

16-year-old female
Indiana

My dream of a perfect society is one where all people are treated the same. . . . Nobody would feel inferior to someone because of the clothes they wear or the car they drive. . . .

Life is supposed to be filled with happiness and some sadness. . . . It would be a beautiful place with trees, green grass, pretty flowers, and a lot of room to run and play. I would want it to be a place where you could go and forget all your problems and troubles.

Paula Whiteaker, 16
Manchester, Minnesota

A perfect family would be one where children can look up to their parents. One where kids are brought up to have good manners.

I wish they would find a cure for arthritis because my dad has it, and it is very painful. . . .

Wayne McDaniel, 16
Red Oak, Texas

My dream of a perfect society is one where people can get along without fighting. . . . Divide everything up equally so no one person is in power over others.

Tom Batcheler, 15
Iowa City, Iowa

I believe dreams run parallel to what's important or relevant in your life. As a child, dreams centered on playing and on family. As you move into the adolescent phase of your life, you gradually begin to dream about sex-related topics. As an adult, I would guess you dream about a job or your spouse. As a senior citizen, I would think you would begin to think about dying or perhaps about when you were young.

John King, 15
Galesburg, Illinois

A perfect family? Now come on! Divorce is everywhere. I've got four parents, and I'm the oldest of four kids (one whole sister and three half-brothers). I rarely see my father or two brothers, my sister (who's 10). . . . Who can talk to their parents? Sure, I love them . . . but what's the definition of a perfect family?

16-year-old female
Arizona

My dreams now are a lot different than my dreams as a child. As people grow older, they begin to see things in shades of gray and not in simple black and white as they did as children. When I was a child, my dreams were simple and selfish. Now I hope for feelings, not things. I dream more for my friends and family, and less for myself.

Jana Riess, 16
Galesburg, Illinois

Tina Church LTHS

Teens and Dreams   *251*

Afterword

Teenagers begin the metamorphosis from wide-eyed naiveté to world-weary experience. In the throws of transformation, they battle to understand the changes in themselves and the lack of changes in their world.

In adults, teenagers witness the seeming inevitability of compromise. They observe a generation—chastized by the failure of the sexual revolution, the "Me generation," and the civil rights movement—abandoning their dreams in exhaustion. In themselves, teens see the seeds of tacit acquiescence. By rejecting adults and adulthood, they attempt to banish a future of compromise.

When adults confront idealistic teenagers, they face dreams failed or dreams abandoned for security, prosperity, or practicality. They reject teenagers to hold their failure at arms length.

Teens understand the message: "Idealism is a luxury. Maturity involves compromise." But teens create dreams out of idealism and innocence, from the perceptions that arise only out of inexperience—the essence of teenagers themselves.

Unfortunately, teens have observed the reality. Government has compromised its democratic ideals for power and control. Families are consumed by self-centeredness. Employers exploit the powerless. Education traps teens between conflicting priorities. Laws ignore the voiceless. Technology proceeds without conscience. Teenagers witness the failure of the American Dream.

Rather than dreaming new dreams, however, teens have adopted the bankrupt goals of prosperity and status. They have retreated from reality and have exiled change from their midst. Though adults compromise, teens ignore. Teenagers are apathetic because they are frustrated by their inability to cause change and to deal with change.

To them, the need for dreams signifies the recognition of failure, the removal of the rose-colored glasses of childhood—the beginning of maturity. The need also implies that the idealized images of self, peers, adults, and the world no longer match the reality. Dreams require the rejection of the status quo.

But dreams also embrace new ways to deal with conflicts. Teenagers and adults have goals—what they need are dreams. Goals are what can be accomplished given the circumstances. Dreams are what should be accomplished regardless of the circumstances. But a world of idealists without pragmatism either leads down a road of chaotic action or to a world of rude, driven neurotics. We do not need a world of dreamers. We do need a world responsive to dreams.

With communication and an open mind, we must hammer away at our rose-colored glass shells. We must discard the pearly, diffuse images of the appearance and stare into the harsh light of reality. We must begin the transformation from wide-eyed naiveté to open-eyed realism, not to steely-eyed cynicism. We must transform our glass shell into a chrysalis of hope.

Greg Jao

National Teenage Research Project staff:
Doug Addison, Chris Anderson, Sara Corrough, Doug Elwell,
Robert Hester, Greg Jao, Michelle Jao, Erik Landahl, Pete Mandik,
Cathy Mau, Gina Nolan, Mark Peaslee, Kim Peirce, Paulette
Polinski, Dave Seng, Diana Slyfield, assistant coordinator; Howard
Spanogle, director.

Copy consultant:
Christine Zrinsky

Research aides:
Kristin Jass and Juanita Spanogle

Summer volunteers:
Neville Bilimoria, Vicki Dominick, Pat Bowlin, Susan Drechsel, Debbie
Elifson, Meaghan Emery, Julio Flores, Jackie Freer, Ruth Grunewald, Peggy
Iffland, Rob Kengott, Bill Karrow, David Markines, Julie Murphy, Dave
Palomares, Andrea Pates, Martha Pates, Lisa Seidlitz, Janice Shoulders,
Forrest Slyfield, Jennifer Sullivan, Jennifer Sweda, Kristin Walz, Jeannie
Wang, Sam Woo

Additional Echo staff, 1985–87; Journalism students, 1986–87:
John Alexis, Amy Baker, Mike Balgemann, Amy Bartt, Viren Bavishi, Shirish Bhatt,
Smita Bhatt, Jeannine Brechin, Tim Burke, Steve Fisher, Jeffrey Freeman, Karen
Glyzewski, Don Gomez, Chris Gorman, Ada Gutierrez, Christie Hart, Brad
Herbert, Carolyn Holland, Jon Johnson, Tasia Katinas, Rebecca Kniebusch,
Christine Kosman, Karen Long, Mark Ludena, Walt Martinez, Chris Morache,
Ginger Murphy, Kathleen O'Connor, Corey Poris, Charlie Reiman, Sean Sampey,
Gerald Shepardson, Debby Stowell, Tammy Thorp, Jon Tyndall, JoAnn Vasbinder,
Gary Wang, Patty Weyburn